Logic-Based Knowledge Representation

MIT Press Series in Logic Programming

Ehud Shapiro, editor
Koichi Furukawa, Fernando Pereira, and David H.D. Warren, associate editors

The Art of Prolog: Advanced Programming Techniques,
Leon Sterling and Ehud Shapiro, 1986

Logic Programming: Proceedings of the Fourth International Conference,
edited by Jean-Louis Lassez, 1987 (Volumes 1 and 2)

Concurrent Prolog: Collected Papers,
edited by Ehud Shapiro, 1987 (Volumes 1 and 2)

Logic Programming: Proceedings of the Fifth International Conference and Symposium,
edited by Robert A. Kowalski and Kenneth A. Bowen, 1988 (Volumes 1 and 2)

Consistency Techniques in Logic Programming,
Pascal van Hentenryck, 1989

Logic-Based Knowledge Representation,
edited by Peter Jackson, Han Reichgelt, and Frank van Harmelen, 1989

Logic-Based Knowledge Representation

Peter Jackson
Han Reichgelt
Frank van Harmelen

The MIT Press
Cambridge, Massachusetts
London, England

This book was printed and bound in the United States of America.

Library of Congress Cataloging-in-Publication Data

Jackson, Peter, 1948—
    Logic-based knowledge representation / Peter Jackson, Han
Reichgelt, Frank van Harmelen.
        p. cm. - - (Logic programming)
    Bibliography: p.
    Includes index.
    ISBN 0-262-10038-X
    1. Expert systems (Computer science) 2. Logic programming.
I. Reichgelt, Han. II. Van Harmelen, Frank. III. Title.
IV. Series.
QA76.76.E95J34   1989
006.3'3--dc19   88-33681
                                                    CIP

Contents

List of Figures   xi

List of Contributors   xiii

Series Foreword   xv

I   AN ABSTRACT ARCHITECTURE FOR BUILDING EXPERT SYSTEMS

1   Introduction   1

1.1   Outline of the book   1

1.2   Problems with current expert system tools   2

1.3   Using logic for knowledge representation   4

1.4   Using meta-level inference for control   5

1.5   Improving meta-level and object-level efficiency   7

1.6   Modal extensions to the predicate calculus   8

1.7   Modal nonmonotonic logic   9

1.8   The scope of the book   10

1.9   Acknowledgements   11

2   A Classification of Meta-Level Architectures   13

2.1   Introduction   13

2.2   Classification of meta-level architectures   14

    2.2.1   Object-level inference systems   16
    2.2.2   Mixed-level inference systems   18
    2.2.3   Pure meta-level inference systems   23

2.3   Other properties of meta-level architectures   27

    2.3.1   Linguistic relation between levels   27
    2.3.2   Declarative or procedural meta-language   28
    2.3.3   Partial specifications   28
    2.3.4   Completeness and strictness   28

2.4   Comparison of the different architectures   30

2.5	Conclusion	35
3	The Architecture of Socrates	37
3.1	The abstract architecture of Socrates	37
3.2	Declaration of the logical representation language	39
3.3	The storage and retrieval mechanism	43
3.4	Declaration of the proof theory	46
3.5	Declaration of the proof strategy	51
3.5.1	Declarative representation	51
3.5.2	Procedural representation	56
3.5.3	The scheduler	60
3.6	Open problems	61
3.7	Summary and conclusion	63
4	Applications of Socrates	65
4.1	Introduction	65
4.2	The INVEST system	65
4.2.1	Partition hierarchy	66
4.2.2	Sort lattice	66
4.2.3	Inference rules	66
4.2.4	Control strategy	67
4.3	The DOCS system	69
4.3.1	Knowledge base structure	69
4.3.2	Control	71
4.4	An office configuration system	72
4.4.1	Assertion-time inference	72
4.4.2	Control	74
4.5	An underground route planner	75
4.5.1	Representation language	76
4.5.2	Control	77
4.6	Schubert's Steamroller	79

4.7   Conclusion   83

II   FURTHER RESEARCH IN REPRESENTATION AND CONTROL

5   The Limitations of Partial Evaluation   87

5.1   Introduction   87

5.2   A description of partial evaluation   87

5.3   Problems of partial evaluation   94
      5.3.1   Changing object-level programs at run time   94
      5.3.2   Lack of static information   96
      5.3.3   Summary of problems   103
5.4   Heuristic guidance to partial evaluation   104
      5.4.1   Summary of heuristics   109
5.5   Related work in the literature   109

6   Assertion-Time Inference in Logic-Based Systems   113

6.1   Introduction   113

6.2   Tableau proof systems   114
      6.2.1   Classical propositional logic   115
      6.2.2   Classical predicate calculus   117
      6.2.3   Soundness   119
      6.2.4   Completeness   123
6.3   Assertion-time inference   124
      6.3.1   Classical propositional logic   125
      6.3.2   Predicate logic   127
6.4   Implementation   136
6.5   Related work   140
6.6   Conclusion   141

7   A Comparison of First Order and Modal Logics of Time   143

7.1   Introduction   143

7.2   Requirements on a temporal logic   144

7.3   A modal temporal logic   148
    7.3.1   A modal temporal language, TM   148
    7.3.2   TM-structures   150
    7.3.3   Interpretations for TM   151
    7.3.4   TM and the criteria   152

7.4   First order temporal logics   154
    7.4.1   The method of temporal arguments   155
    7.4.2   Reified temporal logic   164

7.5   Conclusion   176

8   A General Proof Method for Modal Predicate Logic   177

8.1   Introduction   177

8.2   Proof theory for logics with the Barcan formula   178
    8.2.1   Syntax   178
    8.2.2   Kripke models   179
    8.2.3   World indices   180
    8.2.4   World-unification   181
    8.2.5   M-unification   183
    8.2.6   Proof theory   183
    8.2.7   Examples   185
    8.2.8   Soundness of w-unification   190
    8.2.9   Soundness of proof theory   193
    8.2.10   Concerning completeness   196

8.3   Proof theory without the Barcan formula or its con-
    verse   197
    8.3.1   Kripke models again   197
    8.3.2   Term-indices   198
    8.3.3   Modal term unification   198
    8.3.4   Revised proof theory   199
    8.3.5   Examples   200
    8.3.6   Soundness   201

8.4   Proof theories with either the Barcan formula or its
    converse   203

8.4.1   Proof theory with FB but without BF   203
8.4.2   Proof theory with BF but without FB   205
8.4.3   Correction: BF, FB and symmetry   207

8.5   Implementation   208
8.5.1   Representing sequents and formulas   208
8.5.2   Searching for a proof   210
8.5.3   Assertion-time inferencing   211
8.5.4   Applications and possible improvements   213

8.6   Related work in automated theorem proving   215

8.7   Conclusion   217

8.8   Appendix   219

9   A Modal Proof Method for Doxastic Reasoning   229

9.1   Doxastic theories   229

9.2   The pure proof method   231

9.3   The augmented method   234

9.4   Discussion and related work   236

10   Conclusion   239

10.1   Advantages and disadvantages of an abstract archi-
       tecture   239
10.2   Open problems and further research   241

Bibliography   243
Index   253

List of Figures

2.1   Classification of meta-level systems   15

2.2   Flow of control in reflect-and-act systems   19

2.3   Flow of control in crisis-management systems   20

2.4   Flow of control in subtask-management systems   21

2.5   Properties of meta-level systems   31

3.1   Architecture of Socrates   38

3.2   Logical connectives   42

3.3   Declarative specification of control in Socrates   53

3.4   Sort hierarchy for the meta-level interpreter   54

3.5   Levels of implementation for meta-level control   57

3.6   Procedural specification of control in Socrates   59

4.1   Type hierarchy for the INVEST system   66

4.2   Part of London Underground   76

4.3   Sort lattice for Schubert's Steamroller   80

4.4   CPU time (mmm:ss) and number of nodes visited   82

5.1   An object-level knowledge base in Prolog   91

5.2   A meta-level interpreter in Prolog   92

5.3   The programs after partial evaluation   93

5.4   The programs after restricted partial evaluation   96

5.5   Heuristically limited partial evaluation   107

7.1   Sort hierarchy for TR   166

List of Contributors

Peter Jackson,
McDonnel Douglas Research Laboratories, Dept. 225, Bldg. 105, Level 2, ,Post A1, P.O. Box 516, St. Louis, Missouri 63166, USA.

Han Reichgelt,
Department of Psychology, University of Nottingham, University Drive, Nottingham NG7 2RD, England.

Frank van Harmelen,
Department of Artificial Intelligence, University of Edinburgh, 80 South Bridge, Edinburgh EH1 1HN, Scotland.

Robert Corlett,
Arthur Young Management Consultants, Rolls House, 7 Rolls Buildings, Setter Lane, London EC4A 1NH, England.

Nick Davies,
Dept. of Computer Science, University of Essex, Colchester, Essex, England.

Robin Kahn,
Plessey Research and Technology, Roke Manor, Romsey, Hampshire, England.

Bernie Elfrink,
Insulindeweg 109[III], 1094 PG Amsterdam, The Netherlands.

The research described in this volume was done while Peter Jackson, Han Reichgelt and Frank van Harmelen were at the Department of Artificial Intelligence of the University of Edinburgh, Scotland, Robert Corlett, Nick Davies and Robin Kahn were at the GEC-Marconi Research Center in Great Baddow, Essex, England, and Bernie Elfrink was visiting the University of Edinburgh.

Series Foreword

The logic programming approach to computing investigates the use of logic as a programming language and explores computation models based on controlled deduction.

The field of logic programming has seen a tremendous growth in the last several years, both in depth and in scope. This growth is reflected in the number of articles, journals, theses, books, workshops, and conferences devoted to the subject. The MIT Press series Logic Programming was created to accommodate this development and to nurture it. It is dedicated to the publication of high-quality textbooks, monographs, collections, and proceedings in logic programming.

Ehud Shapiro
The Weizmann Institute of Science
Rehovot, Israel

I AN ABSTRACT ARCHITECTURE FOR BUILDING EXPERT SYSTEMS

1 Introduction

The research described in this volume is an investigation into the usefulness of logic for the representation of knowledge and the control of its application to problem solving. The long-term goal was to design and build an environment for specifying knowledge based systems that was based upon the use of logic as (i) a representation language for domain-specific knowledge, and (ii) a metalanguage for describing task-specific control regimes. The basic idea was that a user should be able to produce a prototype simply by describing both the object-level knowledge of the problem domain and the meta-level knowledge for performing the task. The declarative description language would then be procedurally interpreted to generate the desired behaviours (or not), with bugs in behaviour being corrected by altering the specification. Finally, it should be possible to compile the runnable specification into a more efficient form, e.g. by generating a procedural representation of the declaratively encoded control regime.

1.1 Outline of the book

The work described in Part I provides an abstract knowledge-based architecture (Socrates) which is capable of being specialised and configured for particular applications. Although we confine ourselves to representation languages based on the many-sorted predicate calculus, we strive for as much generality as possible in the specification of control using meta-level inference. This generality does not come without price, but we describe a number of compilation techniques that help to cut the computational cost of meta-level interpretation.

Chapter 2 provides a thorough introduction to the literature on meta-level inference, proposes a scheme for classifying meta-level architectures, and argues in favour of a particular kind of architecture for the Socrates system. Chapter 3 describes the current implementation of this system in detail, indicating how it can be specialised and configured for alternative applications. Chapter 4 outlines a number of applications which have been implemented using Socrates, to illustrate the way in which the system is meant to be used.

Part II reports some novel research which enlarges current theorem proving technology, and which we feel should be incorporated into future versions of the system described in Part I. We examine further techniques for improving efficiency, and show how the predicate calculus base of the representation system can be extended to accommodate modal and nonmonotonic logics.

Chapter 5 assesses the utility of partial evaluation as a device for enhancing the efficiency of meta-level proofs, while chapter 6 examines the potential of assertion-time inferencing for making object-level proofs easier. Chapter 7 compares modal and reified treatments of temporal logic on such grounds as representational and computational adequacy. Chapter 8 presents a sequent based proof method for normal systems of modal predicate logic, while chapter 9 outlines a nonmonotonic version of the proof method for doxastic logic. Chapter 10 summarises the work, and indicates avenues for further research.

The chapters in part II (chapters 5 to 9), although all addressing issues arising out of th ework described in part I, can be read separately, whereas the chapters of part I (describing the Socrates system) should be read together.

In the next sections, we motivate our approach.

1.2   Problems with current expert system tools

Most of the tools that are currently available for constructing expert systems fall into two categories, namely expert system shells and high level programming language environments. Both of these types of tool suffer from a number of shortcomings which limit their usefulness.

The first type of available tools, *shells*, are usually constructed by abstraction from an existing expert system. Thus, a shell normally consists of an inference engine and an empty knowledge base and some debugging and explanation facilities. Buyers of a shell often believe, and manufacturers often claim, that the shell is appropriate for a range of different applications.

However, a large number of people have expressed dissatisfaction with expert system shells. The two most frequently heard complaints (e.g. [Alve83]) are (i) that an inference engine which was successful in one application will not necessarily be successful in another, and (ii) that the knowledge representation scheme suitable for the original domain often makes the expression of knowledge in another domain awkward if not impossible. For example, a production rule language that was designed for solving a classification problem using backward chaining would probably not be very suitable for solving a design or planning problem.

On the other hand, proponents of high level programming language environments (sometimes known as *hybrid systems*), such as LOOPS [Bobr83], KEE [Inte84] or ART [Will83], can be seen as taking a more pluralistic position: instead of providing knowledge engineers with a single pre-fabricated inference engine, one provides them with a large set of tools each of which has proven useful in other applications. LOOPS, for example, provides object-oriented programming with inheritance, a production rule interpreter and active values as well as LISP.

Whilst we accept that hybrid systems are useful as tools for program development, we would claim that they are less useful as tools for building expert systems. Their main problem is that they provide the knowledge engineer with a bewildering array of possibilities and little, if any, guidance as to the circumstances in which any of these possibilities should be used. Unless used by experienced programmers, high level programming environments encourage an ad hoc programming style in which no attention is paid to a principled analysis of the problem at hand to see which strategy is best suited for its solution.

The conclusion that we draw from the problems associated with shells and high level programming language environments is that a number of different architectures are needed for solving different types of problem. When constructing an expert system, a knowledge engineer has to decide what kind of architecture is appropriate to the application at hand. Ideally, a software tool for building expert systems should provide an *abstract architecture* which is capable of being instantiated to derive what we shall call *concrete architecture* suitable for a range of problem solving behaviours.

A concrete architecture has both a static and a dynamic aspect, corresponding to knowledge about the application area plus a strategy that describes how to use this knowledge when solving a problem. This distinction corresponds to a distinction one can make between two different aspects of an expert system. First, there is the *domain* in which the expert system is to solve problems. For example, the domain of an expert system may be electronics, or internal medicine. Secondly, there is the *task* which the knowledge engineer wants the expert system to perform. For example, the task of a system can be diagnosing a faulty electronic circuit or designing a new circuit. It is interesting to note that the problems with shells reflect these two aspects of an expert system. The first complaint about shells concerning the expressiveness of the knowledge representation language is related to the structure of the domain. The second complaint concerning the rigidity of the inference engine is related to the task of the expert system. As pointed out by [Chan83], [Chan85a], [Chan85b], [Chan87] typical expert system tasks such as diagnosis, planning, monitoring etc. seem to require particular control regimes.

Socrates allows the use of a variety of logical languages and a variety of control regimes to address the problem of the lack of flexibility associated with shells.

1.3   Using logic for knowledge representation

Socrates uses a logical language as the main formalism to implement the static aspects of the required concrete architectures for different domains. On the one hand, logical formalisms are rich enough to provide different concrete architectures, while on the other hand the use of logic provides a unifying framework for the system which saves it from the unstructured richness of the hybrid systems. This choice of logic as the main formalism implies that logical languages will serve as the representational scheme, while logical deduction will be the paradigm for the inference engine.

Many advantages come with the use of logic as the main knowledge representation formalism. First of all, unlike most other knowledge representation formalisms, logics come with a formal semantics, giving a precise description of the meaning of expressions in the formalism. Because this precise semantics allows the comparison of different logical languages, it is possible (as argued in [Reic85], [Reic86]) to construct a set of guidelines that correlate characteristics of particular domains and tasks with appropriate logic based representational and inferential mechanisms.

Secondly, again unlike many other knowledge representation formalisms, logics have well understood properties as regards their completeness, soundness, and decidability. For any reasonable logic it is possible to prove that the proof theory is sound. Furthermore, it is possible to establish via formal methods whether a particular logic is complete or not. Finally, it is known whether provability in a logic is decidable or not. It is known that, for any reasonably powerful logic, provability is at best a semi-decidable property. Although these results in themselves are sometimes negative (e.g. *in*completeness, *semi*-decidability), the important point is that these properties are known at all. For many other knowledge representation formalisms no such results have been obtained.

The final, but certainly not the least, advantage in favour of logic is its expressive power. Two aspects of this must be mentioned. Firstly, the language of logic is not restricted to that of standard two-valued, truth functional, first order predicate calculus. Many other logics have been proposed, offering a wide range of expressional and inferential power. A few examples of these are intuitionistic logics, many-valued logics, modal logics, epistemic logics and tense logics. The second important aspect of the expressive power of logic is its ability to express what might be called incomplete knowledge, or information about incompletely known situations [Moor82]. As Levesque and Brachman [Leve85] put it: the expressive power of logic "determines not so much what can be said, but what can be left unsaid". As a result, one is not forced to represent details that are not (yet) known. A few examples may clarify this point. Thus, in classical predicate calculus, one can express the knowledge that an object has a given property without knowing its identity. Or one can express disjunctive knowledge, such as "either my car is red or your car is green". Finally, one can draw a distinction between something not being known, i.e. P not appearing in the set of axioms, and something being known to be false, i.e. $\neg P$ appearing in the set of axioms.

1.4 Using meta-level inference for control

A number of arguments can be given for the explicit and separate representation of control knowledge.

A system with an explicit representation of its control strategies is easier to develop, debug and modify, as argued in [Davi77], [Davi80],

[Bund81], [Clan83a] and [Aiel84]: this explicit representation enables the independent variation of control knowledge and domain knowledge. One can adopt a different strategy in dealing with a particular domain with or without changing the domain knowledge representation, and vice versa. This kind of functional independence is vital. If a first-shot implementation of an expert system performs disappointingly (as is usually the case), then it is important that it is possible to (i) identify where the problem lies in terms of the architecture of the system, and (ii) make the requisite modification to the right module or module interface without having to modify other modules.

A second point is made in [Wiel86]. They note that experts are able to use their domain knowledge for a number of different tasks, eg. finding problems, teaching, communicating new insights, planning solutions. The explicit representation of control knowledge would allow the same domain knowledge to be used for a number of different purposes. [Clan85] formulates this as the possibility to write programs that interpret knowledge bases from multiple perspectives, providing the foundation for explanation, learning and teaching capabilities. A related point is mentioned in [Clan83b]. The separation of control knowledge from object-level knowledge not only makes it possible to use the same object-level knowledge for different purposes, but also the same control knowledge can be used in different domains.

An interesting side-effect of the separation of domain and control knowledge is its usefulness in knowledge elicitation. As is clear from the work of Wielinga and Breuker, a sound epistemological analysis is a prerequisite for successful knowledge elicitation. The distinction between the domain knowledge of experts and the strategies experts use in employing it is a very useful separation in this context.

Finally, [Clan83b], [Clan81] and [Warn84] and [Warn83] stress the importance of explicit control knowledge for the purpose of explanation. By explicitly representing the control knowledge, this part of the system can also be used in explanation. After all, not only should a system be able to explain what piece of knowledge was used, but also how this piece of knowledge was used and why. This enables a much deeper explanation of the behaviour of the system.

The separation of control knowledge from domain knowledge allows domain knowledge to be purely declarative in nature. While formulating domain knowledge we do not have to worry about efficiency, only about the representational adequacy. In the control knowledge on the other hand, the efficiency of the problem solving process is the most prominent aspect (heuristic or computational adequacy).

As argued in many other places in the literature ([Bund85], [Gall82], [Gene83], [Pere82], [Ster82a]), an architecture with a separate object-level and meta-level interpreter can be used to implement the required separation of domain and control knowledge. We take a meta-level architecture to be a system with two clearly separated levels, the meta-level, which is used for representing the control knowledge (or meta-knowledge), and the object-level, which is used for representing the domain knowledge (or object-knowledge).

1.5 Improving meta-level and object-level efficiency

Although the explicit formulation of control knowledge at the meta-level has many advantages, as argued above, a serious problem is inherent in this approach. The extra layer of interpretation that is incurred by a system with an explicit meta-level interpreter (as Socrates is), can amount to as much as an order of magnitude or more. If meta-level interpretation is to be a practical technique, this meta-level overhead should be removed. Some important work has been done in recent years on a technique called partial evaluation which transforms a combination of object- and meta-level program into more efficient code which has much of the meta-level overhead compiled out of it. Many promising results have been reported in the literature (e.g. [Take86] and [Safr86]). Chapter 5 explores this technique in detail, and analyses some of the remaining problems associated with it.

There is also an efficiency problem at the object-level. As Levesque and Brachman [Leve85] point out, there is a trade-off between the expressive power of a knowledge representation language and the computational tractability of an inference engine for the language. Logic is a very expressive knowledge representation language and as a result a logic-based inference engine is potentially rather inefficient. Chapter 6 addresses this problem by investigating the use of assertion-time inference. The rationale is to draw a limited set of inferences when the knowledge base is constructed, rather than doing all the inferencing at retrieval time when the user of querying the knowledge base.

1.6   Modal extensions to the predicate calculus

Modal logics are primarily concerned with the dual notions of necessity and possibility, but they can also provide formal mechanisms for reasoning about knowledge, belief, time and change (see e.g. [Halp85], [Shoh88]). Such mechanisms provide a potential basis for representation languages of great expressive power. In addition to allowing statements about what is or is not the case, modal logic permits us to make more complex and subtle statements about the possible (statements that might be true) and the necessary (statements that must be true). Further, such statements can be given a precise meaning, unlike the expressions of less formal languages, where modal predicates are often employed unsystematically. Many extant problems — in areas as diverse as planning, diagnostic reasoning and natural language understanding — might benefit from the ability to reason about possible, as well as actual, states of affairs in a principled way.

Yet automated reasoning in modal logics is made difficult by two significant problems.

- There is no obvious normal form for expressions containing modal operators. This frustrates the application of relatively efficient, resolution-based techniques to the modal case. Without a normal form, it is not immediately clear under what conditions one would consider two formulas to be complementary.

- Terms occurring within the scope of modal operators are referentially opaque. Consequently, their meaning must be relativised in some way to the context of their occurrence. This further complicates the notion of complementarity so essential to refutation strategies.

Partial solutions to these problems have been put forward in the literature. For example, [Moor85b] proposes a first-order axiomatisation of epistemic S4 in which individual terms are taken to be rigid designators. Thus there are axioms which state the properties of the S4 accessibility relation, and axioms which handle the interaction between modal operators and propositional connectives (and quantifiers). The idea is that modal theorem proving can then proceed within first-order logic. With regard to referential opacity, making individual terms rigid designators requires that every such term have the same denotation in all contexts, and restricts us to models in which the same individuals exist in every possible world.

It is hard to see how such an approach could provide a general solution to either of these problems, or facilitate the implementation of theorem provers for a significant class of modal systems. Many of the first-order axioms required to capture the model theory of modal logics are combinatorially explosive. This is not surprising, since the underlying accessibility relation may share some or all of the properties of equality, such as reflexivity, symmetry and transitivity. These properties render the naive representation of equality notoriously intractable. Insisting that individual terms be rigid designators contains the problem of referential opacity without solving it. The expressive power of modal languages is severely curtailed as a consequence.

Chapter 8 presents a sequent based proof method for modal predicate logic that addresses both of these problems. The inference rules are identical for all modal logics; different logics differ only in the conditions under which two formulas in sequents can be resolved against each other. Yet the conditions for a particular modal logic are closely related to the restrictions on the accessibility relation in the Kripke semantics for that logic.

1.7   Modal nonmonotonic logic

In addition to representing knowledge of some domain, it is also useful to be able to represent belief. The main difference between these two concepts is that belief is defeasible, i.e. one's beliefs can be mistaken, whereas knowledge is often held to be rational, justified, true belief. Beliefs may therefore need to be revised in the face of new evidence, unlike knowledge which has a more permanent character (modulo time and change).

A number of nonmonotonic logics of belief have been proposed. Most are defined in terms of a complete and stable expansion of some set of premises, or base beliefs (e.g. [Moor85a]). Such expansions generally contain all the tautological consequences of the base beliefs and the products of introspection (i.e. believing that one believes, or does not believe, some proposition). Stable expansions are essentially theories of what an ideally rational agent with infinite computational resources might believe. Consequently, they are closed under deduction and introspection, so that an agent must believe all of the logical consequences of his beliefs, as well as being aware of his beliefs.

Rather than attempting to construct the basis of such a theory, which would take exponential time, there is a case for considering nonmonotonic proof methods which only perform deduction and introspection on demand. Chapter 9 presents an augmentation of the modal proof method in chapter 8 for nonmonotonic KD45 which allows an agent to perform introspection incrementally, in response to assertions and queries. The method is explained and justified in terms of Konolige's [Kono85] notion of fulfilment in belief introspection.

1.8   The scope of the book

The research described herein has obviously focused on some problems at the expense of others. The emphasis throughout has been on expressiveness, both in the representation of knowledge ands the specification of control. Neglected topics include knowledge acquisition strategies, the explanation of results and the handling of uncertainty. Each of these topics defines a research area in its own right, and we shall not claim to have made any contribution here. Nevertheless, we can say a little about how each of these topics relates to the Socrates philosophy.

Socrates is really a specification environment for describing and creating prototypes; it is not intended as either a programming language or a delivery vehicle for knowledge based systems. As noted earlier, it attempts to separate the rather different processes of representing knowledge and controlling its application. These processes are often confounded in other expert system tools at the knowledge acquisition stage, with the result that it is difficult to effect changes in one without altering the other.

Socrates generates proofs which justify results; however, such proofs are not really explanations. To provide genuine explanations, one needs some model of what the user knows or believes, as well as some way of making assumptions and control decisions both explicit and intelligible. One advantage of meta-level inference is that, when one line of reasoning is explored in preference to another, much of the information required to explain such a decision is present in the meta-level proof tree, rather than being buried in the object-level interpreter.

The reasoning performed by Socrates is essentially categorical, although there is nothing to prevent the encoding of subjective probabilities at the meta-level. Arguably, this is where such computations belong, since they are usually intended as qualifications of object-level knowledge. Given the increasing number of schemes for handling uncertainty that can be found in the literature, it seems that all a specification environment can do is provide the knowledge engineer with the freedom to experiment or indulge his preferences.

A good deal has been said for and against the use of logic in problem solving (sometimes with the same people appearing for both the prosecution and the defence). The work reported here can be viewed as a largely empirical enterprise, which attempted to see if it was possible to build a credible logic-based knowledge engineering environment. We tend to regard the Socrates system described in Part I as an existence proof that logic has something significant to offer over more heterogeneous styles of representation. However, in the course of this exercise, it became clear that new research was required into both theorem proving methods and compilation techniques if we wanted to combine very expressive logics with the declarative specification of control. The chapters in Part II explore a number of possibilities in this area, with a view to providing a sound basis for further research and development.

1.9 Acknowledgements

The research described in this volume was largely supported by Alvey Project IKBS/031 in which GEC Research, the University of Edinburgh and GEC Avionics were partners. The work at the University was supported by SERC grant GR/D/17151. Ray McDowell and Dave Brunswick have contributed to the work at GEC Research. We thank Lincoln Wallen for useful discussions on chapters 6 and 8 and Yoav Shoham for his comments on an earlier version of chapter 7. Both Leon Sterling and Lincoln Wallen provided useful comments on an earlier draft of this book.

2 A Classification of Meta-Level Architectures

Frank van Harmelen

2.1 Introduction

In this chapter we categorise the meta-level expert systems in the literature on the basis of their crucial architectural features, concentrating on the relation between meta-level and object-level interpreter. We will discuss the communication between these two components and we will distinguish a number of typical architectures. After that we will discuss a number of other, independent properties by which these systems can be distinguished, although they are of secondary importance. Subsequently, we will compare the different types of architectures, and on the basis of this comparison we will argue in favour of one particular type of meta-level system, the so called *bi-lingual pure meta-level inference systems*. This architecture forms the basis of the Socrates system that will be discussed in the next chapter.

The use of meta-level architectures as the basis for building reasoning systems has become widely accepted. The past 10 years have seen the advent of many different systems that in one way or another claim to be a meta-level architecture. The main benefits of meta-level architectures are twofold: meta-level architectures allow the separation of domain knowledge (*what* does the system know), from control knowledge (*how* does the system use its knowledge), and they allow the explicit representation of this control knowledge, as opposed to implicitly building this knowledge into the implementation of the system, or mixing it with the domain knowledge. This separate and explicit representation of control knowledge has a number of advantages, as argued by numerous authors:

- A system with explicitly and separately represented control knowledge is more modular, and therefore easier to develop, debug and modify ([Davi80], [Clan83b] and [Aiel84]).

- It becomes possible to use the same domain knowledge for multiple purposes ([Clan83b]).

- The system can generate explanations of its own behaviour on the basis of the explicit control knowledge ([Warn83]).

- Finally, the separation of control knowledge from domain knowledge allows domain knowledge to be purely declarative in nature.
  While formulating domain knowledge we do not have to worry
  about efficiency, only about the "representational adequacy" (in
  the words of McCarthy). In the control knowledge on the other
  hand, the efficiency of the problem solving process is the most
  prominent aspect ("computational adequacy").

Many systems described in the literature provide ways of explicitly
representing meta-knowledge, and of controlling the inference process.
The systems that were used as the basis for the following categorisa-
tion are (in chronological order) GOLUX [Haye73], MECHO [Bund79],
AGE [Nii79], FOL [Weyh80], MRS [Gene80], TEIRESIAS [Davi80], 3-LISP
[Smit82], PRESS [Bund81], [Ster82b], IMPRESS [Ster82a], NEOMYCIN
[Clan82], [Clan82], the Prolog systems by [Gall79],[Gall82], [Bowe82],
and [Deva86], MLA [Gene83], Centaur [Aiki83], VMT [Hudl84], S.1
[Erma84], OMEGA [Atta84], SOAR [Lair84], BB1 [Haye85], ORBS [Fick85],
PROP [Gall85], LP [Silv86], KRS [Maes86] and PDP-0 [Jans86]. Where
relevant, we will briefly describe some features of these systems.

The goal of this chapter is to develop a classification of this multitude
of different architectures, based on their essential features. Perhaps surprisingly, the diversity of meta-level systems found in the literature can
be classified in a limited number of typical architectures. The advantage
of such a classification is that it will allow us to compare the meta-level
systems at a high level, using only their essential architectural properties, and abstracting away from incidental features.

2.2 Classification of meta-level architectures

The essential characteristic of meta-level architectures is of course that
they consist of two levels, the object-level and the meta-level. Each layer
can be seen as an individual system with a representation language and
an interpreter for expressions in that language. The purpose of the
object-level is to perform reasoning in the application domain of the
system, while the goal of the meta-level is to control the behaviour of

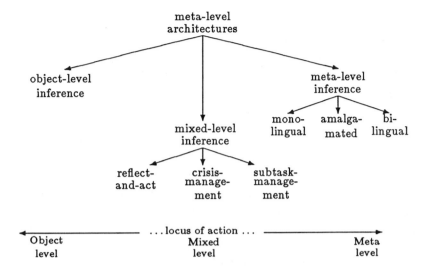

Figure 2.1
Classification of meta-level systems

the object-level.[1] The system as a whole can at any moment in time be active at one of the two levels; either it is interpreting object-level expressions (using the object-level interpreter), or it is interpreting meta-level expressions (using the meta-level interpreter). This leads us to the notion of the *locus of action* (using a phrase coined in [Welh87]): the place in the system which is active at any one point in time. This locus of action can then be either the object-level or the meta-level. It is exactly this locus of action that will form the basis for our main classification of meta-level architectures. We will distinguish a spectrum of systems with, at one end of the spectrum, systems where the locus of action is almost all the time at the object-level, and where meta-level activity takes places only occasionally. At the other end of the spectrum, we will see systems where the converse is true: almost all (or sometimes all) system activity

---

[1]Notice that we restrict our interest in meta-level architectures to those where the meta-level is used to control the search at the object-level. Meta-level architectures can be used for many purposes, such as extending the set of results computable at the object-level, to perform meta-theoretic reasoning concerning consistency and redundancy, learning etc, but these other uses of meta-level architectures are not our primary interest in this chapter.

takes place at the meta-level, and (almost) no activity takes place at the object-level. The systems in the middle of this spectrum exhibit equal amounts of object-level and meta-level activity. This classification, plus further subdivisions, is shown in figure 2.1, and we will discuss each of the types of system in this classification in the following subsections.

2.2.1 Object-level inference systems

On one extreme of the classification shown in figure 2.1 are the systems where the main activity is at the object-level. In fact, these systems do not have a proper meta-level interpreter (ie. an interpreter for meta-level expressions), but only an object-level interpreter that takes the meta-level expressions into account during its computational cycle in order to adjust its behaviour. As a result, the object-level interpreter executes two types of instructions: firstly, the object-level expressions it is supposed to interpret, and secondly the meta-level expressions that affect its behaviour. Typically, the object-level interpreter performs a fixed computational cycle, and the meta-level expressions concern certain fixed points within this cycle. Systems in this category are the Prolog system by Gallaire/Lasserre and Devanbu et.al. and GOLUX.

For instance in the Prolog system developed by Gallaire and Lasserre, a number of meta-predicates can be defined that handle both clause selection and conjunct ordering. These predicates are then used in an interpreter-loop to determine the behaviour of the system. A fixed vocabulary of meta-predicates is available that can express a variety of properties of the object-level propositions that compete for execution. These properties include among others the number of literals in a clause, the presence of a particular literal in a clause, the value of any ancestor of a clause, and the invocation depth of the clause. The object-level propositions that are present in the knowledge base can be specified in the meta-rules by their position in the knowledge base, or by a (partial) specification of their contents. In the Prolog syntax that is used in the system, a clause like

```
order(p(X,Y), [N1, N2, N3, ..., Ni]) :-
    C1, C2, C3, ..., Ck.
```

states that for the resolution of literals that are an instantiation of p(X,Y) the clauses numbered N1, N2, ..., Ni will be used in that order, provided the conditions C1, ..., Ck are met. Notice that the variables X,Y, N1, N2, ..., Ni can be used in the conditions Ci. An example of this would be

```
order(p(X), [1, 2, 3]) :- cond1(X).
order(p(X), [1, 3, 2]) :- cond2(X).
order(p(X), [3, 1, 2]) :- cond3(X).
```

This specifies a different order for the clauses for p(X) for different conditions on the argument X.

An example of content directed conflict resolution is

```
before(p(_), Clause1, Clause2) :-
    length(Clause1,_,N), length(Clause2,_,M),
    N < M.
```

which states that for the resolution of literals of the form p(_) shorter clauses will be used before longer clauses. Replacing p(_) with either a variable or a more specific term (e.g. p([])) would enlarge or reduce the scope of this heuristic. This enables the formulation of both domain dependent and domain independent strategies.

The system also provides a mechanism for conjunct ordering. A clause of the form

```
need(p(X,Y,Z)) :- inst(X).
```

says that for the selection of literal p(X,Y,Z) for execution, it is necessary that variable X has been instantiated.

A literal can be mentioned directly (as the literal p in the example above), or it can be designated indirectly, using an expression like:

```
literal(X, Name, ListOfProperties)
```

This indicates a literal X named by Name that satisfies each of the properties on ListOfProperties. This is a list of pairs (Pi:Vi), where Pi is the name of a property, and Vi is its required value. The properties that are available include such things as ancestor, father, depth and solved. For instance, a meta-level clause like

```
before(T1, T2) :-
    literal(T1, X, [depth:N1]),
    literal(T2, Y, [depth:N2]),
    N1 < N2.
```

specifies a breadth-first strategy for the interpreter. Further restrictions on X and Y would impose such a strategy only on the named literals.

In earlier work along the same lines [Gall79], further facilities were proposed to

- assign priority numbers to competing clauses,

- block backtracking over specified clauses (corresponding to dynamic cut introduction),

- inhibit the execution of literals until they reach some degree of instantiation.

The important point for the classification of meta-level systems is that all these meta-predicates are annotations that are used by a predefined and unchangeable interpreter. In other words, the behaviour of this interpreter (in this case the Prolog interpreter) is parameterised over the definition of meta-level annotations as described above, but cannot be redefined to any further extent. For instance, it would be impossible to specify a forward chaining interpreter in the Gallaire/Lasserre systems, since the hardwired object-level interpreter presumes a backward chaining control regime. It is important to realise that the use and meaning of the predicates described above (such as **order**, **before** and **need**) are fixed by the system by the way they are used in the predefined and hardwired object-level interpreter. It is not possible to extend this set. Thus, object-level inference systems provide only a limited amount of flexibility, and cannot be redefined beyond the scope of the annotations that the object-level interpreter takes into account.

2.2.2   Mixed-level inference systems

In the middle of figure 2.1 we find systems where the computation takes place at both the meta- and the object-level. Object-level and meta-level computations are interleaved, and some mechanism is provided for switching between the two. The computation at the object-level is monitored by the meta-level. We can further subdivide this category of systems halfway the spectrum on the basis of the criterion that is used for switching between object- and meta-level, as shown in figure 2.1.

Reflect-and-act systems.   Sometimes the meta-level is called very frequently, before or after every object-level step. This organisation has

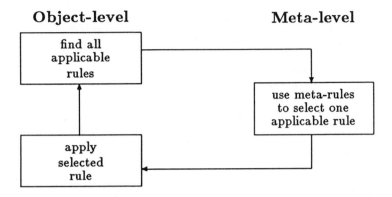

Figure 2.2
Flow of control in reflect-and-act systems

been called a *reflect-and-act* loop, since the object-level "acts", the meta-level "reflects" on the object-level actions and these two together are chained together in a continuous loop. Systems with this architecture are the production rule systems TEIRESIAS and ORBS and the blackboard system BB1.

The flow of control in such reflect-and-act systems can be described as in figure 2.2. The object-level interpreter finds the set of all applicable object-level rules and passes this *conflict-resolution set* on to the meta-level interpreter. The meta-level interpreter uses its control knowledge to select one of these applicable rules, which is then handed down again to the object-level interpreter, which applies this rule. In a system like TEIRESIAS the control knowledge for conflict resolution is written down in meta-rules such as:

```
if   $rule mentions the $current-goal
and  $rule2 does not mention the $current-goal
then $rule1 should be used before $rule2
```

Crisis-management systems. Sometimes the meta-level is called only if a *crisis* or an impasse occurs in the object-level computation, for example when too many or not enough steps are possible at the object-level. PDP-0, VMT and SOAR are examples of this approach.

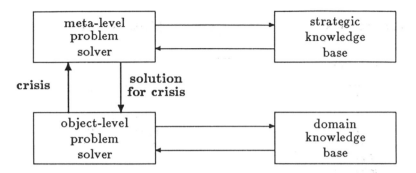

Figure 2.3
Flow of control in crisis-management systems

PDP-0 for instance, is a program that models the behaviour of human problem solvers in the domain of thermodynamics. When the system is given a problem to solve, it selects a problem solving strategy on the basis of characteristics of the input problem. This strategy will be executed by the object-level problem solver. When the program comes to a dead end, for example because none of the known strategies is applicable, or because of the unexpected failure of an applied strategy, this will be noticed by a supervising component. The supervisor will then ask the meta-problem solver to propose an adjustment of the current goal-tree, in order to solve the impasse.

The flow of control in crisis-management systems is summarised in figure 2.3. The object level interpreter uses the domain knowledge to solve a particular problem, and only hands over control to the meta-level interpreter if some kind of crisis occurs which prevents the object-level computation from continuing. The meta-level interpreter then uses its strategic (meta-level) knowledge base to try and solve this crisis. If some kind of solution has been found it is handed down to the object-level interpreter which can then proceed with the computation. Different kinds of crises can occur. One example of a crisis is when no object-level rules can be found that apply to the current subgoal. The meta-level interpreter then has to find a different subgoal for the continuation of the object-level computation. In this way we could implement user-directed backtracking, rather than the built-in standard behaviour of a system like Prolog. Another example of a crisis is when more than

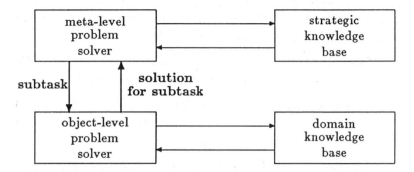

Figure 2.4
Flow of control in subtask-management systems

one object-level rule applies to the current subgoal. The object-level interpreter then turns to the meta-level for conflict resolution. In this way a reflect-and-act system can be simulated in an efficient way by a crisis-management system (efficient since the meta-level is only called if there is indeed more than one applicable object-level rule, rather than in every loop, as in reflect-and-act systems).

Subtask-management systems. Yet another approach is where the meta-level knowledge is used to partition the object-level task into a number of *subtasks*. In such a system, the meta-level interpreter decides on a task to be done, and this task will then be executed by the object-level interpreter. After completion of this object-level task (be it successful or not), the meta-level decides on the next subtask for the object-level. This approach is taken in S.1, NEOMYCIN, MLA, PROP and CENTAUR.

The flow of control in subtask-management systems is described in figure 2.4. The meta-level interpreter first decides upon a subtask to be solved by the object-level interpreter. The object-level interpreter then tries to solve this subtask, and only returns to the meta-level when it has either found a solution or when it has established that it cannot solve the subtask. On the basis of this result the meta-level interpreter can then try to find a new subgoal to be solved. Subtasks are like conventional subroutines in that they can call each other, resulting in a stack-based scheduling of tasks. Subtasks can be either very simple knowledge base partitions that try to solve a particular subgoal, or they can have a more elaborate structure. The subtask concept from NEOMYCIN is a good illustration. Subtasks in NEOMYCIN consist of:

- The focus: this is the argument with which the task is called. This often represents the object to which the task is applied.

- Three sets of meta-rules: the DOBEFORE, DODURING and DOAFTER rules that represent the prologue of the task, the main body and the epilogue respectively.

- The goal that is recorded to show that the task has been accomplished. This can be seen as the result of the task if it exits successfully.

- The end-condition that may abort the task when it becomes true. Whether the task is aborted or not depends on the task-type.

- The task-type, which specifies how the DODURING rules are to be applied. There are two dimensions to the task type: simple vs. iterative, and try-all vs. not-try-all. The combinations give four ways of applying the DODURING rules:

  - Simple, try-all: The rules are applied once each, in order. Each time a metarule succeeds, the end condition is tested.
  - Simple, not-try-all: The rules are applied in sequence until one succeeds, then the process stops.
  - Iterative, try-all: All the rules are applied in sequence. If there are one or more successes, the process is started over. The process stops when all the rules in the sequence fail. Each time a metarule succeeds, the end condition is tested.
  - Iterative, not-try-all: Same as for iterative try-all, except that the process is restarted after a single metarule succeeds.

  These four task-types allow a limited flexibility in the control regime used within a subtask, along the lines of the object-level inference systems described above.

As can be seen from figures 2.3 and 2.4, the architectures for crisis- and subtask-management systems are very similar. The main differences are in the the kind of data that is passed between the object-

and the meta-level, and in the place where the computation starts: the systems communicate either in terms of crises and their solutions or in terms of subtasks and their solutions; furthermore, crisis-management systems initiate their computations at the object-level, while subtask-management systems start their computation at the meta-level.

2.2.3 Pure meta-level inference systems

On the right side of the spectrum in figure 2.1 we see systems where the computation mainly takes place at the meta-level. In these systems the behaviour of the object-level is fully specified at the meta-level. Using this description of the object-level, the meta-level can completely simulate the object-level inference process. This means that there is no longer a need for an explicit object-level interpreter. As a result, the object-level interpreter is no longer present in the system, and its behaviour is completely simulated by the execution of its specification at the meta-level. Systems from this category are MECHO, PRESS, IMPRESS, the Prolog system by Bowen and Kowalski, and Socrates.

As an example of pure meta-level inference systems we consider PRESS. This system performs symbolic algebraic manipulations. One of the main features of PRESS is that the system proceeds in its problem solving process by trying to prove theorems at the meta-level, producing object-level proofs as a side effect. The key idea of pure meta-level inference is that strategies are considered to be at the meta-level of the domain. That is, the strategies are axioms of a meta-theory. For example, consider the following meta-level axiom from PRESS

```
singleocc(X, L=R) &
position(X,L,P)    &
isolate(P, L=R, Ans)
-> solve(L=R, X, Ans).
```

This can be considered procedurally as a strategy to solve an equation: to solve an equation L=R in X giving answer Ans, satisfy the subgoals on the left. However, it also has a declarative meaning in the meta-theory. The declarative meaning is

> If L=R contains exactly one occurrence of X, and the position of this occurrence in L is P, and if the result of isolating X in L=R is Ans, then Ans is a solution to the equation L=R, with X as the unknown.

Note that this description refers to properties such as position and number of occurrences of X. These are meta-theoretic syntactic features.

The inference of PRESS occurs at the meta-level. Some of the meta-level predicates are of the form

New is the result of applying Rule to Old.

To satisfy such a predicate, the rule Rule is applied to the expression Old to produce New. As a result of this, an algebraic transformation has occurred at the object-level, the expression Old has been transformed into New: the object-level strategies are executed by performing inferences in the meta-theory, and affect the object-level via statements of relations between the object-theory and the meta-theory (also called reflection principles). Performing inference at the meta-level and using reflection simulates the behaviour of the object-level. Thus, search at the object-level is replaced by search at the meta-level. This works well because, as described in [Silv86], the meta-level search space is much better behaved than the object-level space. In particular, the branching rate of the meta-level space is much lower, and most wrong choices lead to dead ends rapidly. The use of meta-level inference moves the search process from the object-level to the meta-level, and thereby transforms an ill-behaved search space to a better behaved one. If the meta-level space is still too complex, it is possible to axiomatise the control of this level, i.e. to produce a meta-meta-level. This process can in theory be continued until the control process of the highest level becomes trivial. This usually happens very early, so only two levels are needed.

Systems that have been constructed in different domains using a methodology similar to PRESS are MECHO [Bund79], IMPRESS [Ster82a] and LP [Silv86].

The important difference between pure meta-level inference systems and object-level inference systems as discussed above is that the meta-level predicates of a system like PRESS are interpreted by an independent meta-level interpreter. The set of meta-level predicates (as `singleocc`, `isolate` etc) is therefore fully extendible and redefinable, unlike the meta-level predicates in object-level inference systems, which are a fixed set.

The problem of choosing between the various strategies that are axiomatised at the meta-level and that are applicable at a point in the problem solving process now depends on the proof procedure that is used for the meta-level interpreter. The systems mentioned here use different techniques for this task. PRESS relies on the built in, fixed behaviour of a Prolog interpreter for this task, while MECHO uses a special purpose interpreter. The system described in [Take85] is a re-implementation of PRESS. It does allow reasoning about the selection of strategies, rather than using a hardwired interpreter.

An important subdivision of pure meta-level inference systems can be made on the basis of the relation between the object-level language L and the meta-level language M used by the system. On the one hand, there are the systems that we will call *monolingual*. In these systems M and L are the same language, and no syntactic distinction is made between object-level and meta-level expressions. An examples of these systems is the Gallaire/Lasserre system. In this system Prolog is used for both M and L. On the other hand there are the *bilingual* systems that support two strictly separate languages L and M. In order to provide upwards and downwards communication between L and M, the languages are related via a naming convention which translates sentences, sets of sentences and other linguistic entities of L into variable free terms of M. This choice between monolingual and bilingual systems has a profound effect on the structure of meta-level interpreters. Taking a Prolog system as an example, we can program a simple meta-level Prolog interpreter in Prolog as follows:

```
solve([]).
solve([G|Gs]) :-
    clause(G, B),
    append(B, Gs, NewGs),
    solve(NewGs).
```

This is a monolingual meta-level interpreter which relies on the mixing of object-level terms and meta-level terms for the communication between the two levels. Object-level predicates are regarded as meta-level function symbols, but variables at both levels are represented as Prolog variables, thereby not making a distinction between object-level variables (ranging over object-level terms) and meta-level variables (ranging over object-level formulas). As a result, the built-in unification algorithm of Prolog can be used at both levels. A bilingual version of the same Prolog interpreter in Prolog would look like

```
solve([], []).
solve([G|Gs], S) :-
    clause(G, C),
    rename_vars(C, [G|Gs], C1),
    head(C1, H1),
    unify(G, H1, S1),
    body(C1, B1),
    append(B1, Gs, NewGs),
    instantiate(NewGs, S1, NewGsPlusS1),
    solve(NewGsPlusS1, S2),
    compose(S1, S2, S).
```

This version of the Prolog meta-interpreter in Prolog allows for a separate representation of object- and meta-level variables. Only meta-
level variables are represented by Prolog variables, and object-level
variables correspond to particular variable free meta-level terms. As
a result, an object-level formula such as $\forall x \forall y f(x,y)$ can be represented by *all(var(1),all(var(2),f(var(1),var(2))))*. Simpler naming relations are also possible, such as the standard quoting relation, where
each object-level term is represented by a single meta-level atom:
"$\forall x \ \forall y \ \exists z \ f(x,y,z)$". A third approach is presented in [Bowe82], and
consists of *amalgamating* L and M. In this approach L and M are
in fact the same language, but the naming convention is employed as
above, so that each object-level expression has a variable free term as its
name associated with it. (Since this variable free term is itself again a
syntactically correct object-level expression, since $L = M$, it again must
have another variable free term as its name, ad infinitum).

This concludes our classification of meta-level architectures according to their locus of action. This distinction corresponds roughly to
a distinction made by Silver [Silv86] between *"object-level driven"* and
"meta-level driven" systems. Systems at the left end of the spectrum
shown in figure 2.1 are object-level driven, since their main computation takes place at the object-level, and systems at the right end of the
spectrum are meta-level driven.

2.3   Other properties of meta-level architectures

In this section we will discuss some more properties of meta-level architectures that can be used to further classify them, beyond the classification on the basis of the locus of action as described in the previous section. Some of the properties discussed in this section are found implicitly in the literature. The aim of this section is to sharpen these criteria, and to make them explicit. Figure 2.5 at the end of this section will summarise the position of all the systems mentioned above with respect to all of these properties.

2.3.1   Linguistic relation between levels

The distinction between monolingual, bilingual and amalgamated systems used to subdivide pure meta-level inference systems in the previous section can in fact be used more generally, to apply also to object-level inference and mixed-level inference systems.

Object-level inference systems can have their meta-level instructions to the object-level interpreter expressed in a language that is either the same as or different from the object-level language. The Gallaire/Lasserre system relies on the two languages being the same, whereas GOLUX separates the two languages, providing an explicit *quoting mechanism* to give meta-level names to object-level expressions (using this mechanism, the ground terms at the meta-level that are used as the names of object-level expressions are always atomic constants).

The distinction between monolingual, bilingual and amalgamated systems also applies to mixed-level systems. TEIRESIAS is a bilingual system: although both object-level and meta-level language ar production rule languages, they are quite different languages, properly separated; the languages are of the same type, namely production rule languages, but they are not identical. This is similar to GOLUX, where both meta-level and object-level language are of the same type (first order predicate calculus), but are in fact separate languages. The same remark holds for MLA. NEOMYCIN and S.1 are bilingual systems. In both these systems the meta-level language is not only different from the object-level language, but also of a different type: Both NEOMYCIN and S.1 use production rules at the object-level, but use some special purpose language at the meta-level: the task-language in NEOMYCIN and the so called control-blocks in S.1.

2.3.2   Declarative or procedural meta-language

The control knowledge of the meta-level can be either expressed in a *declarative* or a *procedural* language. Expressions in a procedural language can only be understood in terms of the *behaviour* of the meta-level interpreter, the actions it takes, the order in which it does things etc., whereas a declarative language states true facts that can be understood without reference to the behaviour of the meta-level interpreter. For example, the meta-level expressions of GOLUX are purely declarative descriptions of properties of object-level proof trees, whereas something like the control knowledge of S.1 is purely procedural in nature, talking about the order in which to perform actions, sequences and loops of instructions, etc. Yet other systems (such as PRESS) have a meta-level language that has both a declarative and a procedural reading.

2.3.3   Partial specifications

An important property of some of the systems mentioned above is that they allow the *partial specification* of meta-level knowledge. Such systems (like GOLUX, Gallaire/Lasserre, MLA, 3-LISP, KRS and Bowen/Kowalski) provide a *default specification* of the behaviour of the system that can be totally or partially overwritten by the user to modify the systems default behaviour. In some of these systems the default definition is explicitly available for inspection in the system (3-LISP, KRS, Bowen/Kowalski), whereas the other systems (GOLUX, Gallaire/Lasserre, MLA) only contain an implicit definition of their default behaviour.

2.3.4   Completeness and strictness

One of the main purposes of having a meta-level architecture at all is to allow the object-level to be purely declarative, without having to worry about procedural aspects. Thus, for any given query, the object-level (implicitly) specifies a set of answers[2]. It is the task of the meta-level interpreter to determine which of these possible answers is going to be actually computed, and in which order. Furthermore, in some systems,

---

[2]This is clearest if the object-level consists of a logical theory plus a set of logical inference rules, but similar notions exist for other declarative representation languages.

it is possible for the meta-level to extend the set of answers derivable from the object-level theory, using meta-theoretic devices like *reflection principles* [Fefe62], implemented for instance in FOL [Weyh80]. We call a meta-level architecture *complete* if it computes *all* the results derivable from the object-level theory (i.e. the meta-level does not *suppress* any object-level results). We call a meta-level system *strict* if it computes *only* results derivable from the object-level theory (i.e. the meta-level does not *extend* the object-level results). Notice that it is possible for a meta-level architecture to be both *in*complete and *un*strict, namely if the meta-level suppresses some of the object-level results, but also computes extra ones. We use the term *exact* when a meta-level system is both complete and strict: an exact system computes all and only those results derivable from the declarative object-level theory.

With these definitions it is clear that completeness of a meta-level system is not always a desirable property. The whole point of a meta-level architecture is often to prune parts of the object-level search space, thereby suppressing certain object-level results because they are too expensive to compute. Whether strictness of a meta-level system in the above sense is always a desirable property is less clear. In the context of using meta-level systems for control, we probably do not want to extend the results of the object-level theory, but one possible use of a meta-level architecture (although not our interest here) is exactly to try and extend the results of the object-level theory. [Wall83] used the term "positive heuristic" in connection with the concept of completeness: a positive heuristic is

> a heuristic that prefers certain object-level computations over others, but that does not prohibit certain computations altogether.

In other words, a system that only allows positive heuristics is automatically complete.

A system like the Gallaire/Lasserre Prolog system is one of the few systems mentioned above that is complete: its only concern is the ordering of clauses and literals, thereby affecting only the order in which the object-level computation takes place, but not its ultimate outcome[3].

---

[3]Strictly speaking, this is only true for those versions of their system that do not allow dynamic cut-introduction. This corresponds to dynamically removing object-level backtrack-points, thereby potentially suppressing certain object-level results.

A system like GOLUX is certainly not complete. For instance, we can force proofs in GOLUX to be deterministic, thereby pruning alternative solutions. However, GOLUX is strict in the above sense: no new object-level results can be introduced through meta-level computation. This is not true in meta-level inference systems like KRS and 3-LISP: since their meta-levels completely specify the object-level computation, it is well possible to extend the object-level behaviour in order to produce extra results.

This concludes our discussion of different properties to distinguish meta-level architectures. The table in figure 2.5 summarises the position of all the systems mentioned above on these properties. This table also contains data on the Socrates system, which will be described in the next chapter. However, for convenience, we already include Socrates in the table here.

2.4   Comparison of the different architectures

In this section we will compare the architectures discussed above, and we will conclude that the one based on pure meta-level inference is most promising. The other approaches all have major problems associated with them. Pure meta-level inference does not suffer from these problems, while it offers several advantages.

The most obvious problem is associated with the object-level-inference systems. The meta-level does not have a separate place in the architecture of these systems, and is not stated as explicitly as would be necessary in order to achieve the advantages of a meta-level architecture (better explanation, re-usability and ease of development and debugging). The main structure of the control strategy of these systems is only implicit in the system. Although possibly available for inspection, it is never available for modification, and only a restricted number of aspects of the control strategy can be changed. For instance in the Gallaire/Lasserre system, it is possible to change the clause- and literal-selection strategies, but the fact that the system is chronologically back-tracking and backward chaining is hardwired.

The mixed level systems do not suffer from this problem, but they have other problems associated with them, which can best be discussed

System	Architect. type	linguistic relation	declarative/ procedural	partial spec.	strict & complete
TEIRESIAS	reflect-act.	bi-ling.	decl.	yes	C− ; S+
S.1	task-man.	bi-ling.	proc.	?	C− ; S+
BB1	reflect-act.	bi-ling.	proc.	yes	C− ; S+
MLA	task-man.	bi-ling.	decl.	yes	C− ; S+
KRS	meta-inf.	mono-ling.	$-^1$	yes	C− ; S−
NEOMYCIN	task-man.	bi-ling.	proc.	$-^2$	C− ; S+
PRESS	meta-inf.	mono-ling.	decl.&proc.	$-^2$	$-^3$; S+
GOLUX	object-inf.	bi-ling.	decl.	yes	C− ; S+
PDP-0	crisis-man.	?	?	$-^2$	?
Gallaire	object-inf.	mono-ling.	decl.&proc.	yes	$C+^5$; $S-^4$
Bowen	meta-inf.	amalgam.	decl.&proc.	yes	C− ; $S+^6$
3-LISP	meta-inf.	mono-ling.	proc.	yes	C− ; $S-^4$
Socrates	meta-inf.	bi-ling.	decl.&proc.	no	C− ; S−

Legend:

?	=	unknown, cannot be determined from available literature.
$-^n$	=	not applicable, see note n.
C+/−	=	completeness enforced/not enforced.
S+/−	=	strictness enforced/not enforced.

Notes:

1. It is unclear how the object-oriented paradigm relates to the distinction declarative vs. procedural.
2. The possibility of partial specifications does not occur in this system since it is a program built for a particular task, containing a full specification of one appropriate control regime.
3. The notion of completeness does not apply to PRESS, since the object-level knowledge is not stated independently from the meta-level knowledge: the object-level is *only* represented by its axiomatisation at the meta-level.
4. The system can be made unstrict because the confusion between object-level and meta-level language (monolingual) allows the meta-level predicates to introduce arbitrary bindings for the object-level variables.
5. The system is only complete without the facility of dynamic cut-introduction.
6. The system is only strict if (i) the predicates used in the definition of the demo-predicate are specified precisely enough, for instance member must compute the membership relation, and (ii) if redefinition of these predicates in order to change the behaviour of the system is only possible within the limits of such a specification. In other words, the specification should allow us to change the procedural reading of these predicates, but not their declarative reading.

Figure 2.5
Properties of meta-level systems

using the subcategories from section 2.2:

A problem that is associated with both the crisis-management systems and the reflect-and-act systems is that the search in the solution space is still performed at the object-level. As a result, the meta-level knowledge is only used as a preference criterion over the separate object-level search space, whereas in systems that are more meta-level driven the meta-level knowledge is used to completely specify the whole structure of the search space of the system. This means that no full advantage is taken from the fact that the meta-level search space is better behaved than the object-level search space.

A problem associated with the task-management systems is what could be called the black-box effect: after the meta-level has decided on a task to be performed by the object-level, the object-level is no longer under the control of the meta-level, and again no full benefit is gained from the differences between meta-level and object-level search.

None of the mixed-level inference systems makes all the control knowledge in the system explicit: reflect-and-act systems only deal with conflict resolution strategies, crisis-management systems know how to solve impasses in the computation and subtask-management systems represent the selection of goals and subgoals, but none of them contains a full description of the object-level computation.

Meta-level inference systems do not suffer from these problems. In meta-level inference systems, the meta-knowledge is not just used as preference criteria over the separate object-level search space, but it is used to completely specify the whole structure of the search space. Meta-level inference systems perform their search in the meta-level search space and thereby gain the full benefit of the nicer properties of the meta-level search space. Furthermore, meta-level inference systems contain a full specification of the inference strategy of the system, thereby allowing the user to change any part of this strategy, and not just only a few predefined aspects of it.

This leaves us with the choice between the different subtypes of meta-level inference systems: monolingual, bilingual and amalgamated systems. A number of reasons can be given why it is important for the meta-level language to be separated from the object-level languages, thus ruling out both the mono-lingual and the amalgamated systems. First of all, there is an epistemological reason. [Reic85], [Reic86] and [Chan83],[Chan85a],[Chan85b], [Chan87] argue that different domains require different representation languages. Since the object-level and the meta-level deal with widely different domains (the object-level deals with the application domain of the system, while the meta-level deals with the issue of controlling the object-level), it follows that these two levels of the system do indeed need different representation languages to suit their different needs.

A second argument concerns the modularity of the system. One of the advantages of separating control knowledge from domain knowledge is that the two can be changed independently. The same domain knowledge can be used for different tasks under different control regimes, and the same control knowledge can be used to solve similar tasks in different domains. However, this ability to vary the two levels independently would be greatly reduced if control knowledge and domain knowledge were represented together in one and the same language. Furthermore, the lack of syntactic distinction between the two languages makes it possible for the machine to perform unintended operations, burdening the user with extra debugging efforts.

The third argument is one about explanation. As is argued in [Warn84], the explanations given by expert systems should not only include *what* the system is doing, but also *why* it is doing a particular action and not another one. In other words: the control knowledge should be an identifiable part of the explanations given by the system. In order to enable the system to include control knowledge explicitly in its explanations, it is important for both the human reader and the automated explanation generator that control knowledge can be syntactically distinguished from domain knowledge. This would not be possible if one and the same language were used for both levels.

These arguments are in direct contradiction with [Haye77], where it is claimed that:

> We need to be able to describe processing strategies in a language at least as rich as that in which we describe the external domains, and, for good engineering, it should be the same language.

Good engineering might lead us to choosing languages at the object-level and the meta-level that have the same *structure*, but the above reasons argue that they should nevertheless be *different* languages.

A further problem associated with the amalgamated approach is the

recursive application of the naming convention. Each ground term in the
meta-level language that is the name of an object-level formula is itself
again an object-level formula (since the two languages are the same), and
thus has some ground term as its name, etc. This introduces the possibility of self-referential sentences, which is necessary for introspection,
or for incompleteness proofs in the manner of Gödel (the self-referential
capability is used in exactly this way in [Bowe82]). However, if we
are not interested in these aspects of meta-level reasoning, this added
complexity is not needed, and we can get away with the much simpler
construction of separate languages.

Thus having narrowed our choice down to bi-lingual meta-level inference system, we still have to discuss the best position on the other
properties of meta-level systems described in the previous section: the
possibility of partial specifications, a declarative versus a procedural
meta-level language, and enforcing strictness and completeness on the
meta-level.

The possibility of writing only partial specifications of the control
strategy of the system is obviously attractive for the development of
a system. We can gradually refine the control strategy of the system,
without overcommitting ourselves at any point, postponing decisions
until we understand enough of the domain. However, a high price needs
to be paid for this possibility, resulting in a severe restriction of the
system's architecture. In order for the system to be able to "fill in the
gaps" of the partial specification of the control regime by the user, it is
necessary that this partial specification is of a particular format, so that
it is possible for the system to identify which parts of the control regime
are underspecified, and need to be filled in with default values. This
restricts the possible range of control regimes that can be formulated by
the user.

The question of a declarative versus a procedural meta-level language
is not very clear. This issue will return again in the next chapter, where
we will describe the meta-level architecture of the Socrates system.

Concerning the issues of strictness and completeness we can say the
following: For reasons discussed before, we would not want to enforce
completeness on a meta-level architecture, since often the whole point
of having a meta-level is to be able to avoid the expensive computation
of certain object-level results. Whether strictness, ie. not allowing the
meta-level to extend the set of results that can be computed by the

meta-level, is a desirable property, is less clear in general, and depends on the purpose for which the architecture will be used.

2.5 Conclusion

In this chapter we have categorised the meta-level systems described in the literature, and have distinguished the following types:

- object-level inference systems

- mixed-level inference systems, which can be divided into

    - reflect-and-act systems
    - crisis-management systems
    - subtask-management systems

- pure meta-level inference systems, which can be divided into

    - mono-lingual systems
    - bi-lingual systems
    - amalgamated systems

Furthermore, a number of secondary properties of meta-level architectures were identified:

- Is the meta-level language declarative or procedural?

- Does the system allow partial specifications of the control regime?

- Does the system enforce strictness and completeness of the control regime?

We have compared these systems, and have argued in favour of bilingual, pure meta-level inference systems. The next chapter will present Socrates, a system built on this basis.

3 The Architecture of Socrates

Rob Corlett   Han Reichgelt
Nick Davies   Frank van Harmelen
Robin Khan

3.1   The abstract architecture of Socrates

This chapter describes the architecture of the Socrates toolkit for building expert systems. We describe the abstract architecture for the toolkit which embodies a combination of logic and meta-level inference. This architecture can be instantiated to create a concrete architecture that is specialised for a particular application. This specialisation process can be seen as a methodology for building expert systems. The three stages of this methodology are discussed in detail (sections 3.2, 3.4 and 3.5), along with descriptions of how the Socrates toolkit supports them. Finally, a number of open problems are discussed (section 3.6).

As argued in many other places in the literature an architecture with a separate object-level and meta-level interpreter can be used to implement a separation of domain and control knowledge (see, among others, [Bund79], [Davi82], [Pere82], [Clan83a], [Clan85], [Gene83], [Ster84], [Silv86], [Welh87]). This architecture is shown in figure 3.1. The two-layer architecture of object-level and meta-level interpreter is extended in Socrates with a third level, the scheduler, to be discussed in section 3.5.3. Each of the three interpreters communicates with the knowledge base in order to store and retrieve logical propositions. As will be described in section 3.2 the knowledge base can be organised into a number of partitions, each of which can be hierarchically organised into subpartitions.

The Socrates architecture distinguishes between front-ends to be used by the *end-user* and the *knowledge engineer*.[1] Knowledge engineers and end-users will need different tools for communication with the system. For example, an end-user, when asking for an explanation, will not want to see the entire proof tree, but rather "edited highlights". A knowledge

---

[1] The end-user is the person who uses the expert system application built with the Socrates toolkit, whereas the knowledge engineer is the person building such an application system.

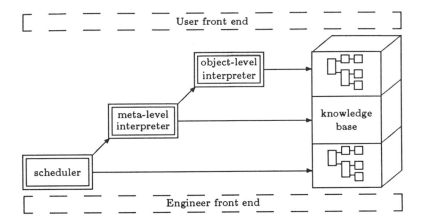

Figure 3.1
Architecture of Socrates

engineer, on the other hand, may want to be able to monitor the reasoning process much more closely and may require the full proof tree. Similarly, a knowledge engineer will need tools for adjusting the behaviour of the interpreters and for editing the knowledge base, whereas an end-user only needs to browse in a read-only manner through the knowledge base. Furthermore, the levels of abstraction at which the system communicates will differ between end-user and knowledge engineer.

This general, application independent architecture needs to be *configured* for a particular expert systems application, given the characteristics of the domain and the task of that application. The use of logic as the underlying framework for the system gives a very specific meaning to the process of configuring the system for a particular application. Rather than having to choose between arbitrary representational schemes and inference methods (as is the case in the hybrid systems), the configuration process now consists of three well defined stages, namely the declaration of a *logical language*, the declaration of a *proof theory* for that logical language, and the declaration of a *proof strategy*. In the remainder of this chapter we will discuss each of these stages in detail, thereby describing the main features of the Socrates system.

3.2   Declaration of the logical representation language

As the first step in the process of configuring a system for a particular application, the knowledge engineer defines the logical language that will be used for representing the domain knowledge. In the context of a knowledge based system, where the logical language is to be used for representational purposes, the *syntactic* declaration of the language has to be augmented with a mechanism for *storage and retrieval*. In this section we discuss the declaration of the language, whereas the next section focusses on the storage and retrieval mechanism.

As the first part of the declaration of the logical representation language, the knowledge engineer has to declare the *vocabulary* of the language. The predicate-symbols, function-symbols and constants that are going to be part of the representation language have to be defined.

Socrates uses *many-sorted logics* of the kind proposed by [Walt84], making use of typed quantification, where the sorts are organised in a hierarchy. Each sort is used to represent a non-empty set of individuals belonging to that sort. In such logics the sort hierarchy is defined by a partial ordering on the set of sorts, corresponding to a lattice structure with the **universal** sort as the maximal and the **empty sort**[2] as the minimal element in the set. This lattice is more general than a tree structure, since it allows sorts to have more than one supersort, thereby increasing the expressiveness of the sort system. The use of many-sorted logics over unsorted logics brings a number of advantages.

First of all, the reformulation of axioms in a many-sorted logic reduces both the number and the complexity of the axioms needed to formalise a given problem. For example, the unsorted expression:

$$\forall x \exists y [human(x) \rightarrow human(y) \ \& \ mother(y, x)]$$

can be rewritten, after the declaration of **human** as a sort, as[3]

$$\forall x{:}human \ \exists y{:}human[mother(y, x)]$$

As another example, the unsorted expression:

---

[2] The empty sort, notation ∅, is the only sort representing an empty set of individuals, and as such does not fulfill any representational role. The reason why sorts must correspond to non-empty sets will be discussed below.

[3] The notation x:t is used to indicate that variable x is of sort t.

$$\forall x[greek(x) \rightarrow human(x)]$$

can be encoded in the sort hierarchy by declaring **greek** $\subset$ **human**, i.e. **greek** is a subsort of the sort **human**. This reduction in number and complexity of axioms not only improves the readability of the knowledge base, but it also causes a significant decrease in the size of the search space for proofs. [Cohn85] (in the context of a resolution based theorem prover), and [Davi87] (in the context of a natural deduction system) show that this reduction can amount to as much as an order of magnitude.

Secondly, the sort hierarchy allows the knowledge engineer to represent what [Clan83b] calls *structural knowledge*, representing the taxonomic hierarchy of the application domain. Structural knowledge consists of the hierarchically organised abstractions that are used to index the domain knowledge. In unsorted logics, this structural knowledge has to be encoded as part of the domain knowledge, where it is no longer separated from other knowledge.

However, a point of caution is in order. It is not always advisable to encode every unary predicate in the language as a sort in the sort hierarchy. In order to satisfy the constraints on the sort hierarchy discussed below (sorts must be unique, non-empty and closed under intersection), the encoding of a sentence such as

$$\forall x[person(x) \rightarrow boy(x) \ \lor \ dog\_owner(x)]$$

(every person is a boy or a dog owner)

forces the introduction of a great number of additional sorts such as **non_dog_owning_boys**, **dog_owning_non_boys**, etc. This interaction occurs because the sorts **boy** and **dog_owner** do not have a subset-relation (as opposed to the example above, where **greek** $\subset$ **human**). Furthermore, if a unary predicate can represent an empty set then it cannot be represented as a sort.

In sorted logics, the unification algorithm has to take the sort hierarchy into account. The rules for unification in a sorted logic are:

- a constant $c_1{:}t_1$ unifies with a constant $c_2{:}t_2$ if $c_1 = c_2$ and $t_1 = t_2$

- a variable $x{:}t_1$ unifies with a constant $c{:}t_2$ if $t_2 \subset t_1$

- a variable $x{:}t_1$ unifies with a variable $y{:}t_2$ if $t_1 \cap t_2 \neq \emptyset$

The third rule results in restricting the sorts of both variables to $t_3 = t_1 \cap t_2$. In order to guarantee that t_3 can be computed and is itself a legal sort, it is necessary that the system knows the values of all pairwise intersections of all sorts, and that sort-intersection is closed over sorts. In other words, if T is the set of all sorts (including $\emptyset$), then

$$\forall t_1 \forall t_2 [t_1 \in T \ \& \ t_2 \in T \rightarrow t_1 \cap t_2 \in T]$$

Furthermore, in order to guarantee that t_3 is uniquely defined, we require that no two sorts are used to represent the same set of individuals. If this were allowed, the unification algorithm would no longer be able to return a unique most general unifier.

The knowledge engineer declares the sorts of the logic by declaring first the set of sorts, and then the hierarchy of sorts using set-theoretic primitives such as equality, subset, superset, intersection, union, set-difference, complementation and disjointness. After this has been done, the system automatically checks whether the sort hierarchy satisfies the following criteria:

- No two sorts are equal

- No sort except $\emptyset$ is empty

- Intersection is closed over sorts

If any of these constraints is violated, or if the constraints are not satisfied by the current declarations (because the knowledge engineer has underspecified the sort hierarchy), the system asks the knowledge engineer for different or additional declarations.

The sorts of the constants of the logical language can be declared in two ways. The simplest way is by simply enumerating the constants of a particular sort (*extensional* definition of types). However, for some sorts, enumeration is not feasible, either because the set of constants of that sort is not known in advance, or because this set is too large, or indeed infinite. For these cases it is possible to define constants by declaring a *recognition procedure* for the sort. Every object for which the recognition procedure succeeds will be assumed to be a constant of that particular sort (*intensional* definition of types). The definitions of the recognition procedures must be supplied in the implementation language of the system. This allows an interface between the logical

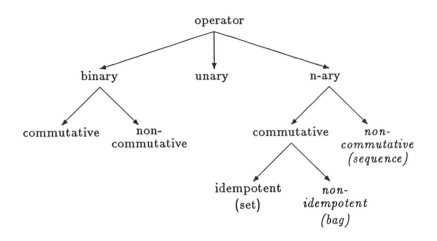

Figure 3.2
Logical connectives

representation language and the computational data types supplied by the implementation language of the system. An example of a sort that can be declared via this mechanism is the sort of all **integers**, or as a second example, for any given sort T, the sort T^* consisting of all lists of elements of sort T.

As part of declaring the vocabulary of the logical representation language, it is possible to exploit what [Weyh80] calls *semantic attachment*. This is done by declaring a special class of predicates called *evaluable predicates*. When one of these predicates is encountered in a proof, it is possible (depending on the control decisions made by the meta-level interpreter to be discussed in section 3.5) to execute a procedure defined for this predicate to determine its truth value and possibly provide bindings for any variables. These predicates provide an interface between the logical representation language and the computational environment of the system, enabling external systems interaction, input/output for interacting with the end-user, and the access of the facilities provided by the implementation language of the system.

At this stage the representation language consists only of a sort hierarchy and a set of predicates, constants and functions. We still need to extend our language with *logical connectives* such as implication, disjunction, etc, and possibly non-standard operators[4] such as modal and temporal operators. As part of the declaration of these logical connectives the knowledge engineer can declare their properties with respect to commutativity and associativity. These declarations will be used to configure a unifier for the defined logical language (see the section on the declaration of the proof theory for a more detailed discussion of this subject).

Socrates distinguishes between different kinds of logical connectives as shown in figure 3.2. *Unary* connectives take one argument. *Binary* connectives take two arguments, and can be divided on the basis of their commutativity. Implication ($\rightarrow$) is an example of a *non-commutative binary* connective, whereas equivalence ($\leftrightarrow$) is an example of a *commutative binary* connective. If connectives are both commutative and associative (such as for instance conjunction), they are treated as so-called *set*-connectives. This amounts to them taking any number of arguments in any order. Furthermore, set connectives are assumed to be idempotent: all multiple occurrences of an argument can be reduced to only one occurrence.

The hierarchy from figure 3.2 also shows the other possible connectives which are not currently implemented in Socrates: *bag* operators which are associative and commutative but not idempotent (i.e. the order of arguments does not matter, but multiple occurrences of an argument cannot be reduced), and *sequence* operators, where the order of the arguments is significant, and multiple occurrences cannot be reduced.

3.3   The storage and retrieval mechanism

Now that the vocabulary of the logical language is complete, we need to declare a storage and retrieval mechanism for expressions in the language. This is what is typically called the "knowledge base" of the system. The knowledge base of Socrates is not a flat space of assertions in the declared logical language, but can be divided into a number of *partitions*. Each of these partitions can have a separate logical language associated with it (but see further down for a restriction on this). This facility serves a number of different purposes.

First of all, it allows the knowledge engineer to use mixed language

---

[4]We use the terms logical connective and logical operator synonymously.

representations of the domain. Different types of knowledge or different aspects of the domain can be represented in separate logical languages. A particular example of this will be described in section 3.5, where we discuss the control knowledge of the system. This meta-level knowledge is expressed in a different language from the object-level knowledge. Nevertheless, it can be stored in the same knowledge base, using the partitioning mechanism to separate the two.

Secondly, the partition hierarchy can be used to reduce the search that needs to be done both by the retrieval mechanism and by the inference machinery. In many problem solving situations, only a subset of all the available knowledge is applicable at any one time to a given problem. Partitioning allows useful subsets to be applied while others are ignored. In this way, Socrates can be used to model a blackboard architecture, with each of the partitions simulating the contents of a knowledge source.

An important aspect of the partitions in the knowledge base is that they can be recursively divided into subpartitions, and that these subpartitions are organised hierarchically. Partitions lower down in this hierarchy inherit all the propositions from partitions higher up in the hierarchy, but not vice versa. A particular example of this could be the use of a single working memory for a number of different subsets of domain knowledge, where the working memory would be represented in the top node, and the subsets of domain knowledge represented in subpartitions. The results of reasoning done within one subpartition can in this way be communicated to the other partitions via the working memory. Again, this feature can also be used in the modelling of a blackboard system in Socrates, since the blackboard needs to be visible from all knowledge sources, but not vice versa. Since partitions can be created dynamically at runtime, another application for the partition hierarchy in the knowledge base is hypothetical reasoning, sometimes known as "what-if" reasoning. Each time a new hypothesis is generated, a new subpartition can be created containing this hypothesis, and inheriting all existing propositions from higher partitions.

The inheritance mechanism puts restraints on the logical languages that can be used within subpartitions. Because subpartitions inherit propositions from superpartitions, all the partitions in a partition hierarchy must be associated with the same logical representation language. (Strictly speaking, it is only necessary that the language of a subpartition is an extension of the language of its superpartition, but Socrates does not support this type of language inheritance). Thus, the knowledge base can be seen as a set of trees of partitions. Within each tree, all partitions must have the same language, but each separate tree can be associated with a different language.

A final facility supported by the knowledge base is the annotation of propositions. Each proposition can be annotated with arbitrary information using a slot-value mechanism. This allows us to associate extra-logical information with propositions. This information can be used for a wide range of purposes, of which a few examples are: natural language descriptions to be used in explanations, control information to be used by the meta-level interpreter, certainty values, etc. This slot-value mechanism could be used to model a truth-maintenance system in Socrates, by storing each derived proposition in the knowledge base together with annotations that contain the premises that were used in its derivation.

Socrates uses a discrimination net technique for retrieval of propositions [Char80]. The optimal criteria that the net should use for discrimination depend on the particular application, and Socrates therefore allows the knowledge engineer to adjust these discrimination criteria to suit the particular ways in which the knowledge base retrieval mechanism will be used. For example, if the main control regime for a particular application is some form of backward chaining, then propositions of the form *left-hand-side* $\rightarrow$ *right-hand-side* will be retrieved from the knowledge base on the basis of the patterns in the *right-hand-side* argument. This implies that the discrimination net should first discriminate implications on the basis of their consequent, rather than their antecedent. As a second example we note that many predicates use a certain number of their arguments as "inputs", while others are used as "output" arguments. A predicate such as `suffers-from(patient, disease)` will typically be used to associate a given `patient` with a `disease`, rather than to try and find all `patients` suffering from a given `disease`. This particular use of arguments indicates that the discrimination net should use the first argument as the main discrimination criterion, rather than the second argument. Because these properties are specific to a particular application, they can only be adjusted by the knowledge engineer who configures the system, rather then being hardwired into the retrieval mechanism of the knowledge base.

In this section and the previous one we have seen that on the basis of all the declarations by the knowledge engineer discussed so far, Socrates configures the following language dependent modules:

- a parser for the logical language that accepts well-formed formulas and converts them to the internal data structures used by the system;

- a unifier, capable of performing a unification algorithm on the well-formed formulas of the logical language, taking into account both the sort hierarchy and the commutativity and associativity of the logical connectives;

- a discrimination net that supports efficient retrieval of propositions from the knowledge base.

3.4   Declaration of the proof theory

The declaration of a logical language together with a storage and retrieval mechanism allows us to represent knowledge, but in order to manipulate this knowledge to derive new conclusions we need rules that tell us what the legal derivations will be. Since we have chosen logic as the representation language for the system, we are committed to logical deduction as the inference process. We therefore need to define a proof theory, i.e. a set of inference rules[5] that tell us how propositions can be manipulated in order to perform a proof. In Socrates we follow [Bled77] in using the natural deduction style of performing proofs rather than for instance resolution. Although natural deduction systems use a relatively large number of inference rules (as opposed to the single inference rule of resolution based systems), and thereby create a potential control problem, a number of reasons can be given in favour of natural deduction. The inference rules of a natural deduction system are more intuitively meaningful than for instance the resolution rule. Furthermore, no normal forms are required for the formulas used in a proof. As a result, the proofs performed by a natural deduction system are easier to follow for a human reader, thereby improving the possibilities for explanation

---

[5]We use the term inference rule in the logician's sense: An inference rule is a rule that describes how true formulas can be inferred from other true formulas, and is of the form $f_1 \ldots f_n \vdash g$, where g is inferred from $f_1 \ldots f_n$. The term inference rule is often incorrectly used to denote formulas of the form $f \rightarrow g$ (i.e. material implications).

facilities. The naturalness of the proof development also makes it easier to identify heuristics to control the problem solving process, in the
manner discussed in section 3.5.

When expressing inference rules, the knowledge engineer can make
use of extra-logical variables that range over well-formed formulas from
the object-level representation language. For instance the rules

$$P, \; P \rightarrow Q \vdash Q$$
$$P \vdash P \vee Q$$

represent the rules for Modus Ponens and Or Introduction. It is important to stress that these inference rules can be used in both a forward
and a backward direction. For instance Modus Ponens can be used to
determine that P and $P \rightarrow Q$ have to be proved in order to prove Q
(backward use), or the rule can be used to infer that Q is true when we
know that both P and $P \rightarrow Q$ are true. Furthermore, because of the associativity and commutativity of some of the logical connectives, a single
inference rule can often be applied in more than one way. For instance,
if disjunction ($\vee$) has been declared as a *set-operator*, Or Introduction
can be applied backward to $(f \vee g)$ in two different ways, binding P to
either f or g, thereby generating either f or g as a subgoal for proving
$(f \vee g)$. However, which of these possible applications of an inference
rule should be used is a control decision, and is therefore a meta-level
issue, which is not decided as part of the proof theory.

Not all the inference rules that the system uses are declared as part
of the proof strategy. First of all, there is a set of inference rules that
tell the system how to deal with typed quantification. These rules:

- $\forall x{:}t_1 \; P[x] \vdash P[c{:}t_2]$ for an arbitrary constant c and all sorts t_1 and
  t_2 with $t_1 \supseteq t_2 \supset \emptyset$

- $P[c{:}t_1] \vdash \exists x{:}t_2 \; P[x]$ for an arbitrary constant c, and all sorts t_1
  and t_2 with $t_2 \supseteq t_1 \supset \emptyset$[6]

- $\exists x{:}t_1 \forall y{:}t_2 \; P[x, y] \vdash \forall y{:}t_2 \exists x{:}t_1 \; P[x, y]$ for all sorts t_1 and t_2

are taken to be of universal validity (that is: across different application areas of the system), and are therefore hardwired into the retrieval
mechanism. A second set of rules that is part of the retrieval mechanism

---

[6]It is exactly because of this rule that in section 3.2 we required all sorts except
$\emptyset$ to be non-empty.

in the knowledge base rather than the proof theory are the rules that
deal with the commutativity and associativity of certain logical connectives. For any operator φ that has been declared as *binary-commutative*,
the inference rule

$$P \varphi Q \vdash Q \varphi P$$

is hardwired into the knowledge base retrieval mechanism, as are, for
every *set-operator*, the additional rules

$$P \vdash P \varphi P$$
$$(P \varphi (Q \varphi R)) \vdash ((P \varphi Q) \varphi R)$$

By taking all these rules out of the explicit declaration of the proof strategy and transferring them to the retrieval mechanism of the knowledge
base, we have given a limited deductive capability to the knowledge
base. In order to decide which inference rules should be included in the
knowledge base retrieval mechanism, we used the following heuristics:

No chaining restriction: As argued in [Fris87], retrieval is intuitively
viewed more as a matching operation than a deductive one. Therefore, only inference rules are included in the knowledge base that
satisfy his no chaining restriction: a query is retrievable only if it
is deducible from a single knowledge base fact.

Control restriction: Only those inference rules should be included in
the knowledge base which would otherwise greatly increase the
control problem, either because they have to be applied very frequently, or because they greatly increase the branching rate of the
proof space, or because they are recursive in nature.

Explanation restriction: Since the deduction steps made by the retrieval mechanism do not appear explicitly in the inference steps of
the system made under the guidance of the meta-level interpreter,
they cannot be included in any explanation given by the system
of its inferential behaviour. Therefore, only those inference rules
must be included in the retrieval mechanism that can safely be
omitted from explanations.

The retrieval mechanism comprises two sequential stages, a syntactic
pattern matcher and a *unifier*. Syntactic pattern matching is effected using the discrimination net technique mentioned above. Given a formula

as a query to the knowledge base, this process will retrieve all formulas with the same pattern of operators and predicates, subject to the commutativity and associativity rules as declared for the particular language. This means that unification will be attempted only on patterns that have a strong possibility of succeeding.

The patterns that can be specified as input to the syntactic pattern matching phase are allowed to contain *meta-logical (propositional) variables* that can match with formulas of the logical representation language rather than with terms. These meta-logical variables will get bound to the corresponding components of the matching expression, using pattern matching under the inference rules governing commutativity and associativity. For example, the pattern *(& f ?P)* will match with a formula like *(& g f)*, binding *?P* with *g* after applying commutativity. To facilitate the retrieval of expressions containing set-operators, a special version of these meta-logical variables is available, the so-called *segment variables*. These segment variables do not match with formulas, but with lists of logical formulas. For example, a formula like *(& f g h)* will match with a pattern like *(& g ?P^segment)*, binding *?P* with the list *(f h)*. Because of the meta-logical variables, the patterns sent to the knowledge base for retrieval are actually schemata, representing whole families of queries rather than just a single query.

In the second phase of the retrieval process the unifier will construct bindings of the logical variables occurring in the query. This is necessary since in the context of expert systems we are interested in performing constructive proofs, and we therefore need the values for the existentially quantified variables in the query for which the query succeeds. In other words, for a query such as $\exists x{:}t_1 \ p(x)$, we want not only a yes/no response, but also the values of x which can be deduced from the contents of the knowledge base. Notice that these bindings might only consist of restrictions on the sort of x, rather than of bindings of x to terms. The sorted unification algorithm might tell us that the query succeeds for all values of x of a certain sort t_2, with $t_2 \subset t_1$. In this way, taxonomic reasoning is performed at retrieval time.

There are three potential problems with using unification. The first problem is that to use unification requires that the formulas are in skolemised form. This might at first sight seem to restrict Socrates to only those languages in which such a skolemised form exists, thereby excluding useful logical languages such as many of the modal languages.

However, [Reic87] describes how this restriction can be lifted by dealing
with the reified version of such languages.[7]

The second problem is in the handling of associativity and commutativity.   As soon as a function symbol is allowed to be declared as
associative and not commutative, the matching operation can result in
an infinite set of most general unifiers [Siek86]. For this reason, we restrict associativity and commutativity declarations to the connectives of
the logical languages. This ensures that only a finite set of most general
unifiers exists. The reason for this is that the only variables that can
match with the arguments of a logical connective are the meta-logical
variables in the query pattern, and these meta-logical variables can only
occur in the query pattern (and not in the propositions in the knowledge base). Thus, as far as the logical connectives are concerned, the
retrieval process is a one way matching process for meta-logical variables,
and matching (rather than unification) does not suffer from the problem
of an infinite set of matches under associativity and non-commutativity.

The third problem concerns quantification and the unification algorithm. In order to be able to use unification for retrieving propositions
from a knowledge base, one has to skolemise the knowledge base assertions and the query. However, whereas knowledge base assertions can
be skolemised in the normal way, queries have to be interpreted as being implicitly negated. Because skolemisation can only take place after
the formula has been transformed into prenex normal form, this means
that in queries existentially quantified variables become free variables,
while universally quantified variables become skolem constants. As a
consequence, existentially quantified variables in the query and universally quantified variables in the assertion are represented in the same
way, as are universally quantified variables in the query and existentially quantified variables in the assertion. But, if a variable is returned
in the unifier, it is important to know whether it should be translated
back into an existential or a universal variable (since the skolemisation
is only done internally for the retrieval process, invisible to the other
parts of the architecture). This problem is discussed in [Shep84] with
regard to the same problem in Prolog. Our solution to this problem is

---

[7]Reified logics are logics in which what would normally be propositions appear
as terms. The process of reification can be used to represent the semantics of non-
standard first order logics (such as modal logics) in the language of standard first
order logic. This technique can then be used to simulate deductions in the non-
standard logic within the standard logic. See also chapter 7.

to mark each variable, before skolemisation, with its source (query or knowledge base proposition). It is thus possible to translate variables returned in the unifier back to the correct quantifier.

A final point to be made about the declaration of the proof theory concerns the soundness and completeness of the set of inference rules. In order to guarantee soundness of the proof theory, the knowledge engineer should not be allowed to declare arbitrary inference rules, but only to select inference rules from a predefined (and sound) set.[8] This selection process will of course affect the completeness of the system. However, the loss of completeness in the context of expert systems is not serious, since one does not want to infer *all* facts that follow from the available knowledge, but only those facts that one is interested in.

3.5   Declaration of the proof strategy

At this point, the knowledge engineer has declared both a logical language and a corresponding proof theory. From a purely logical point of view, no further declarations are necessary. The combination of language and proof theory determines all the possible inferences that the system can make. However, in order to create a practical computer system, we have to take one more step. Proving statements in any non-trivial logical language is a search intensive problem. The logical language and proof theory together define a search space for the proof process. What remains to be done is the specification of the strategy that the system should use to traverse this space while searching for a proof. For this task, Socrates provides a declarative language for representing such a control strategy. This language is described in section 3.5.1.

Because such a declarative language has certain disadvantages associated with it, a more procedural language has also been investigated, as described in section 3.5.2.

3.5.1   Declarative representation

Socrates allows the knowledge engineer to explicitly specify a control strategy. This control strategy provides the system with a description of its desired behaviour, and is interpreted at run time by the meta-level

---

[8]Such a selection procedure has not been provided in the current implementation of Socrates.

interpreter. As a result, the meta-level interpreter executes this control strategy, and thereby guides the search through the space of all possible proofs. The language that is used to express the control strategy is a many sorted version of Horn Clause Logic. This language, although also a logical representation language, should be distinguished from the logical languages used to represent the domain knowledge. Unlike the object-level languages, the language used at the meta-level has a fixed set of logical connectives, namely exactly those connectives needed in Horn Clause Logic: conjunction, implication and negation, plus disjunction. All these connectives are declared as non-commutative, non-associative. This is done because the procedural interpretation (i.e. the way in which the meta-level interpreter executes expressions of the language) is also fixed. The procedural interpretation of the language is the standard interpretation for Horn Clauses, the standard depth-first proof procedure as found in Prolog systems. The reason why Socrates does not allow the knowledge engineer to change the control regime of the meta-level interpreter (which would amount to providing a meta-meta-level interpreter[9]) follows from the analysis of [Reic85] and [Reic86]. As indicated there, typical expert system tasks such as diagnosis, planning, monitoring etc. are related to particular control regimes. The meta-level controls the behaviour of the object-level interpreter according to the expert system task. The variation in control is achieved by changing the meta-level knowledge base. There is no need to change the interpreter which always has the same task, namely controlling the behaviour of the object-level interpreter by using the data in the meta-level knowledge base.

The parts of the meta-level language that are still subject to declarations made by the knowledge engineer are therefore the set of constants, predicates and function symbols, the sort hierarchy, and the set of *evaluable predicates*. Figure 3.3 shows an example of a description of a local-best-first non-exhaustive backward chaining control strategy. For this control strategy a sort hierarchy was defined as shown in figure 3.4. In this example, clause [1] states that in order to prove a non-compound expression F on the basis of the contents of knowledge base partition P giving a substitution S as a result, the system should either try to see if

---

[9]The notion of a meta-meta-level interpreter should not be confused with the scheduler, as discussed in section 3.5.3: the relation between meta-level interpreter and scheduler is very different from the relation between object-level and meta-level interpreter.

[1] (∀F:non-evaluable-formula, P:partition, S:substitution,
      Next:non-empty-list-of-formulas,
      SomeNext:non-empty-list-of-formulas)
     [kb-lookup(F, P, S)
        ∨ (object-level-interpreter(F, P, backward, Next) &
            select-inferences(Next, SomeNext) &
            infer(SomeNext, P, S))
        ∨ ask-user(F, P, S)
      → proof(F, P, S)
     ]

[2] (∀Inferences:non-empty-list-of-formulas, P:partition,
      S:substitution, Best:formula, Rest:list-of-formulas)
     [best(Inferences, Best, Rest) &
     (proof(Best, P, S)
        ∨ infer(Rest, P, S))
      → infer(Inferences, P, S)
     ]

[3] (∀List:non-empty-list-of-formulas, Best:formula,
      Rest:list-of-formulas)
     [highest-certainty-value(List, Best, Rest)
      → best(List, Best, Rest)
     ]

[4] (∀F:compound-formula, P:partition, S:substitution,
      Lhs:formula, Rhs:formula, LhsSubst:substitution,
      RhsSubst:substitution)
     [split-compound-expression(F, Lhs, Rhs) &
     proof(Lhs, P, LhsSubst) &
     proof(Rhs, P, RhsSubst) &
     combine(LhsSubst, RhsSubst, S)
      → proof(F, P, S)
     ]

[5] ∀F:evaluable-formula, P:partition, S:substitution,
     [evaluate(F, P, S) → proof(F, P, S)
     ]

Figure 3.3
Declarative specification of control in Socrates

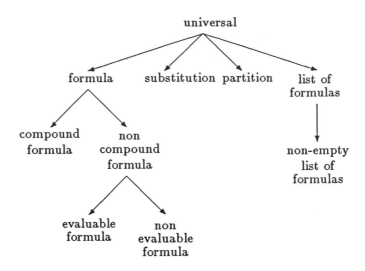

Figure 3.4
Sort hierarchy for the meta-level interpreter

the formula is a known fact in the knowledge base, or the system should try to infer the formula on its own, or it should ask the end-user. Trying to infer the formula means generating all possible inferences, selecting some of these possible inferences, and continuing with clause [2]. That clause chooses the best of all selected possible steps, and tries to continue the proof with this selection. If this succeeds, the proof terminates (i.e. non-exhaustive), if this fails, the proof continues with the next best step. Clause [3] states the criterion used in the best-first search, while clause [4] describes what needs to be done in order to prove a compound expression: prove both left- and right-hand sides of the compound expression, and combine the results. Clause [5] states that all evaluable predicates encountered in a proof should be evaluated without any further control scheduling.

This example shows how the different aspects of this strategy can be changed if needed for a particular application. For example, the order of the disjuncts in clause [1] might be changed to ask the end-user for solutions before the system tries a proof itself, or the ask-user disjunct might be deleted altogether. The criterion used for the best-first scheduling could be changed, or a new decision for scheduling the order in which conjuncts are proved in clause [4] could be introduced. More thorough changes to the strategy could also be made, but they would amount to writing a completely new proof strategy rather than changing the one shown in this example.

Of the evaluable predicates mentioned in figure 3.3 (such as `ask-user`, `kb-lookup`, `combine`), the predicate `object-level-interpreter` is the most important one. This predicate encapsulates the interface between the meta-level interpreter executing the control strategy, and the object-level interpreter handling the logical representation language and the corresponding proof theory. The input of this predicate is an object-level formula F, the name of a knowledge base partition P and a direction in which to apply inference rules (either `forward` or `backward`), and returns as output the result of applying all inference rules specified as part of the proof theory for partition P to the input formula F in the indicated direction. In terms of the proof search space, this amounts to generating all nodes that are accessible from the current node as represented by F. Thus, the predicate `object-level-interpreter` allows the meta-level interpreter to access an explicit representation of the object-level search space, and to choose which branches of the object-level proof tree will be expanded on the basis of the control regime provided by the knowledge engineer.

The two layered architecture of Socrates reflects the separation between the declarative aspects of the system (the logical language and the proof theory) on the one hand, and the procedural aspects of the system (the proof strategy) on the other. This separation corresponds closely to Kowalski's slogan [Kowa79]

$$\text{algorithm} = \text{logic} + \text{control}$$

The object-level (language + proof theory) has a purely declarative reading, and is provided with its procedural interpretation by the declaration of the control strategy at the meta-level.

Unlike many logic-based meta-level architectures proposed in the literature, (such as [Silv86], or the Prolog system described in [Gall82]), Socrates completely separates the languages used at the object-level from the language used at the meta-level. Even when the object-level representation language happened to be defined as sorted Horn Clause Logic, the two languages would still be syntactically separate. The meta-level

language and the object-level languages are connected through a *naming
relation*. The meta-level language contains names for all object-level expressions. In Socrates, the name of an object-level sentence corresponds
to a constant in the meta-level language. Other meta-level constants
are used to denote bindings for object-level variables. If required, meta-
level expressions could range over any of the extra-logical properties of
object-level expressions such as truth values, certainty factors, justifications, etc. In this way, Socrates could for instance be configured to
deal with certainty values by specifying as part of the control strategy
how certainty values should be used in a proof. This corresponds to
the approach suggested in [Shap83], with the important difference that
Socrates makes a correct distinction between meta-level and object-level
languages, whereas Shapiro mixes the two, and uses Prolog for both.
The reasons why it is important to separate the meta-level language
from the object-level language were discussed in chapter 2.

3.5.2 Procedural representation

The approach to the specification of a proof strategy described in section
3.5.1 is based on the use of a declarative meta-level language. Although
the declarative style of control of reasoning has its attractions there
are also disadvantages. Two problems in particular are caused by the
use of a declarative language, and in an attempt to overcome these
problems, Socrates provides an alternative, more procedural language
for specifying control regimes. The two problems are the following.

First of all, the extra layer of interpretation that is incurred by the
explicit meta-level interpreter is expensive because of the declarative
nature of the meta-level language. A procedural meta-level language
would be much closer to the underlying implementation language and
machine architecture, and therefore cheaper to execute.

Secondly, much of the knowledge expressed in the meta-level language
is procedural, rather than declarative. For example, one often wishes to
apply knowledge of the form "try method-1 before method-2" or "in
order to achieve goal-1, achieve subgoal-1 to subgoal-n". In the declarative meta-level language this type of procedural knowledge has to be
expressed by either relying on the hardwired control regime for the meta-
level interpreter, or by using semantic attachment. Neither of these ways
of expressing procedural knowledge is very desirable, since they encode
knowledge implicitly rather than represent it explicitly. A more pro-

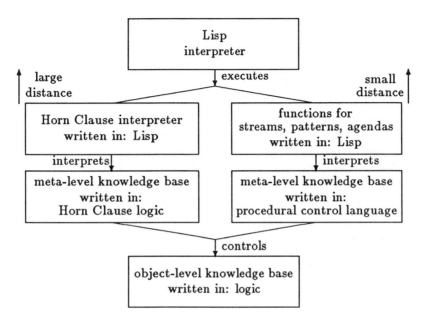

Figure 3.5
Levels of implementation for meta-level control

cedural language provides a more natural medium for expressing the procedural control knowledge.

Our approach to procedural control is therefore to provide a *meta-level programming language* rather in the vein of ML [Gord79] in its relationship to LCF. That is, we provide high level primitives that make the writing of control regimes easier. It is important to note that a procedural control language is only an alternative way of implementing the separation of control knowledge from object-level knowledge. The procedural approach still clearly separates control knowledge from object-level knowledge. The difference is that rather than putting the control knowledge into a declarative knowledge base with its own interpreter, we propose implementing a special purpose meta-level interpreter that incorporates the control knowledge. The three stage process of building systems is retained. One particular point to note is that we retain the explicit declaration of inference rules and provide primitives to apply inference rules. The procedural meta-level language consists

of the implementation language of the system (CommonLisp), extended
with primitives implementing standard AI techniques that have been
found useful in writing interpreters. Figure 3.5 shows how the levels of
implementation for the declarative control regime as described in section
3.5.1 are preserved in the more procedural approach.

Central to the system is the use of lazy evaluation. The procedural
meta-level language provides facilities for the manipulation of lazily evaluated lists (also called streams — see [Abel85, chapter 3] for a detailed
discussion), for example for creating, accessing, mapping and filtering
such lists. This forms the basis of a backtracking mechanism, as well as
allowing some degree of coroutining in control regimes. A good example of the use of lazy evaluation is in a "generate and test" algorithm,
where potential solutions are generated lazily, and a particular solution
is tested before the next one is generated.

Agenda based reasoning is a powerful control technique in AI and the
procedural meta-level language includes an agenda facility, based on the
use of demons for inserting items onto agendas, selecting the next item
to be processed, etc. This technique allows the knowledge engineer to
experiment with several different control strategies often only needing
to change the way the demons behave without changing the rest of the
control regime code. A good example is changing between breadth-
first, depth-first and best-first control strategies, since only the agenda-
selection demon has to be changed each time (LIFO for breadth-first,
FIFO for depth-first, and random-access for best-first).

One often wants to examine the structure of object-level expressions
in order to make a control decision. The procedural meta-level language includes a pattern matcher which provides the basis of pattern
directed invocation of proof methods. This pattern matcher is different
from the unification-based pattern matching performed by the declarative meta-level language, since it does not treat object-level expressions
as constants, but can examine their structure.

It is important to realise that in this procedural approach it is still the
case that the only inference rules are those declared explicitly during the
declaration of the proof theory, as described in section 3.4. Language
primitives are provided to apply the declared inference rules.

Figure 3.6 shows an example of a control regime formulated in the
procedural meta-level language. This code is the procedural equivalent
of the declarative prover given in figure 3.3. The main function is called

```
(defun proof (Goals Part Subst &aux NewGoals NewSubst)
 (if Goals
     (foreach (NewGoals . NewSubst)
       in (or (any-of (order-infs (evaluate (first Goals)
                            :partition Part :subst Subst))
                      (order-infs (lookup (first Goals)
                            :partition Part :subst Subst))
                      (select-infs
                        (gen-backw-infs (first Goals)
                            :partition Part :subst Subst)))
                      (ask-user (first Goals)
                            :partition Part :subst Subst))
         generate-each (proof (append NewGoals (cdr Goals))
                            Part NewSubst))
     (list Subst)))
```

Figure 3.6
Procedural specification of control in Socrates

proof and performs the same function as the predicate of that name.
Being stream-based, **proof** returns a stream of substitutions that prove
the goals in the GoalList argument. Thus if the GoalList is empty
there is one such proof, given by the Subst argument. If the GoalList
is not empty then the inference rules are applied to the first goal in
GoalList. The **any-of** macro is a way of lazily combining streams. Thus,
in this example, we generate all the possible inferences using **evaluate**
(and put them in a preferred order), then all the possible inferences using
lookup (again in preferred order), followed, finally, by a selection of the
possible inferences generated using all the inference rules. If and only
if no possible inferences are generated by this procedure then **ask-user**
is applied to obtain possible inferences. Each inference rule application
generates three things: a set of new goals to be proved in order to
prove the goal (bound to the variable NewGoals); a new substitution,
bound to the variable NewSubst; a justification which merely describes
which inference rule has been applied and is effectively ignored by this
prover. The **foreach** macro itself generates a stream of answers. Thus,
if at some later stage in the proof there is a need to backtrack the next
inferences will be generated only then. Note that, unlike the declarative

prover which generates only the first proof, the procedure **proof** returns a stream of proofs and thus generates the set of all proofs (lazily).

It was noted at the beginning of this section that much control knowledge seems very procedural in nature (such as the execution of a sequence of goals). However, sometimes control knowledge is declarative in nature (for instance a set of criteria used in the ordering of conjuncts). The architecture of Socrates is such that even with procedural control it is still possible to invoke a declarative meta-level interpreter that is implemented using the techniques described in section 3.5.1.

3.5.3   The scheduler

A third level in the architecture of Socrates as shown in figure 3.1 is the *scheduler*; this level is not actually implemented in the current Socrates architecture. The main notion that is treated at this level is that of a *subtask*. As shown in [Reic86], many expert systems perform not just one simple task, but a composite one that can be thought of as consisting of a number of elementary tasks (MYCIN, R1 and VM are among the systems discussed in that paper). It is unlikely that one appropriate control regime can be found that would be suitable for these composite tasks. Rather, the composite task should be split up into its constituent subtasks, and a proper control regime can then be chosen for each of the subtasks.

The subtasks that would be the end results of this decomposition process are the kind of prototypical tasks proposed in [Reic86], [Chan87] and [Wiel86] like classification, monitoring, simulation, design, etc. The scheduling level of the Socrates architecture is meant to deal with this subdivision of the major task into prototypical subtasks. Each of these prototypical subtasks can than be solved using the appropriate meta-level control strategy. (By using the knowledge base partition mechanism, it is possible to equip a Socrates configuration with more than one control strategy). For engineering purposes it would be easiest to equip the scheduling level with a language similar to (but again syntactically separate from) the language used to describe the control strategy at the meta-level. However, early experience indicates that the type of knowledge to be expressed at the scheduling level is of a very procedural nature (even more so than the knowledge expressed at the meta-level), and therefore a language with more conventional procedural primitives such as sequences, conditionals, loops and subroutines might be more appropriate.

It is important to stress that the relation between scheduler and meta-level interpreter is not the same as the relation between meta-level interpreter and object-level interpreter. As discussed above, the meta-level interpreter controls the execution of the object-level interpreter, but its control regime in turn is fixed. Thus, the scheduler is not a meta-meta-interpreter, since it does not control the execution of the meta-level interpreter. Rather, the scheduler controls *which* meta-level interpreter will be used to control the object-level interpreter (or more precisely, which meta-level theory will be used by the meta-level interpreter to control the object-level interpreter). Thus, the scheduler controls the usage of individual meta-level theories, but not the way these theories are executed. The relation between the scheduler and the meta-level interpreter is aptly characterised by the category of subtask-management systems, described in chapter 2, section 2.2.2, whereas the relation between meta-level and object-level interpreter is that of a pure meta-level inference system (section 2.2.3).

3.6   Open problems

Of the three stages of the configuration process, the third one (declaring a proof strategy) is by far the most problematic. An important open question here is the choice of a good language for specifying such a control strategy. As described above, the system primarily uses a declarative logical language to do this, but a procedural language has also been investigated. Apart from the type of language used at the meta-level, a related problem is the required vocabulary of such a language. At the moment, the vocabulary of the system is specified by the knowledge engineer, and although this is to a certain extent inevitable, since part of the vocabulary will be application-specific, one would hope that at least a central core vocabulary can be distinguished that can be preprogrammed into the system. The example of a control regime discussed above suggests predicates to do with manipulating substitutions and formulas and with generating the object-level search space, but a more extensive and more exactly defined vocabulary is needed in order to alleviate the task of the knowledge engineer.

A second problem associated with the explicit meta-level interpreter

is that of meta-level overhead. Although the flexibility in defining the
appropriate control strategy at the meta-level can considerably reduce
the object-level search space, the price we have to pay for this is the fact
that the object-level inference process is completely simulated by the
meta-level interpreter. This is obviously much more expensive than an
object-level interpreter that has the appropriate control strategy hardwired into it. This problem could be solved by taking the explicit formulation of a control regime, and compiling it into an interpreter that has
the particular control regime hardwired into it. This compilation process (whose first stages could be similar to that described in [Altm87])
has been simulated in Socrates by hand coding a number of hardwired
control strategies. Experience with these hardwired strategies in both
the DOCS system and in solving Schubert's Steamroller (both described
in chapter 4) indicates that the meta-level overhead can indeed be reduced to an acceptably small amount. This problem is the subject of
ongoing research [Harm87].

A further problem with the system in general and with the meta-level
interpreter in particular is the issue of soundness. As already discussed in
section 3.4, the current system allows the knowledge engineer to declare
arbitrary sets of inference rules for the propositional part of the object-
level logic (the quantificational part of the proof theory is hardwired in
the knowledge base retrieval mechanism). This enables the knowledge
engineer to declare potentially unsound sets of inference rules, an obviously undesirable situation. As described in section 3.4, it is possible
to the restrict the declaration of the proof theory to a process of selection of subsets from sets of sound inference rules, thereby making it
impossible to introduce unsoundness in the proof theory. However, this
approach breaks down when the knowledge engineer introduces new logical connectives that are not included in the library of predefined sets
of inference rules. A further source of unsoundness is the meta-level
interpreter. Not only do the control strategies at the meta-level affect
the completeness of the system (as they are intended to do in order to
cut down the search space), but unfortunately they can also affect the
soundness. Taking the example of figure 3.3, we can change clause [4]
into:

[4a]   ($\forall$F:compound-formula, P:partition, S:substitution,
    Lhs:formula, Rhs:formula,)
[split-compound-expression(F, Lhs, Rhs) & proof(Lhs, P, S)
$\rightarrow$ proof(F, P, S)
]

and thereby reducing the proof of a compound expression to the proof of
the left-hand side of that expression only. This would obviously produce
an unsound system, but the knowledge engineer is in no way prevented
from making mistakes like this. Again, we could introduce a library
system, and allowing the knowledge engineer only predefined strategies
from this library, but this would severely restrict the flexibility and power
of the system. Other approaches are possible, such as the one in the
LCF/ML system [Gord79], where a type system enforces the soundness of
the system. Research going on in Edinburgh [Harm87], partly inspired
by [Eshg86], is investigating alternative approaches to the problem of
unsoundness introduced by the meta-level interpreter.

3.7 Summary and conclusion

A version of the Socrates architecture as described above has been implemented in approximately 15K lines of CommonLisp code. The system
currently runs in a number of CommonLisp implementations on Unix
based systems. In one of these CommonLisp systems, the Poplog system,
a graphics-based knowledge engineer interface has been constructed, allowing interaction with the system via menus, browsers, graphers, etc.

A substantial number of different control strategies have been written as meta-level programs, including backward and forward chaining,
exhaustive and non-exhaustive search, user guided or automatic conflict resolution, best-first, depth-first, breadth-first search, branch and
bound type algorithms, generate and test procedures, elimination and
confirmation strategies, etc.

The work described in this chapter is an attempt to create an environment for building expert systems based on the following principles:

- an epistemological analysis of the domain and task of a particular application guides the choice of the appropriate knowledge
  representation language and the appropriate control regime.

- logic is used as the main underlying formalism.

- control knowledge is represented explicitly and is separated from the domain knowledge.

When configuring the Socrates environment into a particular expert system, a knowledge engineer can vary the architecture along three dimensions:

- the representation language: a knowledge engineer can define his own logical representation language, including first order logics (possibly many-sorted), modal logics, temporal logics, etc.

- the inference rules for the logical language: the set of rules that determine the possible inferences made in the logical language can be changed by the knowledge engineer.

- the control regime under which the inference rules will be used to perform proofs in the logical representation language.

An implementation of the Socrates abstract architecture and a number of applications of the system have proved the feasibility of this approach. Some of these applications will be described in detail in the next chapter.

4 Applications of Socrates

Nick Davies
Robin Khan

4.1 Introduction

In this chapter, we describe some of the AI application systems which have been implemented (or re-implemented) in Socrates. We point out where the Socrates approach has been particularly helpful in the implementation of these systems.

We begin by describing the INVEST system, a toy system in the domain of financial investment advice which nevertheless demonstrates how theorem proving in Socrates corresponds to problem solving in an expert system. We then discuss a more significant expert systems application in the domain of chest pain symptom diagnosis. Of particular interest in this system is the way the separation of control in Socrates allowed the implementation of a control strategy which checked the knowledge base for certain types of inconsistency. Next a forward reasoning application is described, the application being a demonstration system for configuring office furniture. A simple route planning system is then discussed, showing how a number of standard AI techniques can be exploited in the Socrates system. Comparisons are made with Prolog's less flexible theorem proving capability. The computational tractability of Socrates' representation and inference mechanisms is demonstrated in the final application discussed: the solution of a well-known hard theorem-proving problem, Schubert's Steamroller.

4.2 The INVEST system

The INVEST expert system gives financial advice. It is not intended to be used as a serious system but was created in order to demonstrate Socrates.

Users can be taken through the various stages of creating an expert system in Socrates: from defining the knowledge representation language, through declaring the set of logical inferences that can be used in the domain, to creating a strategy for executing and controlling these

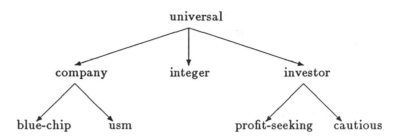

Figure 4.1
Type hierarchy for the INVEST system

inferences. To make it suitable for naive users, INVEST exploits as many of the system building facilities contained within Socrates as possible. These include:

4.2.1 Partition hierarchy

The logical propositions constituting the knowledge of the system are stored in an *invest-rules* partition. Since this is declared as a sub-partition of a *working* memory partition, it inherits all (temporary) run-time assertions, which are made in the *working* partition.

4.2.2 Sort lattice

INVEST makes use of the sort lattice which indicates taxonomic relations between objects in the domain as in figure 4.1.

4.2.3 Inference rules

Since the INVEST knowledge base uses just three logical operators (implication, conjunction and disjunction), the system only needs a few of the normal inference rules to prove its goals. These are Modus Ponens, And Introduction and Or Introduction. These rules can be represented as follows:

- Modus Ponens: $P, P \rightarrow Q \vdash Q$

- And Introduction: $P, Q \vdash P \;\&\; Q$

- Or Introduction: $P \vdash P \vee Q$

Besides these rules, INVEST uses rules for retrieving known propositions from the knowledge base (strictly speaking, for unifying a goal
with a proposition in the knowledge base)[1], for evaluating predicates
that have pieces of code associated with them (semantic attachment),
and for asking the user a question associated with a predicate (this can
also be seen as a form of semantic attachment, where the truth or fal-
sity of an expression is not determined by a procedure but by the user).
Each of these rules may return bindings for variables, giving the context
in which the goal succeeded.

4.2.4 Control strategy

INVEST is a straightforward backward-chaining expert system. The initial goal to be proved is always: does there exist a company in which the
user can invest? A user profile is first established: the user is asked his
or her name, how much is to be invested and whether safe or high-profit
investments are sought. These are asserted in the *working* partition of
the knowledge base. The system then begins backward chaining. A
brief example is given below to show how a logical proof in Socrates
corresponds to the problem-solving process of an expert system.

For a user called Bill, the initial goal would be represented as the
proposition:

($\exists$(*c:company*) (*invest-in c Bill*))

When the predicate *invest-in* exists as the right-hand side of an implication, by applying Modus Ponens the goal can be replaced with the
left-hand side of the implication.

For example, suppose we have the following proposition in the knowledge base

($\forall$ (*c:company i:investor*)
    ($\rightarrow$ (& ($\vee$ (*buy-shares-in c i*)
                 (*buy-gold-from c i*))
            (*candidate-for-saving i*))
      (*invest-in c i*)))

A specialisation of this proposition (that is, a more specific instance of
it, derived by the inference rules that deal with quantification) is:

---

[1] These are the inference rules that deal with quantification, which are hardwired
into the retrieval mechanism, as discussed in chapter 3.

$(\exists \quad (c\text{:}company)$
$\quad (\rightarrow \quad (\& \quad (\vee \quad (buy\text{-}shares\text{-}in\ c\ Bill)$
$\qquad\qquad\qquad\qquad (buy\text{-}gold\text{-}from\ c\ Bill))$
$\qquad\qquad\quad (candidate\text{-}for\text{-}saving\ Bill))$
$\qquad\quad (invest\text{-}in\ c\ Bill)))$

After application of modus ponens, the new goal to be proved would thus be:

$(\exists \quad (c\text{:}company)$
$\quad (\& \quad (\vee \quad (buy\text{-}shares\text{-}in\ c\ Bill)$
$\qquad\qquad\quad (buy\text{-}gold\text{-}from\ c\ Bill))$
$\qquad\quad (candidate\text{-}for\text{-}saving\ Bill))$

By applying the And-Introduction rule to this, effectively splitting the &, the new goals to be proved are

$(\exists \quad (c\text{:}company)$
$\quad (\vee \quad (buy\text{-}shares\text{-}in\ c\ Bill)$
$\qquad\quad (buy\text{-}gold\text{-}from\ c\ Bill))$

and

$(candidate\text{-}for\text{-}saving\ Bill)$

If the fact *(candidate-for-saving Bill)* were in the knowledge base, this could then be removed from the goal list, leaving

$(\exists \quad (c\text{:}company)$
$\quad \vee \quad (buy\text{-}shares\text{-}in\ c\ Bill)$
$\qquad\quad (buy\text{-}gold\text{-}from\ c\ Bill)))$

as the outstanding goal.

The goals continue to be refined in this way until either there are no goals left to prove, meaning that we have proved the original goal or until we cannot refine any of the current goals any further, in which case we have failed to find a proof of the original goal. Note that the proof of the original goal will typically involve a binding for the existential variable c, so that the answer the system gives is not simply that there is a company which *Bill* should invest in but also which company he should invest in. Often there may be more than one such binding (company).

The rules *lookup*, *ask-user* and *evaluate* constitute a special class of inference rule in that these are the rules which actually make the list of goals shorter. If a goal list contains a goal g and we can find that goal in the knowledge base (as in the case of *(candidate-for-saving Bill)* in the example above), or if we can confirm the goal's truth by asking the user, or confirm its truth by running a procedure associated on some way with the goal then we can simply delete the goal from the goal list. It is by the application of these rules that a goal list eventually becomes empty and a proof hence succeeds.

4.3   The DOCS system

Socrates has been used to reimplement an existing expert system under the name of DOCS (Diagnosis Of Chest pain Symptoms), developed by GEC-Marconi Research in collaboration with Westminster Hospital, London. The DOCS system addresses the following problem: when patients suffering from chest pains arrive at hospital, they are assessed with the aid of various tests. On the basis of the results of these tests, patients are assigned into one of six categories: high risk, medium risk or low risk cardiac and similar risk categories for non-cardiac. It has been observed that many patients are mistakenly ascribed to high risk categories thus using valuable resources needlessly. The aim of the DOCS systems is to help reduce erroneous decisions and time taken in selecting the appropriate risk category.

The system consists of 130 rules. Its reimplementation demonstrates several of the facilities available in Socrates, including: the use of knowledge base partitions to structure the knowledge base; the way in which a simple explanation system can be constructed for an expert system developed in Socrates; the use of strategic knowledge to guide the search for a solution (proof); the way in which Socrates facilitates some degree of knowledge base validation; and the capability for graphical interaction with a system implemented in Socrates.

4.3.1   Knowledge base structure

The 130 rules can be divided into two types: *barn door* rules and *elimination* rules. The barn door rules attempt to identify prototypical cases for the different risk categories directly. An example of such a rule is:

```
(if ((site_rough=upper_left) or (site_rough=upper_right))
    and (pulse_rate > 120)
    and chest_constricted
 then high_risk_cardiac)
```

As can be seen, barn door rules attempt to identify risk categories on the basis of a few key symptoms. When the risk category cannot be identified on this basis, however, the use of elimination rules may be appropriate. The elimination approach involves dividing the diseases from which the patient may be suffering into some 50 "similarity of indicant" sets. (An indicant is a symptom or some other piece of relevant information such as the age of the patient). These sets are divided into smaller sets, which are in turn divided into further sets on the basis of the indicants known. There are five levels of such sets. Elimination rules can be characterised as being of the form:

```
(if <patient has a disease in set-disease1>
    and <patient has indicants>
 then <patient has a disease in set-disease2>)
```

Set-disease1 and set-disease2 are sets of diseases where set-disease2 is a subset of set-disease1. So each rule application reduces the set of possible diseases for the patient until each of the possible diseases for the patient fall into one and only one of the risk categories, at which point the diagnosis is complete.

The strategy used by the system is to first identify the site of the pain (probably the most important indicant). A series of human chests are drawn on the screen, each of which has a particular site of pain shaded in. The user is then asked to select the appropriate site using the mouse button. This mouse activity is associated, via semantic attachment, with a site predicate. Information about the site of the pain is thus entered into the knowledge base.

The next step is to try and identify the patient as belonging to the barn door, prototypical cases first. If this fails, then the elimination rules are attempted. The two types of rules are stored in two separate knowledge base partitions. This improves efficiency, since only relevant rules are accessed during the two stages of the problem-solving process. Furthermore, the partition hierarchy is organised so that these two partitions can use data from a common working memory partition. This means that information obtained from the first stage is not lost in the second and also facilitates the deletion of temporary data (which is all held in the working memory partition). The use of two partitions also shows how strategic knowledge can easily be exploited in Socrates. The strategic knowledge in this case is "First identify the site of the pain; next look for a prototypical case; then use a process of elimination". A proof is first attempted in the partition using the barn door rules. If this fails, the partition is changed to that containing the elimination rules, effectively changing the portion of the knowledge base visible to the theorem prover.

4.3.2 Control

The theorem-prover itself is fairly straightforward. The knowledge base consists entirely of implications, the consequents of which are predicate expressions. The antecedents are more complex formulae, involving negation, conjunction and disjunction. The theorem prover in the DOCS system thus acts very similarly to a standard backward chaining rule-based system. The inference rules used are modus ponens and De Morgan's Laws. A simple heuristic used by the theorem prover is to discard any goal it encounters if it has previously tried and failed to prove it.

The clear separation of the control strategy from the object-level knowledge base in Socrates facilitates the writing of new theorem provers to perform different tasks without the need to interfere with the object level knowledge.

A good example of the use of a *verification theorem prover* on an expert system knowledge base can be seen in DOCS. For the elimination rules described above, it is straightforward to write a new control regime which checks that for every rule, `set-disease1` is indeed a proper superset of `set-disease2`. In systems where control and object-level knowledge are mixed, or where the object-level knowledge has a procedural interpretation, this would not have been possible.

If the proper superset relation does not hold, there are 3 possibilities: firstly, `set-disease1` and `set-disease2` might be the same set, in which case one should be removed and replaced by the other everywhere in the knowledge base. Secondly, `set-disease1` might be a proper subset of `set-disease2` in which case the rule, rather than eliminating possibilities, is introducing them and should be checked with the expert. Thirdly, the intersection of the two sets might be empty, in which case an inconsistency in the knowledge base seems likely, since this implies that the presence of one set of diseases is suggesting the presence of another, entirely disjoint, set of diseases which is at odds with the elimination strategy being used. This case should again be checked with the expert.

The implementation of a verification meta level for this diagnosis expert system knowledge base was quite straightforward and could be used to detect the three different types of error. Several rules were found to be incorrect using this approach.

The system includes a simple explanation facility which records which rules are used in the path to a proof. A trace of the rules is then printed out if explanation is requested. Also stored is information about the different disease sets used in the elimination rules and this can also be accessed by the explanation mechanism.

4.4   An office configuration system

The office configuration domain is an example of a forward chaining system in Socrates. It uses a method that can be called "constrain and generate" to determine a configuration. Essentially, the problem as given is highly underconstrained. Thus, there are usually many possible solutions to a given problem. We therefore assume that there are often several choice points, in a partial solution, that are undecided. We let our configurer make a choice and then propagate the effect of that choice through the system, thus further constraining any future choices.

4.4.1   Assertion-time inference

The system is implemented by the technique of assertion-time inference. That is, when an assertion is made it immediately tries to deduce as much as possible from that fact. Consider the following assertion in the knowledge base:

$$(xor \quad (type\text{-}of \; (main\text{-}desk \; fred) \; single\text{-}pedestal) \tag{4.1}$$
$$(type\text{-}of \; (main\text{-}desk \; fred) \; double\text{-}pedestal))$$

It states that Fred's main desk must either be of the single or double pedestal type (but cannot be both). If we then assert:

$$(type\text{-}of\ (main\text{-}desk\ fred)\ single\text{-}pedestal) \qquad (4.2)$$

we can immediately deduce that:

$$(not\ (type\text{-}of\ (main\text{-}desk\ fred))\ double\text{-}pedestal) \qquad (4.3)$$

In this particular implementation, this type of deduction is made as soon as possible. Thus when 4.1 is asserted the system immediately looks to see if expression 4.2 or expression 4.3 (or a number of others) are present in the knowledge base and if so immediately makes the relevant deduction. When assertion 4.2 is put in the knowledge base it immediately looks for expressions similar to 4.1 (and for several other types of expression) and can immediately deduce 4.3.

The reason for making these deductions immediately, rather than scheduling, them is that we want the system to be maximally constrained. Delaying the deduction would run a risk of an inconsistent solution being derived. For example, if we did not immediately propagate any information upon receipt we might assert expressions 4.1 and 4.2 and

$$(type\text{-}of\ (main\text{-}desk\ fred)\ double\text{-}pedestal) \qquad (4.4)$$

which is, of course, a contradiction (since expression 4.1 states explicitly that one cannot have both expression 4.2 and 4.4 true at the same time). Thus at all times we want all known constraints to be available, since then we would have known not to assert 4.4 since 4.3 would have been in the knowledge base.

The assertion time inference mechanism uses mainly forward deduction. Given a fact it applies relevant inference rules that enable to determine which new deductions it can make. Some potential inferences require additional facts to be known before they can be made. In such cases, a simple goal-directed theorem prover is invoked to try and prove the required additional facts. Consider for example the following assertion:

$$(\rightarrow \quad (\&\ (has\ fred\ (main\text{-}desk\ fred)) \qquad (4.5)$$
$$(has\ fred\ (terminal\text{-}table\ fred)))$$
$$(preferred\text{-}type\ (chair\text{-}of\ fred)\ swivel))$$

This states that if fred has a main desk and a terminal table then his preferred type of chair is a swivel chair. If we assume that:

$$(has\ fred\ (main\text{-}desk\ fred)) \tag{4.6}$$

is then asserted, the inference rules state that, in order to deduce:

$$(preferred\text{-}type\ (chair\text{-}of\ fred)\ swivel) \tag{4.7}$$

it must first be proved that:

$$(has\ fred\ (terminal\text{-}table\ fred)) \tag{4.8}$$

We could invoke a full backwards chaining theorem prover to do this. But as noted above we have already propagated forwards all possible deductions and so all we need actually do is try to satisfy 4.8 either by unifying it with a proposition in the knowledge base or by using semantic attachment.

4.4.2 Control

When the system is run, a number of fixed questions are asked. The control strategy then attempts to deduce additional assertions that do not contradict existing constraints until a solution is provided.

We initially have to find out the names of all the people in the office. This allows us to make additional assertions regarding total shelving requirements and total filing cabinet requirements. Thus, if the only occupants in the office are Fred and Bill then their total shelving requirements are the sum of their individual requirements. Other pertinent facts about people are the number of books and units of filing cabinet space required, whether the person is junior or senior in rank, and whether the person will have a computer terminal.

From asserting these facts some deductions can be made. However, these may not be enough to solve the problem. The next step is to look for assertions that assert preferences for people. Assertions 4.5 and 4.7 above are examples of such assertions.

Constraints may make some preferences impossible and this is checked for. For example, the knowledge base contains the assertion that no one can have both a swivel chair and a double pedestal main desk. Thus, as soon as one of these two possibilities is selected the other preference is disabled. Since we are sure that all possible assertions regarding what is possible and what is not have been made at this point (through asserting all such constraints via assertion time inference), we can use the fact that if the negation of a preference is not in the knowledge base then we can assert that preference as fact.

Even after asserting preferences we cannot be sure we have solved the problem. Thus, we look for each object that a person "has" and check to see if we know its "kind". For example, if we find that a person requires a terminal table then we check to see if we know if it is a table or a single pedestal desk. If we do not know, then we look for assertions of the form:

$(xor\ (type\text{-}of\ \langle object\rangle\ \langle kind\rangle)\ \ldots)$

since this is the way of expressing various "object kind" restrictions. Assertion 4.1 is of this type. Again we check if an object-kind assertion is known to be impossible before asserting it. When this process is complete then we have sufficient information to print out the configuration.

4.5 An underground route planner

The STATIONS system is a simple application that demonstrates how a number of AI techniques can be exploited in the Socrates system. The following techniques are incorporated: explicit control of reasoning, use of heuristics, breadth-first search, agenda-based reasoning and the use of logical functions as data structures. Some interesting comparisons are drawn between Socrates' approach with Prolog's more limited and less flexible theorem proving capability. The problem is one of finding a route between two stations on the London Underground. The knowledge base is intentionally kept simple, but could easily be extended. In fact, it contains a single "rule" and a large number of facts. We have reduced the number of stations and lines to the minimum required to display interesting behaviour. Figure 4.2 shows the map of the stations we have included and their lines.

Consider the problem of getting from Wimbledon to Embankment. The trivial solution is to go by the District line direct. However, there are other solutions. For example: District to Notting Hill Gate, then Circle to Embankment; District to South Kensington, Circle line to Baker Street, Waterloo line to Embankment. Clearly, we want the shorter solutions first. Furthermore we wish to avoid stupid solutions such as: District to Notting Hill Gate, District to Embankment (using the same

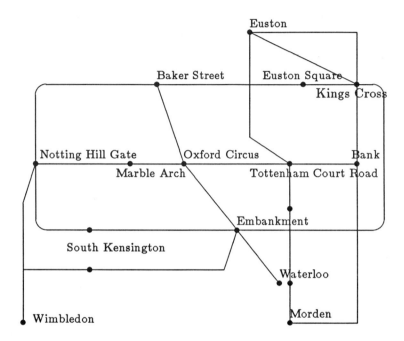

Figure 4.2
Part of London Underground

line twice); District to Notting Hill Gate, Circle to Notting Hill Gate (again!), Central to Oxford Circus, Bakerloo to Embankment (using the same station twice).

4.5.1   Representation language

Recall that Socrates' knowledge representation scheme is based on sorted first-order predicate calculus. The sort lattice in this example is quite straightforward, consisting of just three disjoint subsorts of the universal sort, namely route, line and station.

Two predicates are used: *on* and *can-get-to*. The first of these is used to record which stations are on which lines. Thus, (on circle kings-cross) states that Kings Cross is on the circle line. The predicate *on* is sorted (that is, its arguments have their sorts restricted) so that the first argument can only be an object of sort *line*, and its second argument can only be of sort *station*. The second predicate *can-get-to* is used to represent that it is possible to get to a given station using a given route. The route is represented by two things: the constant *start*, which represents the null route; and the logical-function *change* which takes three arguments. The first argument is a route (an object of sort *route*), the second is a *line*, the third is a *station*. The interpretation is that *(change X Y Z)* represents the route that consists of following the route *X*, then changing onto the line *Y* and going to station *Z*. Thus,

(*change* (*change start district notting-hill-gate*) *circle embankment*)

represents the route of starting at somewhere on the District line, following the district line to Notting Hill Gate, changing onto the Circle line and going to Embankment. This is an example of how in Socrates logical functions can be used as data structures.

The single rule used is:

(∀ (*R:route L:line X:station Y:station*)
  (→ (& (*can-get-to X R*) (*on L X*) (*on L Y*))
    (*can-get-to Y* (*change R L Y*)))))

4.5.2 Control

Given a starting point and a required destination, the theorem prover first asserts that one *can-get-to* the starting station using the route *start*. Then it puts the goal:

(∃ (*R:route*) (*can-get-to* ⟨*destination*⟩ *R*))

onto an agenda. A demon is activated that works on each agenda item in turn. Each agenda item consists of a list of goals that have to be proved in order to solve the problem, thus the agenda represents a list of partial solutions.

There are several heuristics we can incorporate into the agenda mechanism to make the theorem prover more efficient. The first efficiency improvement we can make is to order the goals in the agenda items. The goals in each agenda item are ordered so that any involving operators go first. Then those involving the *on* predicate with the station argument known (instantiated). Then those involving the *on* predicate with the station argument unknown (uninstantiated), and finally those involving the *can-get-to* predicate.

This ordering will improve the efficiency of the theorem prover for the following reasons. Those goals that involve an operator must involve &

(since this is the only operator) and should be immediately broken up into their subgoals. Thus, goals of this form should be solved first. We also know that *on* goals can only be solved by a direct look up. Thus, we handle these next. We prefer to handle goals where the station name is known first, since these will have only few possible bindings for the line argument. That is, stations tend to be on only a small number of lines, but lines tend to have many stations on them. By searching this way we reduce the number of branches that have to be explored. Finally, goals of the form of a *can-get-to* predicate are dealt with last. If they were dealt with first they could cause an infinite loop (as they would in Prolog, using Prolog's built in depth first theorem prover). This can happen when replacing a *can-get-to* goal with a new *can-get-to* goal, which then gets replaced by another, and so on, without binding any variables.

The *can-get-to* goals are a second place where heuristics can be applied. Before a *can-get-to* goal is expanded it is checked that the route that it specifies does not contain any loops (i.e. no stations or lines being revisited). When a *can-get-to* goal is expanded it is not further explored, but instead placed back onto the agenda for further investigation. There is a demon that decides where this new task will be placed. In this theorem prover the demon puts the task at the end of the agenda, effectively searching in a breadth-first fashion. This means that it finds the shortest routes first. By changing this demon we can perform a depth-first search instead (or more complex search strategies if required).

The example demonstrates how the control of reasoning can be clearly separated from the domain knowledge. The rule defines what forms the accessibility of stations by routes, it is simply that we can ignore certain routes as unsatisfactory. We also improve the efficiency of the theorem prover and change the order in which it finds solutions without changing the rule itself (cf. Prolog, in which the rule would have to be changed in order to do this and where the loop protection would have to be implemented by careful ordering of the goals in the antecedent of the rule).

4.6   Schubert's Steamroller

Schubert's Steamroller has become well known as a challenging puzzle for theorem provers and until recently no automated solution had been found, although the problem has now been solved using resolution-based theorem provers [Walt84]. Our natural deduction theorem prover exploits a number of features of the Socrates system for improving its efficiency in finding a proof.

The problem below is taken from [Walt84]. It was first proposed by L. Schubert and is known as Schubert's Steamroller. It has become well known as a problem which humans can solve after some thought, but which is difficult for automated theorem provers to solve because of the huge search space it generates.

> Wolves, foxes, birds, caterpillars, and snails are animals, and there are some of each of them. Also there are some grains, and grains are plants. Every animal either likes to eat all plants or all animals much smaller than itself that like to eat some plants. Caterpillars and snails are much smaller than birds, which are much smaller than foxes, which in turn are much smaller than wolves. Wolves do not like to eat foxes or grains, while birds like to eat caterpillars but not snails. Caterpillars and snails like to eat some plants. Therefore there is an animal that likes to eat a grain-eating animal.

Recently, a number of authors ([Cohn85], [Walt84]) have reported success using resolution theorem provers and many-sorted axiomatisations. As far as we are aware, ours is the first natural deduction proof found by an automated theorem prover.

An axiomatisation of the problem in standard first order predicate calculus is:

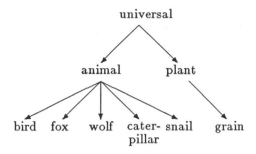

Figure 4.3
Sort lattice for Schubert's Steamroller

$$(\exists(x1\ x2\ x3\ x4\ x5\ x6)(w(x1)\&f(x2)\&b(x3)\&c(x4)\&s(x5)\&g(x6)))$$
$$(\forall(x)((w(x)\lor f(x)\lor b(x)\lor c(x)\lor s(x))\to a(x)))$$
$$(\forall(x)(g(x)\to p(x)))$$
$$(\forall(x)(a(x)\to(\forall(y)(p(y)\to eats(x,y))$$
$$\lor(\forall(y)((a(y)\&mst(y,x)$$
$$\&(\exists(z)(p(z)\&eats(y,z))))\to eats(x,y))))$$
$$(\forall(x\ y)((c(x)\&b(y))\to mst(x,y)))$$
$$(\forall(x\ y)((s(x))\&b(y))\to mst(x,y)))$$
$$(\forall(x\ y)((b(x)\&f(y))\to mst(x,y)))$$
$$(\forall(x\ y)((f(x)\&w(y))\to mst(x,y)))$$
$$(\forall(x\ y)((f(x)\&w(y))\to\neg eats(y,x))))$$
$$(\forall(x\ y)((g(x))\&w(y))\to\neg eats(y,x))))$$
$$(\forall(x\ y)((b(x)\&c(y))\to eats(x,y)))$$
$$(\forall(x\ y)((b(x)\&s(y))\to\neg eats(x,y)))$$
$$(\forall(x)(s(x)\to(\exists(y)(p(y)\&eats(x,y)))$$
$$(\forall(x)(c(x)\to(\exists(y)(p(y)\&eats(x,y)))$$

We are trying to prove:

$$(\exists(x\ y)(a(x)\&a(y)\&(\forall(z)(g(z)\to(eats(x,y)\&eats(y,z))))))$$

In order to recast this into our sorted logic, we must first declare a sort
lattice. The sort lattice used, which is effectively a taxonomic representation of the animals and plants occurring in the problem, is shown in
figure 4.3.

Our new (sorted) axiomatisation (in Socrates' prefix notation) is:

1. $(\forall(a1\text{:}animal\ a2\text{:}animal\ p1\text{:}plant\ p2\text{:}plant)$
   $(\vee(eats\ a1\ p1)(\rightarrow(\&(mst\ a2\ a1)(eats\ a2\ p2))(eats\ a1\ a2))))$
2. $(\forall(f\text{:}fox\ w\text{:}wolf)(mst\ f\ w))$
3. $(\forall(b\text{:}bird\ f\text{:}fox)(mst\ b\ f))$
4. $(\forall(s\text{:}snail\ b\text{:}bird)(mst\ s\ b))$
5. $(\forall(c\text{:}caterpillar\ b\text{:}bird)(mst\ c\ b))$
6. $(\forall(g\text{:}grain\ w\text{:}wolf)(\neg(eats\ w\ g)))$
7. $(\forall(f\text{:}fox\ w\text{:}wolf)(\neg(eats\ w\ f)))$
8. $(\forall(b\text{:}bird\ c\text{:}caterpillar)(eats\ b\ c))$
9. $(\forall(b\text{:}bird\ s\text{:}snail)(\neg(eats\ b\ s)))$
10. $(\forall(s\text{:}snail)(\exists(p\text{:}plant)(eats\ s\ p)))$
11. $(\forall(c\text{:}caterpillar)(\exists(p\text{:}plant)(eats\ c\ p)))$

Our goal is now:

$(\exists(a1\text{:}animal\ a2\text{:}animal)(\forall(g\text{:}grain)(\&(eats\ a1\ a2)(eats\ a2\ g))))$

The solution to the problem is:

$(\forall(a1\text{:}fox\ a2\text{:}bird\text{:}grain)(\&(eats\ a1\ a2)(eats\ a2\ g)))$

The reduction in complexity in the formulas resulting from the adoption of a sorted representation can be clearly seen: the first three formulas of the unsorted axiomatisation are now captured by the sort lattice. In the other formulas, all expressions containing the unary predicates w, f, b, c, s, g and p have been simplified since these predicates are now incorporated in the sort lattice. For example, all propositions of the form:

$(\forall(x)(\rightarrow(t\ x)P))$

where t is now a sort have been replaced by

$(\forall(x\text{:}t)P),$

eliminating all but one implication.

A second way in which the efficiency of a natural deduction system can be improved is by the omission of unnecessary inference rules. For the purposes of the Steamroller problem, the required inference rules were selected by constructing a hand-written proof.

The inference rules used in this hand-written proof were then included in the mechanical prover. (In expert system domains it is in general

	No Pruning	Pruning
Best-first search	24:55; 716	2:06; 204
Breadth-first search	> 970:00; > 3000	10:37; 980

Figure 4.4
CPU time (mmm:ss) and number of nodes visited

much easier to select appropriate inference rules than in a hard logical
problem of this nature).

Another optimisation we have adopted is to embed certain inference
rules into the many-sorted unification algorithm which is used as the
knowledge base retrieval mechanism. We have declared the connectives
& and ∨ to be associative and commutative. This means that the following inference rules for & (and equivalent ones for ∨) are included in
the unifier:

$(\& \ P \ Q) \vdash (\& \ Q \ P)$
$(\& \ (\& \ P \ Q) \ R) \vdash (\& \ P \ (\& \ Q \ R))$

The automatic application of these commonly used rules by the unifier
removes the overhead of applying them explicitly via the theorem prover.

A fourth way to enhance the efficiency of a system written in Socrates
is to provide a proof strategy which controls the application of inference
rules and hence determines the course of the proof.

Several different proof strategies have been used to attempt to solve
Schubert's Steamroller. A comparison of the results of using these strategies shows the significant gains in efficiency which can be achieved by
the use of meta-level guidance of the proof (see table 4.4).

The first of these strategies is probably the most obvious: to exhaustively search the proof tree in a breadth-first manner. The second proof
strategy is to modify this breadth-first strategy in a simple way to a
best-first strategy.

Another way in which the search can be constrained is by pruning
branches of the proof tree which have no chance of yielding a solution.
One such class of useless branches can be identified by examination of
the inference rules and the axiomatisation.

The time taken to find a proof using these different strategies reveal
that the use of even relatively simple meta-level guidance of the proof
can dramatically reduce the computational resources required to find a

solution in terms of both time and run-time storage. The importance of the use of meta-level control in expert systems is widely recognised. In Socrates, the identification of suitable heuristics is facilitated by the use of a logic-based scheme and in particular the explicit representation of both the inference rules to be used for a particular application and of the logical formulas which these inference rules will manipulate. The use of a natural deduction prover, wherein logical formulas are not rewritten into clausal form, also makes it easier to identify effective heuristics.

To summarise, the Socrates techniques which have enabled a solution of this difficult (for automated theorem provers) problem are: the use of a sorted logic, the need only to incorporate relevant inference rules, the inclusion of a certain class of inference rules into the unifier and the use of heuristics to guide the proof.

A more detailed discussion of Schubert's Steamroller and its solution in Socrates can be found in [Davi87].

4.7 Conclusion

We have described a number of applications of the Socrates system. These applications covered a number of different tasks in different domains, indicating that the Socrates abstract architecture can indeed be instantiated into different concrete architectures that deal with different applications. The DOCS application performed a diagnosis task in a domain with a strong hierarchical structure, the office configuration system solved a constraint-satisfaction problem using forward inferencing, and Schubert's steamroller was a theorem proving task.

Various aspects of the Socrates architecture have facilitated the solutions described above. A hierarchical domain structure could be expressed using many-sorted logic (as in DOCS), knowledge base partitions were used to separate working memory from long-term knowledge (again as in DOCS), and the efficiency of the control regime could be improved without changing the domain knowledge (Schubert's steamroller and the route planner). All these applications used first order logic for the representation of object-level knowledge, but chapter 7 will discuss the use of a modal temporal logic in Socrates.

II FURTHER RESEARCH IN REPRESENTATION AND CONTROL

5 The Limitations of Partial Evaluation

Frank van Harmelen

5.1 Introduction

Although many of the papers in the literature dealing with the use of meta-level interpreters for control issues acknowledge the inefficiency that is inherent in the multiple layers of interpretation, very few of them offer any solutions to this problem. An important section of the limited work on reducing meta-level overhead in recent years has been based on the idea of specialising the general purpose formulation of the meta-level control regime with respect to the particular object-level knowledge that is being used in the system. Most of the work on this idea is based on the use of *partial evaluation* as an optimisation technique.

Work reported in for example [Venk84], [Take86], [Take85], [Safr86], [Levi88] and [Gall86], is all based on this technique. In this chapter we will first describe this technique, and its application to meta-level interpreters in logic-based systems. In the second part of this chapter we will explore some of the limitations of this technique in the context of meta-level interpreters for logic-based expert systems, which remain largely undiscussed in the literature.

5.2 A description of partial evaluation

The main goal of partial evaluation is to perform as much of the computation in a program as possible without depending on any of the input values of the program. The theoretical foundation for partial evaluation is Kleene's S-M-N theorem from recursive function theory [Klee52]. This theorem says that given any computable function f of n variables ($f = f(x_1, \ldots, x_n)$), and k ($k \leq n$) values $a_1, \ldots, a_k$ for $x_1, \ldots, x_k$, we can effectively compute a new function f' such that

$$f'(x_{k+1}, \ldots, x_n) = f(a_1, \ldots, a_k, x_{k+1}, \ldots, x_n).$$

The new function f' is a specialisation of f, and is easier to compute than f for those specific input values. A partial evaluation algorithm can be regarded as the implementation of this theorem, and is in fact slightly more general in the context of logic programming: it allows not only that a number of input variables are instantiated to constants, but also that these variables can be partially instantiated to terms that contain nested variables. Furthermore, a partial evaluation algorithm allows k in the above theorem (the number of instantiated input variables), to be 0, that is, no input to f is specified at all. Even in this case a partial evaluation algorithm is often able to produce a definition of f' which is equivalent to f but more efficient, since all the computations performed by f that are independent of the values of the input variables can be precomputed in f'. Thus, a partial evaluation algorithm takes as its input a function (program) definition, together with a partial specification of the input of the program, and produces a new version of the program that is specialised for the particular input values. The new version of the program may then be less general but more efficient than the original version.

A partial evaluation algorithm works by symbolically evaluating the input program while trying to (i) propagate constant values through the program code, (ii) unfold procedure calls, and (iii) branching out conditional parts of the code. If the language used to express the input program is logic, then the symbolic evaluation of the program becomes the construction of the proof tree corresponding to the execution of the program.

A special case of partial evaluation is when none of the values for the input variables $x_1, \ldots, x_k$ are given (in other words, $k = 0$). In this case, the partial evaluation algorithm cannot do as much optimisation of the input program, and as a result the new program will not be as efficient. However, the new program is no longer only a specialisation of the original program, but indeed equivalent to it. Thus, in this way partial evaluation can be used as a way of reformulating the input program in an equivalent but more efficient way.

As a simple example of partial evaluation, consider the following function in Lisp:

```
(defun assoc (key alist)
      (cond ((null alist) nil)
            ((eq key (caar alist)) (car alist))
            (t (assoc key (cdr alist)))))
```

This function accesses the standard Lisp assoc-list data-structure. If we specify a partial input, such as

```
alist = '((key1 . val1)(key2 . val2))
```

then we can partially evaluate `assoc`, using the following call to the partial evaluator:[1]

```
(peval '(assoc key '((key1 . val1)(key2 . val2))))
```

to return the derived program `assoc'`:

```
(defun assoc' (key)
      (cond ((eq key 'key1) '(key1 . val1))
            (t (cond ((eq key 'key2) '(key2 . val2))
                     (t nil)))))
```

One problem with partial evaluation in general is that the partial evaluator has to handle uninstantiated variables. This is because the input of the source program is only partially specified and some of the variables in the source program will not have a value at partial evaluation time. In most programming languages it is hard to deal with uninstantiated variables, and the partial evaluator has to be very careful about what it evaluates, and what not.

This is exactly the reason why logic programming is especially suited for partial evaluation. Unification is a fundamental computational operation in logic programming, and handling uninstantiated variables in unification is no problem at all. In fact, uninstantiated variables arising from partially specified input[2] can be treated like any other term. For instance, in the example above, care had to be taken not to further evaluate the `eq`'s and `cond`'s, since the variable `key` was uninstantiated at partial evaluation time. However, in Prolog, the program `assoc`:

---

[1]This call to the partial evaluator only specifies half of its input: the partially specified input to the source program. The other half of the input to the partial evaluator (the actual definition of the source program) is assumed to be globally available in the execution environment of this call. This argument could be made explicit in the obvious way.

[2]In the context of logic programming G' is a partial specification of G if G' is subsumed by G. We also say that G' is an *instantiation* of G (notation: $G' \leq_{inst} G$): there exists a substitution θ for variables in G such that θ applied to G gives G': $G' = \theta G$. G' is a *strict instantiation* of G (notation: $G' <_{inst} G$) if there is a non-empty substitution θ for variables in G such that $G' = \theta G$.

```
assoc(_, [], []).
assoc(Key, [[Key, Value]|_], Value).
assoc(Key, [_|Alist], Value) :-
assoc(Key, Alist, Value).
```

plus a call to the partial evaluator:

```
:- peval(assoc(Key, [[key1, val1], [key2, val2]], Val)).
```

partially evaluates into:

```
assoc'(key1, [[key1, val1], [key2, val2]], val1).
assoc'(key2, [[key1, val1], [key2, val2]], val2).
assoc'(_, [[key1, val1], [key2, val2]], []).
```

without having to worry about evaluation at all, since even with an
uninstantiated variable Key, the procedure evaluates to the equivalent
specialised code, which now contains no further calls to be executed at
run time.

This technique of specialising a program with respect to its (partial)
input to derive a more efficient version, can also be applied in the special
case when the source program is itself the definition of an interpreter
(i.e. a meta-level program). This will then produce a version of the
meta-level interpreter which is specialised for the particular object-level
program that was given as input specification.

Example in Prolog: Consider an object-level knowledge base, called
invest, as in figure 5.1 and a meta-level interpreter that specifies how
to use these clauses, as in figure 5.2.

This meta-level interpreter assumes a Socrates-like architecture, as
described in chapter 3, where the predicate object_level_interpreter
generates all possible formulas derivable from the input formula using
the available object-level inference rules[3]. A full instantiation of the
input to the meta-level interpreter consists of the object-level knowledge
base, plus the top goal that should be proved. So, if the above meta-level
program is partially evaluated with the arguments:

---

[3]Actually, the meta-level interpreter from figure 5.2 does not quite follow the
Socrates architecture. For the sake of simplicity this interpreter mixes object- and
meta-level language, so that object-level substitutions do not have to be handled
explicitly by the meta-level interpreter. However, this simplification does not effect
any of the arguments in this chapter, and only serves to scale down the examples.

```
theory(invest,
      [cautious(usr) &
       growth_potential(X)
       => buy_shares_in(X, usr),

       profit_seeking(usr) &
       rerating_potential(X)
       => buy_shares_in(X, usr),

       might_take_over(_, X)
       => rerating_potential(X),

       might_take_over(gec, plessey),

       profit_seeking(usr)
      ]).
```

Figure 5.1
An object-level knowledge base in Prolog

```
Goal = buy_shares_in(X, usr)
Theory = invest
```

with the following call to the partial evaluator:

```
:- peval(proof(buy_shares_in(X, usr), invest)).
```

then, assuming that the inference rules Modus Ponens and And Introduction are in the object-level inference rules, the derived version of the meta-level program becomes:

```
proof(buy_shares_in(plessey, usr), invest).
```

However, we do not want to specify the top goal of the query, since we cannot predict which goal we will want to prove. So, we underspecify the input to the source program (the meta-level interpreter): we leave the query uninstantiated, and only specify the object-level knowledge base that we want to use. In the example above we would call the partial evaluator with

```
:- peval(proof(Goal, invest)).
```

```
[1] proof(Goal, Theory) :-
        lookup(Goal, Theory).
[2] proof(Goal, Theory) :-
        object_level_inference(Goal, Theory, New_Goals),
        proof(New_Goals, Theory).

[3] proof([],_).
[4] proof([Goal|Goals], Theory) :-
        proof(Goal, Theory),
        proof(Goals, Theory).
```

Figure 5.2
A meta-level interpreter in Prolog

giving us the remarkably transformed source program as shown in figure
5.3. This program contains the direct results for all the successful proofs
that could be performed by the meta-level interpreter, namely:

- clauses [1]-[5] contain all the results derived via clause [1] of the
  meta-level interpreter (using lookup),

- clauses [6]-[7] contain all the results derivable via application of
  Modus Ponens (via clause [2] of the meta-level interpreter),

- clause [8] contains a precomputed scheme for applying And Introduction (based on clauses [2]-[4] of the meta-interpreter),

- clauses [9] and [10] repeat the code from the meta-interpreter for
  iterating over conjunctive goals. This code will never be used by
  the partially evaluated version, since the iteration over conjunctive
  goals has already been precomputed in clause [8]. The fact that
  this superfluous code still appears in the partially evaluated version
  is due to the difference in status of clauses [1]-[2] and [3]-[4] of the
  meta-level interpreter: clauses [1]-[2] are meant to be called by the
  user of the meta-level interpreter, whereas clauses [3]-[4] are only
  meant to be called by the code itself. If this information had been
  conveyed to the partial evaluator (for instance by introducing a
  new predicate name, clauses [9]-[10] would not have occurred in
  the partially evaluated code.

```
[1]   proof(cautious(usr) & growth_potential(X) =>
             buy_shares_in(X,usr), invest).
[2]   proof(profit_seeking(usr) & rerating_potential(X) =>
             buy_shares_in(X,usr), invest).
[3]   proof(might_take_over(X,Y) =>
             rerating_potential(Y), invest).
[4]   proof(might_take_over(gec,plessey), invest).
[5]   proof(profit_seeking(usr), invest).
[6]   proof(rerating_potential(plessey), invest).
[7]   proof(buy_shares_in(plessey,usr), invest).
[8]   proof(X & Y, invest) :-
         proof(X, invest),
         proof(Y, invest).
[9]   proof([X|Y], invest) :-
         proof(X, invest),
         proof(Y, invest).
[10]  proof([], invest).
```

Figure 5.3
The programs after partial evaluation

The partially evaluated code from figure 5.3 is of course much more efficient than the original code from figures 5.1 and 5.2: Any of the facts
mentioned in clauses [1]-[5] of figure 5.3 can now be proved in 1 logical
inference (one logical inference corresponds roughly to one procedure
call), instead of taking anywhere between 4 and 8 logical inferences (depending on their place in the object-level theory). Similarly, the facts
from clauses [6]-[7] can now be proved in 1 logical inference, instead of
18 and 41 logical inferences respectively. The speedup for conjunctive
goals is 3 logical inferences per conjunction. These speedups may be
quite small as absolute figures, but taken as a proportion of the small
amount of inference done by this toy example it amounts to about an
order of magnitude speedup.

5.3   Problems of partial evaluation

Although the above example indicates the power of partial evaluation, there are some serious problems associated with partial evaluation as a tool for reducing meta-level overhead. Experiments with partial evaluation of small Prolog programs that were executed by a simple meta-level interpreter indicated two main problems. The first of these is related to the definition of the object-level program (which is one of the arguments of the meta-level procedure that is instantiated at partial evaluation time), and the second problem is to do with the amount of information that is available to the partial evaluator.

5.3.1   Changing object-level programs at run time

In partial evaluation, programs are specialised with respect to their (partial) input. This gives a derived program that is specialised with respect to its input, and obviously this specialised program cannot be used to do computations on different inputs.

In our specific case, the only part of the input to the source program (the meta-level interpreter) that is specified is the object-level theory. However, this object-level theory is likely to change while the meta-level interpreter is running. We are likely to want to add to the object-level theory during the proof of a particular query, thereby invalidating the optimised version of the meta-level program. An obvious solution to this problem is to follow [Reic85] and [Reic86] in distinguishing object-level *knowledge* from object-level *data*. The latter is object-level information that is dependent on a particular session (such as information about a the investment profile of a particular user), and therefore will certainly change during a run of the system, whereas the former is object-level information that is not likely to change between sessions, such as general rules containing knowledge about investments. In the above example knowledge-base the predicates `might-take-over` and `profit-seeking` would classify as object-level data, and the other predicates as object-level knowledge. We can now restrict our partial evaluation algorithm to only evaluate code that uses object-level knowledge. The execution of code that uses object-level data on the other hand has to be postponed until run-time.

Furukawa and Takeuchi [Take86] describe an alternative solution for the special case when the object-level knowledge base grows monotoni-

cally. This involves constructing a version of a partial evaluator which
is specialised for the meta-level interpreter plus the current version of
the object-level knowledge base, by applying the partial evaluator to
itself with the meta-level interpreter and object-level knowledge base
as input. When a clause is added to the object-level knowledge base,
the specialised version of the partial evaluator can be used to construct
both a partially evaluated version of the meta-level interpreter for the
increased object-level knowledge base, as well as a new version of the
specialised partial evaluator, which is in turn to be used when the next
clause is added to the object-level knowledge base. Since this process
can be performed incrementally, the overhead of repeated partial evaluation is greatly reduced. However, although this incremental approach
might be useful during the development stages of a system, it is doubtful
whether the price of repeatedly constructing a new specialised version of
both meta-level interpreter and partial evaluator at run time does not
cost more than it gains, especially when the object-level knowledge base
changes frequently. In the context of the problem of changing object-
level knowledge bases, Sterling and Beer [Ster86] talk about "open programs", which are programs whose definition is not complete, for instance because input data for the expert system needs to be provided at
run time. They do not provide a solution for this problem, since they

> assume that a goal which fails during partial evaluation time
> will also fail at run time, that is, we assume that a system
> to be partially evaluated is closed.

Another solution to the problem of run time changes to the object-
level knowledge base would be not to include the object-level knowledge
base in the specialisation process. However, would this leave any input for specialisation of the meta-level interpreter? In a system like
Socrates, we are left with the object-level rules of inference. In terms of
the example meta-level interpreter from figure 5.2 this would mean that
we do not supply the object-level theory from figure 5.1 but that we do
supply the definition of the predicate object_level_interpreter. This
restricted version of the partial evaluation process would not generate a
very efficient program like the one in figure 5.3 but the code in figure 5.4.
Although this code is not as optimal as the code in figure 5.3 (since a lot
of computation is still to be done at run time), it is still more efficient
than the original version from figure 5.2. The new program will not be

```
proof(X,invest) :-
        lookup(X,invest).
proof(X,invest) :-
        proof([Y=>X,Y],invest).
proof(X&Y,invest) :-
        proof([X,Y],invest).
proof([X|Y],invest) :-
        proof(X,invest),
        proof(Y,invest).
proof([],invest).
```

Figure 5.4
The programs after restricted partial evaluation

invalidated by run time changes, since the object-level knowledge base
was not used in the specialisation process (the predicate lookup will
still be executed at run time, and was not precomputed by the partial
evaluator, as it was in figure 5.3. The rules of inference (which were
used in the specialisation process) are not very likely to be the subject
of run time changes.

5.3.2 Lack of static information

An important distinction can be made between so called *static* and *dynamic* information. Static information is information which is part of,
or can be derived from, the program code, whereas dynamic information is dependent on the run time environment of the program. For the
purposes of partial evaluation we include the values of input variables
supplied at partial evaluation time in our definition of static information.
For example, in the following or statement

```
(or (eq x 'a)(eql y 2))
```

under the partial input specification

```
y = 3
```

both argument to the call to eql are statically available (and therefore
so is the result of the call to eql), whereas only one argument to the call
to eq is statically available, since the value of x can only be dynamically
determined.

[Beet87] distinguishes three different types of information that can influence the search strategy:

1. Information that is independent of the current problem and the current state of the problem solving process.

2. Information that is dependent on the current problem, but independent of the current state of the problem solving process.

3. Information that is dependent on both the current problem and the current state of the problem solving process.

Since both the second and the third type of control information will only be dynamically available, search strategies that use such information can not be optimised (or only to a limited extent) by using partial evaluation. Only search strategies that are independent of both the input problem and the current state of the problem solving process can make full use of partial evaluation. However, such search strategies are very weak and general, and do not typically play a very important role in expert systems applications. It is notable that all the examples given in the literature on partial evaluation show programs that employ only the first type of information.

In order to analyse the problem of dynamic information in more detail, we can distinguish three techniques that are used by a partial evaluator to produce more efficient code:[4]

1. branching out conditional parts of the code,

2. propagating data structures,

3. opening up intermediate procedure calls (unfolding).

We will argue that each of these techniques is crucially dependent on a large proportion of the information being statically available. If most of the information is only dynamically available, partial evaluation will generate quite poor results.

---

[4]Sometimes a fourth technique is included in this list, namely the so called "pushing down meta-arguments". This involves transforming a call to meta-level predicate such as `solve(object-level-pred(X),Subst)` into a call to the newly created object-level predicated `object-level-pred(X,Subst)`. However, this technique relies necessarily on the fact that the object-level and the meta-level languages are the same, and is therefore not included in this list.

The first technique deals with *conditional branches in the code*. If the condition for such a branch cannot be evaluated at partial evaluation time, because its value is dependent on dynamic information, the partial evaluator either has to stop its evaluations at this point, or it has to generate code for both branches of the conditional, and leave it to the run time evaluation to determine which of these branches should be taken. Neither of these strategies is very successful: if a partial evaluator has to stop optimising the source code at the first dynamically determined conditional it encounters in the code, the resulting code may be not very different at all from the original code, and hence will not be any more efficient. The other strategy (generating code for all possible branches) is also usually not very attractive, given the high branching rates of most programs. This will result in very bulky output code (possibly exponential in the size of the original code), most of which will not be executed at run time. In the context of Prolog, this will mean a large number of clauses that will have to be tried at run time, even though most of them will fail in most cases.

The second technique (*propagating data structures*) tries to pass on data structures through the code in the program. This passing of data structures can be done both *forward* (for input values), and *backward* (for output values)[5]. Obviously, the forward passing of data structures only works for those parts of the data that have been provided statically as partial input. The backward passing of data structures is typically dependent on the values of the input, and is therefore also blocked if most information is only available dynamically. A special problem occurs with the so called built-in predicates that are provided by the Prolog interpreter. These predicates often depend on the full instantiation of a number of their arguments (e.g. `is`), and can therefore not be executed by the partial evaluator if the argument-values are not available. Other built-in predicates cause side effects that must occur at run time (e.g. `write`), and such predicates must also be suspended by the partial evaluator.

The third technique (*unfolding*) tries to insert code for procedure calls as 'in line code', rather than explicitly calling the procedures at run

---

[5]It is exactly this passing of data structures which makes logic programs so suited for partial evaluation, since both the forward and the backward passing is done automatically by the unification mechanism that is provided by the standard interpreter for the language.

time. This technique runs into trouble as soon as the source program contains recursive calls. Although a particular recursive program may in practice always terminate at run-time, this is not necessarily the case at partial-evaluation time, due to the lack of static information. In the case of a logic program this means that the proof tree may contain infinite paths for some uninstantiated goals, and the partial evaluation would be non terminating. Since these infinite computations only arise from the lack of information at partial-evaluation time, and do not occur at run time, we will use the phrase *pseudo-infinite* computation. Two different types of pseudo-infinite computation can be distinguished. The first type, *pseudo-infinitely deep* computation, is caused by programs whose recursive clauses always apply (at partial evaluation time), but whose base clauses never apply, due to the lack of static information. This gives rise to a proof tree with infinitely long branches. The second type, *pseudo-infinitely wide* computation, is caused by programs whose recursive clauses always apply, but whose base clauses also apply sometimes. This gives rise to a proof tree with infinitely many finite branches. A mixture of both types of pseudo-infinite computation is of course also possible. Pseudo-infinitely deep computation corresponds to a program that needs an infinite amount of time to compute its first output, and pseudo-infinitely wide computation corresponds to a program that computes an infinite number of answers (on backtracking, in the case of Prolog). A good example of both problems is the predicate num-elem given below, which selects numeric elements from a list:

```
num-elem(X, [X|_]) :- number(X).
num-elem(X, [_|L]) :- num-elem(X,L).
```

If this predicate is partially evaluated with no input specified, then the base case will never apply, and an infinitely deep computation will result. If this predicate is partially evaluated with the first argument bound to a specific number, but the second argument still unbound, then the base case will always apply, but so will the recursive clause, resulting in an infinitely wide computation. (Notice that when this predicate is partially evaluated with the second argument bound, then none of these problems occur).

In certain cases, the occurrence of infinitely wide computation does not need to lead to problems during partial evaluation, in particular if it is known at partial evaluation time how many outputs are required of the source program. If it is known that at most n different outputs are needed from the source program, then the partial evaluator can unfold the proof tree of the source program until the base clauses have applied n times. A realistic example of this is where a predicate P is immediately followed by a cut in a Prolog program:

$$Q_1, \ldots, Q_i, P, !, Q_{i+1}, \ldots, Q_k$$

or more generally

$$Q_1, \ldots, Q_i, P, Q_{i+1}, \ldots, Q_j, !, Q_{j+1}, \ldots, Q_k$$

where all the conjuncts $Q_{i+1}, \ldots, Q_j$ are known to be deterministic (that is: given an input, they compute exactly one output). In such a case $n = 1$, i.e. only 1 output will ever be required from P. This sort of analysis does of course presuppose that the partial evaluation algorithm has knowledge about properties of cut and of determinateness of predicates in the source program.

In the more general case, where such information about n is not known, or for pseudo-infinitely deep programs, it is necessary for a partial evaluation program to select a finite subtree from the infinite proof tree, in order to guarantee termination of the partial evaluation algorithm. Let π be a source program, θ an input substitution to π, $P(\pi, \theta)$ a partial evaluation procedure, and let $\pi(\theta) \downarrow$ mean that π terminates on input θ, then we would at least require P to terminate whenever π would terminate on θ (or on some instantiation of θ). Formally:

$$\forall \pi \forall \theta : (\exists \theta' \leq_{inst} \theta : \pi(\theta') \downarrow) \rightarrow P(\pi, \theta) \downarrow .$$

This can of course always be achieved by trivial means, such as not unfolding recursive predicates at all, or only unfolding them once (as in [Venk84]), or in general only unfolding them to a fixed maximum depth. However, a more sophisticated solution would be to incorporate a stop criterion in the partial evaluation procedure that will tell us whether a branch of the proof tree for $\pi(\theta)$ is infinite. Thus, we need a stop criterion S such that:

$$\forall \pi \forall \theta : (\forall \theta' \leq_{inst} \theta : \pi(\theta') \uparrow) \leftrightarrow S(\pi, \theta). \tag{5.1}$$

As soon as S becomes true on a branch for $\pi(\theta)$, the partial evaluation procedure should stop. The problem with such a criterion S is that it amounts to solving the halting problem for Prolog, and that therefore it is undecidable. The halting problem for a given language L is to find a predicate H_L that will decided whether an arbitrary program P written in L will halt on an arbitrary input I or not:[6]

$$\forall P \forall I : P(I) \uparrow \leftrightarrow H_L(P, I) \tag{5.2}$$

One of the fundamental theorems of the theory of computation states that this problem is undecidable for any sufficiently powerful language L. Prolog is certainly sufficiently powerful, since it is Turing complete [Tarn77]. Since having S from (5.1) would also give us H_{Prolog} from (5.2), S must also be undecidable. This means that the best we can hope for regarding a stop criterion for partial evaluation is one that is either too strong or too weak. A stop criterion which is too strong will satisfy the $\leftarrow$ direction of (5.1), but there will be some π_0 and θ_0 such that

$$S(\pi_0, \theta_0) \wedge \exists \theta' \leq_{inst} \theta : \pi(\theta') \downarrow,$$

in other words, S will tell us that π_0 will not terminate on θ_0 (or any instantiation of it), while in fact it would. This would result in stopping the unfolding of the partial evaluation algorithm prematurely, thereby producing suboptimal results. Conversely, a stop criterion which is too weak will satisfy the $\rightarrow$ direction of (5.1), but there will be some π_0 and θ_0 such that

$$\neg S(\pi_0, \theta_0) \wedge \forall \theta' \leq_{inst} \theta : \pi(\theta') \uparrow,$$

in other words, S will tell us that π_0 will terminate on θ_0 (or some instantiation of it), while in fact it would not. This would result in a non-terminating partial evaluation.

In the practical use of a stop criterion, a partial evaluator would keep a stack of goals that are unfolded during the expansion of the input program. If we call the original goal $G = G_0$, and we describe the stack of unfolded goals by $G_i (0 > i > j)$, then a number of useful termination criteria are:

    1. unification: $\exists i < j, \exists \theta : \theta G_j = \theta G_i$. We write $G_j =_{unif} G_i$.

---

[6] The reader should be aware of a possible confusion: the stop criterion S from (5.1) is true not when $\pi(\theta)$ will stop, but when $\pi(\theta)$ will *not* stop, indicating that the partial evaluator *should be stopped*. In analogy, 5.2 has been formulated using $P(I) \uparrow$ instead of the usual $P(I) \downarrow$.

2. instantiation: $\exists i < j, \exists \theta : G_j = \theta G_i$, i.e. $G_j \leq_{inst} G_i$.

3. strict instantiation: $\exists i < j, \exists \theta (non\text{-}empty) : G_j = \theta G_i$, i.e $G_j <_{inst} G_i$.

4. alphabetic variancy: $G_j \leq_{inst} G_i$ and $G_i \leq_{inst} G_j$, i.e. $G_j =_{inst} G_i$ (G_i and G_j are identical up to renaming of variables).

It is not necessary to consider another variation, namely $(G_j >_{inst} G_i)$ where G_i is a strict instantiation of G_j, since any chain of ever more general subgoals (a chain $G_0, \ldots, G_n$ where $G_i <_{inst} G_j$ if $i < j$) will always have a most general goal as its limit, and therefore such a computation must always terminate. However, we can have two different variations of (1), namely unification without occurs-check (1a) and unification with occurs-check (1b). These stop criteria relate to each other as follows:

$$(3 \vee 4) \leftrightarrow 2 \rightarrow 1b \rightarrow 1a$$

Simple examples can show that none of these criteria performs satisfactorily. In particular, none of these criteria deals satisfactorily with pseudo-infinitely wide computations. Consider for example a predicate like:

```
p1(X,Y).
p1(X,Y) :- p1(s(X),Y)
```

which generates on backtracking all terms $s^n(0)$ after the call

```
:- p1(0,Y).
```

None of the above stop criteria is able to prevent a partial evaluator from looping while trying to partially evaluate p1 with the first argument instantiated. The point here is not that we would expect a great optimisation from the partial evaluation (it is not clear what such optimisation could possibly be), but rather that the presence of a predicate like p1 in any code makes the partial evaluation non-terminating. An example that illustrates the difference between some of the termination criteria is partially evaluating the above predicate p1 with no input specified. In this case stop criterion (3) is too weak, and lets the partial evaluator loop infinitely, while criteria (4) (and by implication (2), (1a) and (1b)) properly halt the partial evaluator and reproduce the original code. However, the roles of (3) and (4) swap over on the predicate:

```
p2(0).
p2(s(X)) :- p2(X).
```

which will succeed on any input of the form $s^n(0)$. Partially evaluating p2 with no input specified will be properly stopped by (3) (and by implication also by (2), (1a) and (1b), but not by (4) which will loop forever.

For a more realistic example, we can turn to the example that was used in the previous section to describe the use of partial evaluation for meta-level interpreters, shown in figures 5.1, 5.2 and 5.3. The partially evaluated code in figure 5.3 was computed from the code in figures 5.1 and 5.2 using stop criterion (3) (strict instantiation). Had we used the stronger stop criterion (2) (non-strict instantiation), the partial evaluator would have produced the same code in as figure 5.3 but with clauses [6]-[7] replaced by the following clause:

```
[6a] proof(X, invest) :-
         proof([Y => X, Y], invest).
```

This new clause represents a precomputed version of Modus Ponens, but the partial evaluator has stopped short of actually applying this rule, as in in figure 5.3, due to the stronger stop criterion. As a result, this new code is not as efficient as the code from figure 5.3. An advantage of the stronger stop criterion is that it takes significantly less time to execute the partial evaluator (the difference between the execution times of the partial evaluator with stop criteria (2) and (3) is more than a factor of 100).

A different situation occurred while computing the code for figure 5.4. Fewer bindings for variables were known for that partial evaluation, since the object-level theory was not included in the input specification. As a result, the stronger stop criterion (2) had to be used to produce the result in figure 5.4. Any weaker stop criterion would result in either a non-terminating partial evaluation, or in code with many spurious branches.

5.3.3 Summary of problems

Summarising, we can say that although in principle a powerful technique, partial evaluation is rather restricted in its use for optimising meta-level interpreters for two reasons.

- Firstly, if the object-level theory is going to be changed at run time, at least part of the object-level theory cannot be included as input to the partial evaluation algorithm, thereby negatively affecting the optimisations achieved by partial evaluation.

- Secondly, if most of the information in a program is only dynamically available (i.e. at run time), partial evaluation suffers from the following disadvantages:

  - If the source code contains conditional expressions, then a partial evaluator will either have to stop the optimisation process at that point, or produce very bulky code.
  - Data structures cannot be propagated throughout the code.
  - If the source code contains recursive procedures, then, unless specific termination criteria are programmed for particular predicates, a partial evaluator will either produce suboptimal code, or termination of the partial evaluator is no longer guaranteed.

It has to be stressed that although the above discussion quotes examples in Prolog, the problems are not due to this choice, and are fundamental to the concept of partial evaluation.

5.4   Heuristic guidance to partial evaluation

Although the problems discussed above seriously limit the applicability of partial evaluation as a tool for reducing meta-level overhead, a number of heuristics solution can be found to alleviate the problems to a certain extent. The heuristics discussed below are all based on the idea that we will try to build a specific partial evaluator for a particular application, rather than a general, application independent one. More precisely, we can maintain the general framework for a partial evaluator as discussed above, but identify specific places in the algorithm where a user can tune the algorithm to suit a particular application. In particular, we will point out a number of places in the partial evaluation algorithm where we can insert specific knowledge about the behaviour of components of the program to be evaluated. In our case these components will be meta-level predicates, ie. predicates occurring in the meta-level interpreter.

An obvious candidate for removing over-generality is the stop criterion used to determine when to stop unfolding recursive predicates. This criterion can never be correct in the general case (since such a criterion would solve the halting problem for Prolog programs, and hence for Turing machines). As a result, any general criterion is either going to be too weak (i.e. not halting on some infinite recursion), or too strong (i.e. halting too early on some finite recursion). However, if we know the intended meaning of particular parts of a program we can construct specialised termination criteria that are just right for these particular procedures. As example, consider the definition of member/2:

```
member(X, [X|_]).
member(X, [_|T]) :- member(X,T).
```

We know that this predicate is guaranteed to terminate as long as the length of the second argument is decreasing. A good specialised stop criterion for this predicate would therefore be:

$$\exists i, j : i > j, \ member_i(X, L_i) \& member_j(X, L_j) \wedge \| L_i \| \geq \| L_j \|,$$

where $member_i$ represents the i-th call to member. This stop criterion would successfully unfold all calls to member/2 where the second argument is instantiated, but will not loop on those calls where the second argument is uninstantiated (due to a lack of static information). This corresponds to the notion that member/2 will be used to test membership of a given list, and not to generate all possible lists containing a certain element. This criterion will even work for partially instantiated second arguments. A call to member/2 like

```
:- member(X, [1,2|L]).
```

will properly partially evaluate to:

```
member(1, [1,2|L]).
member(2, [1,2|L]).
member(X, [1,2,X|_]).
member(X, [1,2,_|T]) :- member(X, T).
```

The partial evaluation has generated all possible results based on the available static information, while stopping short of looping on the uninstantiated part of the input.

The above halting criterion is based on the intended meaning and use of the predicate member/2, and cannot be generally used, since it would again be either too strong or too weak for certain predicates. Consider for instance the predicate nlist/2 which generates a list of length n:

```
nlist(0, []).
nlist(s(X), [_|T]) :- nlist(X, T).
```

(We use terms $s^n(0)$ for representing the number n to avoid problems with the built in arithmetical predicates. More about this below). This predicate should not be stopped when its second argument is increasing in length, as with member/2, but rather when its first argument is increasing in depth. Such metrics should be devised where possible for predicates used in a meta-level interpreter, and the stop criterion should be specialised for these cases.

A second heuristic that we can inject in the partial evaluation algorithm is a special treatment for certain predicates which are known to be easy to compute at run time, but possibly hard or impossible to compute with only static information. This idea is based on the notion of an *operational predicate* as introduced in the explanation-based generalisation algorithm [Mitc86] which turns out to be closely related to the partial evaluation algorithm [Harm88]. The partial evaluation algorithm should stop when encountering such an operational predicate (which is declared as such beforehand), no matter what amount of precomputation could potentially be done using the definition of such a predicate. For instance, it is possible that the definition of such a predicate has a very high branching rate, leading to an explosion of the size of the code generated by partial evaluation, while only one of the many branches would be chosen and computed at low cost at run time, pruning all the other branches. In such a case it is better not to generate the highly branched search space explicitly at partial evaluation time, but to leave it for run time computation.

An example of this specialised treatment of the partial evaluation algorithm for certain predicates is the standard logic programming technique where a predicate, when applied to a list, unpacks the list into its elements, and then takes a specific action for each of the elements in the list. If these specific actions have a very high branching rate, a good strategy for the partial evaluator is to precompute the process of unfolding the list into its elements (a deterministic operation), but to

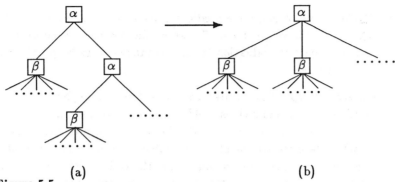

Figure 5.5
Heuristically limited partial evaluation

stop short of partially evaluating the actions taken for the individual elements. These actions will have to be performed at run time, when extra available dynamic information will possibly cut down the branching rate. Graphically, this optimisation process can be depicted as in figure 5.5. Figure 5.5a shows the search tree of original code before partial evaluation, with the α nodes doing the unfolding of the list, and the β nodes doing the highly non-deterministic actions for the individual nodes. If we designate β to be an operational predicate, the limited partial evaluation described above will produce code that has a search space as in figure 5.5b showing that the limited partial evaluation still optimises the search space, but does not get bogged down in the explosive parts of it.

Another heuristic to optimise partial evaluation is *mixed computation*. This involves declaring certain meta-level predicates to be executable at partial evaluation time. If the partial evaluator comes across such a predicate during unfolding, it does not unfold that predicate using its ordinary unfolding strategy, but rather it calls the hardwired interpreter that would normally execute the meta-level code (i.e. in our examples the Prolog interpreter) to execute the particular predicate. The resulting variable bindings are then taken into account during the rest of the unfolding process, but the predicate itself can be removed from the code.

A final heuristic to be embodied in the partial evaluator concerns the evaluable predicates, as typically built into a Prolog system. These predicates can be divided into three types, and for each of the types a different partial evaluation strategy should be used.

- The first type of evaluable predicates are those that perform *side-effects* (e.g. input-output). These predicates can never be performed at partial evaluation time, and must always be postponed until run time.

- The second type of predicates are those that can be partially evaluated if certain conditions hold. These conditions are specific for each particular predicate. For instance, the predicate var/1 (which tests if its argument is a variable), can be partially evaluated (to false, pruning branches from the code) if its argument is not a variable. The reason for this is of course that if the argument is not a variable at partial evaluation time, it will never become a variable at run time, since variables only get more instantiated, not less. On the other hand, if the predicate var/1 succeeds at partial evaluation time, it must remain in the code, since its argument might or might not have become instantiated at run time. Another example is the predicate ==/2 (testing if its arguments are the same Prolog object). This predicate can be evaluated (to true, that is: removed), if it succeeds at partial evaluation time. The argument here is that if it succeeds at partial evaluation time, it will also succeed at run time (since objects that are the same can never become different again), but when the arguments are different at partial evaluation time the predicate should remain in the code, since the objects might or might not have become the same at run time[7]. A third example of this category is the predicate functor/3 (which computes functor and arity of a Prolog term). This predicate can be partially evaluated if either the first or both the second and third arguments are (at least partially) instantiated. Further criteria could be provided for a number of other built in Prolog predicates.

- fully evaluated (if they are fully instantiated at partial evaluation time), or translated into a number of simplified constraints. A good example of this class of predicates are the arithmetic predicates. Obviously, a goal like X is 5+4 can be fully computed at partial evaluation time, as well as goals like 9 is X+4 and

---

[7]This criterion for ==/2 is quite different from that used in the partial evaluator described in [Prie87], where it is incorrectly treated the same as =/2 (unification), which can always be performed at partial evaluation time, unlike ==/2.

X>10, X<5 (although a somewhat more sophisticated algorithm is required). In general a goal like X is Y ⟨op⟩ Z, where ⟨op⟩ is any of the functions +, - and * can be fully computed at partial evaluation time if at least 2 out of the 3 arguments are instantiated. Some types of calls cannot be fully computed at partial evaluation time, but can be transformed into simplified conditions, for instance X<10, X<11 can be reduced to X <10, and the integer division 4 is X/3 can be transformed into X>11, X<15. The partial evaluator incorporated in the PROLEARN system [Prie87] implements these heuristics.

5.4.1 Summary of heuristics

The partial evaluator can be tailored to specific applications by

- incorporating specialised stop criteria for certain recursive predicates

- using knowledge about operational predicates to stop the partial evaluation process

- using knowledge about the branching factor of certain predicates to stop the partial evaluation process

- allowing execution during partial evaluation, the so called mixed computation

- using specialised knowledge to deal with evaluable predicates, dividing them in three ways:

  - predicates that can never be partially evaluated (predicates with side effects).

  - predicates that can only be evaluated if certain conditions hold

  - predicates that can be transformed into simpler constraints.

5.5   Related work in the literature

Much related work has been done in the last few years on partial evaluation and its application to meta-programming (e.g. [Bjor87] and

[Lloy88]). Some of these papers analyse and discuss the limitations of partial evaluation in a similar way as we have done in this chapter, and we will discuss two of these papers in particular.

A well known problem with the use of negation in logic programming is that it is only sound when applied to fully instantiated goals. If applied to partially uninstantiated subgoals, the negation is said to "flounder" [Lloy84], and produces unsound results. This problem is particularly urgent during partial evaluation. A partial evaluation algorithm cannot unfold a negated subgoal if it is not fully instantiated. However, due to the lack of dynamic information at partial evaluation time, many negated subgoals will not be fully instantiated, thus hampering the performance of partial evaluation. As a result, the partial evaluation algorithm given in [Lloy87] is restricted to either evaluate negated subgoals completely (if they are fully instantiated), or not at all otherwise. To solve this problem, [Chan88] gives two techniques for dealing with negated subgoals. This solution is based on two separate techniques for eliminating negation from a program, or at least splitting up into smaller pieces, so that the partial evaluation algorithm can optimise larger parts of the source program.

A second paper that explores the limitations of partial evaluation is [Owen88]. Owen applied partial evaluation to a number of meta-interpreters that were developed for a particular application, and compared the results of this with hand-coded optimisations of the same set of interpreters. This careful analysis revealed many problems with the practical use of partial evaluation, some of which have also been discussed in this chapter:

- Partial evaluation should not always suspend built-in meta-logical predicates (see section 5.4).

- Partial evaluation causes significant fruitless branches in the object-level program (see section 5.3.2).

- Partial evaluation systems always suspend the execution of Prolog's cut, even when this is not necessary.

In order to deal with these problems, Owen proposes a number of enhancements to the partial evaluation algorithm. The most significant of these is what he calls a *folding transformation*, which folds a sequence of conjuncts into a new, uniquely named procedure. This is the opposite of the unfolding operation described in section 5.2. The main goal of this extra operation is to control the branching rate of the code produced by partial evaluation. However, the introduction of this new operation makes a partial evaluation algorithm non-deterministic (the algorithm will have to choose between different possible operations at each step), whereas this was not the case before. This introduces a search component in the partial evaluation procedure that was not present without the folding operation. Further extensions that Owen proposes to the partial evaluation algorithm are the merging of clauses with identical heads, or with heads that only differ in positions containing local variables, and rules that allow the treatment of cuts in certain under certain conditions at partial evaluation time. Unfortunately, even with these an many other special purpose extensions to his partial evaluation algorithm, Owen found the results of partial evaluation on his meta-level interpreters suboptimal, and it would require open ended theorem proving and consistency checking to achieve the same results as his hand-code optimisations.

6 Assertion-Time Inference in Logic-Based Systems

Bernie Elfrink
Han Reichgelt

6.1 Introduction

Many have argued for the use of logic as a knowledge representation language (e.g. [Haye77], [Moor84]). One of the problems that anybody who subscribes to this view faces is the potential inefficiency of a logic based inference engine. [Brac87] mentions different possible solutions. They include restricting the language, or restricting the set of inference rules. Another possibility is the judicious use of meta-level reasoning to prune unpromising branches in the proof tree early on, or the use of hybrid representation languages. We propose yet another way: assertion-time inference.

The problem was studied in the context of Socrates (see chapter 3). The motivation behind the proposal is that in an expert system you want maximal speed at retrieval time when a user is querying the system, even at the cost of lesser speed at assertion time when a knowledge engineer is constructing a knowledge base. The problem is of course that one could in principle draw an infinite number of inferences from a given set of assertions. Our system avoids this problem by using tableau type inference rules.

Tableau type proof theories are very similar to Gentzen type natural deduction proof theories. As [Bled77] points out, systems of this type have, among others, the advantage that they are more natural for humans than resolution-based systems. For example, propositions do not first have to rewritten in conjunctive normal form, but can be used in whatever syntactic form is most natural. Obviously, this argument is even more forceful in the context of expert systems. An expert system should be able to explain its reasoning, and an inference engines whose behaviour is natural and can easily be explained is therefore at a premium.

We first discuss tableau type systems in some detail. Then we show how these rules can be used to construct a system that does assertion time inference. We prove the correctness of the various algorithms. This chapter is an extended version of [Elfr88].

6.2   Tableau proof systems

Tableau proof systems are essentially due to [Beth59]. [Smul68] presents a more elegant notation for proof systems of this type. In this chapter we use Smullyan's notation.

In a tableau, every formula is signed with a T or an F. The intuitive reading of $T\phi$ is ϕ *is true*, while $F\phi$ intuitively means ϕ *is false*. There is an inference rule for each combination of sign (i.e. T or F) and connective. In order to construct a proof of a formula ϕ one signs it with an F and applies the available inference rules until either no more rules can be applied, in which case ϕ is not provable, or until one can show that there is a formula ψ that would have to be signed both with a T and an F. Intuitively, this is a *reductio ad absurdum* argument: one assumes that the formula to be proven is false, and one then derives a contradiction from it.

The formal definition of a proof in a tableau type proof system is as follows. A *signed formula* is an ordered pair consisting of a sign (T or F) and a formula. Rather than writing $\langle T, \phi \rangle$ and $\langle F, \phi \rangle$ we will write $T\phi$ and $F\phi$ respectively. A *sequent* is a set of signed formulas. A sequent is *closed* if there is a formula ϕ such that both $T\phi \in S$, and $F\phi \in S$. A formula ϕ is provable if there is an ordered set of sequents, which we call a *proof tree*, such that

1. $F\phi$ is the first sequent,

2. every sequent is obtained from a previous sequent by applying an inference rule, and

3. every sequent to which no other inference rules are applied is closed.

A signed formula to which an inference rule has been applied is called a *reduced formula*. A sequent which contains no unreduced formulas is called *final*. We will use the term *final set of sequents* to denote a set of final sequents.

Below we will discuss tableau proof theories for classical propositional and predicate logic. However, similar proof systems can be defined for other logics. [Fitt69] presents a proof system for intuitionistic logic and for various modal logics. [Swar80] contains proof systems for many more modal logics. The basic ideas are thus applicable to a wide range of logics.

6.2.1   Classical propositional logic

We first define the inference rules for classical propositional logic. In the following definition S denotes a sequent, $S[\sigma]$ denotes a sequent S containing the signed formula σ and S, σ is a shorthand for $S \cup \{\sigma\}$.

$$\frac{S[T\phi \rightarrow \psi]}{F\phi, S \mid T\psi, S} \quad \frac{S[F\phi \rightarrow \psi]}{T\phi, F\psi, S} \quad \frac{S[T\phi \,\&\, \psi]}{T\phi, T\psi, S} \quad \frac{S[F\phi \,\&\, \psi]}{F\phi, S \mid F\psi, S}$$

$$\frac{S[T\phi \vee \psi]}{T\phi, S \mid T\psi, S} \quad \frac{S[F\phi \vee \psi]}{F\phi, F\psi, S} \quad \frac{S[T\neg\phi]}{F\phi, S} \quad \frac{S[F\neg\phi]}{T\phi, S}$$

The $\mid$ signifies a split in the proof tree. Applying a split inducing inference rule leads to the introduction of two new sequents in the proof tree. The intuitive motivation behind rules of this kind can be illustrated by considering rule $F-\&$. As said before, the intuitive reading of $F\phi\&\psi$ is that $\phi\&\psi$ is false. Now if $\phi\&\psi$ is false, then there are two possibilities: either ϕ is false, or ψ is false. We need to keep both possibilities in mind, and hence the need for splits.

Formulas to which inference rules have been applied are also present in the output sequents. It is therefore in principle possible to apply the same inference rule to the same formula more than once.

The following illustrates the proof system

$$F(\phi \rightarrow \psi) \rightarrow ((\psi \rightarrow \pi) \rightarrow (\phi \rightarrow \pi))$$
$$T(\phi \rightarrow \psi), F(\psi \rightarrow \pi) \rightarrow (\phi \rightarrow \pi)$$
$$T(\phi \rightarrow \psi), T(\psi \rightarrow \pi), F(\phi \rightarrow \pi)$$
$$T(\phi \rightarrow \psi), T(\psi \rightarrow \pi), T\phi, F\pi$$

$F\phi, T(\psi \rightarrow \pi), T\phi, F\pi$	$T\psi, T(\psi \rightarrow \pi), T\phi, F\pi$	
closed	$F\psi, T\psi, T\phi, F\pi$	$T\pi, T\psi, T\phi, F\pi$
	closed	*closed*

As said before, in the above formulation of inference rules, every reduced formula, every formula to which an inference rule has been applied, remains in principle available for further applications of the same inference rule. However, it can be proven that in the propositional calculus, there is nothing to be gained from applying the same inference rule to the same formula twice: everything that is provable when you apply inference rules more than once to the same formula is also provable when you apply the inference rule just once. A formal proof of this proposition is based on the observation that, if an inference rule can be applied to a sequent S to give as output sequent S', then applying the same inference rule to S' gives as output S' as well. Applying one of the above inference rules to the same formula twice will result in the same (less complex) formulas being added twice to a sequent. But as a sequent is a set of formulas, applying an inference rule to the same formula more than once, will not add any new signed propositions to a sequent.

One can strengthen this observation. It is actually possible to delete reduced formulas altogether. Everything that is provable when reduced formulas are not deleted is also provable when they are. Rather than prove this result formally, we will give a proof sketch. Suppose that the result did not hold. Then this would imply that we can find closures in branches of the proof tree because some non-atomic formula occurs signed both T and F in this branch. We prove by induction that if there is a such a closure, then all the branches obtained from this branch from exhaustively applying the inference rules are closed as well. The following illustrates this for a conjunction $\pi \& \psi$. We assume that there is some branch which contains this conjunction signed both T and F:

$$
\begin{array}{c}
S, T\pi\&\psi, F\pi\&\psi \\
S, T\pi, T\psi, F\pi\&\psi \\
\hline
\end{array}
$$

$$
S, T\pi, \overline{T\psi, F\pi} \quad \Big| \quad S, T\pi, T\psi, F\psi
$$
$$
\textit{closed} \qquad\qquad\quad \textit{closed}
$$

The assumption that the final sequents are closed is of course guaranteed by the induction hypothesis. The reader can verify that the induction step holds for other non-atomic propositions as well.

The above result is important because it enables us to define an effective proof procedure for classical propositional calculus: reduce all signed formulas and delete them. When no more inference rules can be applied, search each sequent for a formula that is signed both T and F. If for all final sequents there is a such a formula, then the formula is provable.

A final observation: exhaustively applying the inference rules to a formula effectively amounts to rewriting the formula in a disjunctive normal form, i.e. as a disjunction of conjunctions. Each of the final

branches of a proof tree is one disjunct, i.e. a conjunction of atomic
formulas or their negations. Each formula signed with a T corresponds
to an atomic formula, and each formula signed with an F corresponds
to a negated atomic formula. We will prove this formally for the proof
theory for classical predicate calculus which we introduce now.

6.2.2   Classical predicate calculus

There are two ways in which the above system can be generalized to
classical first order predicate calculus.   The first way, and the one
that is usually taken by logicians, is to add the following four inference
rules to the above set, two for the universal quantifier, and two for the
existential

$$\frac{S[T(\forall x)\phi x]}{T\phi a, S} \quad \frac{S[F(\forall x)\phi x]}{F\phi a, S} \quad \frac{S[T(\exists x)\phi x]}{T\phi a, S} \quad \frac{S[F(\exists x)\phi x]}{T\phi a, S}$$

with the restriction on the rules F-$\forall$ and T-$\exists$ that a is a
constant not appearing in the formula ϕ, or in any of the
propositions in S.

The disadvantage of this method is that the rules T-$\forall$ and F-$\exists$ may
have to be applied more than once. As noted above, a formula remains
available when a inference rule has been applied to it. Therefore, one
could apply the rules T-$\forall$ and F-$\exists$ to the same formula. Unlike the
propositional case, applying the same inference rule to the same formula
more than once will lead to new signed formulas being added. This is of
course the consequence of the fact that each new application of one of
these rules lead to the introduction of a new constant. Because of this,
there is no effective way of deciding when to stop applying inference
rules to a given branch. This of course is in accordance with the fact
that there is no effective decision procedure for classical predicate calculus. [Wall85] describes a method adapted from [Bibe82a], [Bibe82b] for
determining an order in which formulas should be reduced. A necessary,
but not sufficient, condition for a formula to be provable, is that this
ordering be acyclic. For more details, the reader is referred to the papers
by Bibel and Wallen.

We have developed an alternative way of generalizing the propositional
system to predicate logic. The basic idea is that rather than always
replacing the quantified variable in a quantified formula by a constant,

the quantified formula is skolemised during the search of a proof. This approach can be called *skolemising by need.*

The skolemising by need approach involves three extensions to the proof theory for propositional logic. First, we add four inference rules.

$$\frac{S[T(\forall x)\phi x]}{T\phi y, S} \quad \frac{S[F(\forall x)\phi x]}{F\phi f, S} \quad \frac{S[T(\exists x)\phi x]}{T\phi f, S} \quad \frac{S[F(\exists x)\phi x]}{F\phi y, S}$$

where y is the first variable not occurring free in ϕx or S, and where f is a new functional term constructed from a new function symbol and all free variables in ϕx except for x itself.

A second complication concerns the way one deals with free variables in formulas that are reduced by the split inducing inference rules T-$\lor$, T-$\rightarrow$ and $F - \&$. Before such a rule can be applied the variables and the skolem constants/functions in the to be reduced formula need to be replaced, provided they occur in formulas on both sides of the split, by what we will call *wide scope* variables and *wide scope* skolem terms. If x is a variable, then we use the notation x^w to denote a wide scope variable; similarly, if a is a skolem term then a^w is a wide scope skolem term. The intuitive motivation is that a wide scope term has wider scope than the disjunction that is implicitly introduced when a split is introduced. Thus, before the application of an inference rule that introduce a split in the proof tree, every free variable and every skolem term in the formula that is to be reduced is first replaced by a wide scope variable.

The final complication is a change in the definitions of closed sequents and closed trees. A sequent is closed if it contains two formulas ϕ and ψ that unify with one being signed T and the other F. This unification may return bindings for wide scope variables. A proof tree is closed if

1. all the sequents that cannot be reduced any further are closed,

2. the unifications for the wide scope variables that are returned by final sequents are compatible with each other.

We illustrate the need for wide scope variables by comparing two formulas, one of which is valid in classical predicate calculus, the other of which is not. First consider the formula $(\forall x)(\phi x \& \psi x) \rightarrow (\phi a \& \psi b)$. The following is a successful proof of this formula

$$F(\forall x)(\phi x \& \psi x) \rightarrow (\phi a \& \psi b)$$
$$T(\forall x)(\phi x \& \psi x), F(\phi a \& \psi b)$$
$$T(\phi x \& \psi x), F(\phi a \& \psi b)$$
$$T\phi x, T\psi x, F(\phi a \& \psi b)$$

$T\phi x, T\psi x, F\phi a$	$T\phi x, T\psi x, F\psi b$
closed	*closed*

The above proof is entirely satisfactory because both final sequents are closed and the unifications for the wide scope variables are compatible, (there are no such unifications).

In contrast, consider the formula, $(\forall x)(\phi x \vee \psi x) \rightarrow (\phi a \vee \psi b)$, which is not valid.

$$F(\forall x)(\phi x \vee \psi x) \rightarrow (\phi a \vee \psi b)$$
$$T(\forall x)(\phi x \vee \psi x), F(\phi a \vee \psi b)$$
$$T(\phi x \vee \psi x), F(\phi a \vee \psi b)$$
$$T(\phi x \vee \psi x), F\phi a, F\psi b$$

$T\phi x^w, F\phi a, F\psi b$	$T\psi x^w, F\phi a, F\psi b$

The proof fails because although both sequents can by themselves be closed, the unifications that they give for the wide scope variable x^w, x^w/a and x^w/b respectively, are incompatible.

In the skolemisation by need approach, there is no longer any need for keeping reduced formulas around. They can just be deleted. The reader can verify that if one applies the same inference rule to a quantified formula in a sequent S to give sequent S', then applying the same inference rule to S' will give the same sequent S''. So, applying the same inference rule twice to the same formula will not add any further signed formulas. Moreover, the reader can check that every branch that closes because a non-atomic formula is signed both T and F will also closed if the formulas are further reduced. As a result, one can use basically the same algorithm as was used for the propositional case except that there needs to be an additional check to ensure that that the wide scope variable bindings which result from closing individual final sequents, are compatible.

6.2.3 Soundness

It can be shown that the above proof systems are both complete and sound. For the proof for the original proof theory the reader is referred to [Smul68].

We prove soundness for the revised proof theory by formulating a translation algorithm that rewrites sets of sequents into formulas and proving that if the input to an inference rule is true, then the rewritten output is true as well. The translation algorithm can be formulated as follows:

Rewriting algorithm.   Let $S = S_1, \ldots, S_n$ be a final set of sequents. Then, to find the corresponding formula, go through the following steps:

1. for every signed formula σ in $S_i, 0 < i < n + 1$, if $\sigma = T\phi$, then replace it by ϕ, else replace it by $\neg \phi$.

2. for each sequent, conjoin the rewritten formulas.

3. deskolemise every formula ϕ in the rewritten sequents as follows: if it contains wide scope variables and skolem terms, or skolem terms with wider scope, then leave those; rewrite the other variables and skolem terms by replacing the free variables by universally quantified variables, and skolem functions by existentionally quantified variables, respecting their relative scopes, i.e. if the skolem function contains an occurrence of a free variable, then the universally quantified variable that replaces the free variable should have wider scope than the existential variable replacing the skolem function.

4. form a disjunction of the rewritten sequents.

5. rewrite the wide scope variables and the remaining skolem functions in the same way as in step 3.

The following illustrates the rewriting algorithm:

$$T(\forall x)\big((\exists y)(\phi xy \,\&\, \psi y) \rightarrow \neg(\pi x \vee \chi x)\big)$$
$$T(\exists y)(\phi xy \,\&\, \psi y) \rightarrow \neg(\pi x \vee \chi x)$$

$$
\begin{array}{c|c}
F(\exists y)(\phi x^w y \,\&\, \psi y) & T\neg(\pi x^w \vee \chi x^w) \\
F(\phi x^w f(x) \,\&\, \psi f(x)) & F(\pi x^w \vee \chi x^w) \\
\hline
F\phi x^w f(x)^w \mid F\psi f(x)^w & F\pi x^w, F\chi x^w
\end{array}
$$

The set of final sequents can the be given as input to the rewriting algorithm:

$$\{\{F\phi x^w f(x)^w\}, \{F\psi f(x)^w\}, \{F\pi x^w, F\chi x^w\}\}$$
$$\{\{\neg\phi x^w f(x)^w\}, \{\neg\psi f(x)^w\}, \{\neg\pi x^w, \neg\chi x^w\}\}$$
$$\{\{\neg\phi x^w f(x)^w\}, \{\neg\psi f(x)^w\}, \{(\neg\pi x^w \,\&\, \neg\chi x^w)\}\}$$
$$\neg\phi x^w f(x)^w \vee \neg\psi f(x)^w \vee (\neg\pi x^w \,\&\, \neg\chi x^w)$$
$$(\forall x)(\exists y)(\neg\phi xy \vee \neg\psi y \vee (\neg\pi x \,\&\, \neg\chi x))$$

Step 3 of the rewriting algorithm was not applicable. The reader can check that the output of the rewriting algorithm

$$(\forall x)(\exists y)(\neg \phi xy \vee \neg \psi y \vee (\neg \pi x \& \neg \chi x))$$

is equivalent to formula that we started with

$$(\forall x)((\exists y)(\phi xy \& \psi y) \rightarrow \neg(\pi x \vee \chi x)).$$

We will now prove that this is always the case.

THEOREM 1 Let ϕ be a formula, let $rew(\phi)$ be the result of applying the rewriting algorithm to the final set of sequents obtained from $T\phi$. Then $rew(\phi) \leftrightarrow \phi$.

Proof The proof is an induction proof over the number of sequents. Below we prove the base cases where there is one sequent. The induction step is straightforward. Note that each set of sequents is rewritten as a disjunction. The induction step then follows because $\pi \leftrightarrow \psi$ implies $(\pi_1 \ldots \vee \ldots \vee \pi \vee \ldots \vee \pi_n) \leftrightarrow (\pi_1 \ldots \vee \ldots \vee \psi \vee \ldots \vee \pi_n)$.

We first prove the result for the propositional rules. Thus, suppose that $S = \pi_1, \ldots, \pi, \ldots, \pi_n$, with as wide scope variables and skolem terms $x_1, \ldots, x_n$, then we have the following where each left hand side rewrites the input sequent, and each right hand side the output sequent(s).

$$Qx_1, \ldots, Qx_n(\pi_1 \& \ldots \& \neg(\phi \rightarrow \psi) \& \ldots \& \pi_n) \leftrightarrow$$
$$Qx_1, \ldots, Qx_n(\pi_1 \& \ldots \& \phi \& \neg \psi \& \ldots \& \pi_n)$$

$$Qx_1, \ldots, Qx_n(\pi_1 \& \ldots \& (\phi \rightarrow \psi) \& \ldots \& \pi_n) \leftrightarrow$$
$$Qx_1, \ldots, Qx_n((\pi_1 \& \ldots \& \neg \phi \& \ldots \& \pi_n) \vee (\pi_1 \& \ldots \& \psi \& \ldots \& \pi_n))$$

$$Qx_1, \ldots, Qx_n(\pi_1 \& \ldots \& (\phi \& \psi) \& \ldots \& \pi_n) \leftrightarrow$$
$$Qx_1, \ldots, Qx_n(\pi_1 \& \ldots \& \phi \& \psi \& \ldots \& \pi_n)$$

$$Qx_1, \ldots, Qx_n(\pi_1 \& \ldots \& \neg(\phi \& \psi) \& \ldots \& \pi_n) \leftrightarrow$$
$$Qx_1, \ldots, Qx_n((\pi_1 \& \ldots \& \neg \phi \& \ldots \& \pi_n) \vee (\pi_1 \& \ldots \& \neg \psi \& \ldots \& \pi_n))$$

$$Qx_1, \ldots, Qx_n(\pi_1 \& \ldots \& \neg(\phi \vee \psi) \& \ldots \& \pi_n) \leftrightarrow$$
$$Qx_1, \ldots, Qx_n(\pi_1 \& \ldots \& \neg\phi \& \neg\psi \& \ldots \& \pi_n)$$

$$Qx_1, \ldots, Qx_n(\pi_1 \& \ldots \& (\phi \vee \psi) \& \ldots \& \pi_n) \leftrightarrow$$
$$Qx_1, \ldots, Qx_n((\pi_1 \& \ldots \& \phi \& \ldots \& \pi_n) \vee (\pi_1 \& \ldots \& \psi \& \ldots \& \pi_n))$$

$$Qx_1, \ldots, Qx_n(\pi_1 \& \ldots \& \neg\phi \& \ldots \& \pi_n) \leftrightarrow$$
$$Qx_1, \ldots, Qx_n(\pi_1 \& \ldots \& \neg\phi \& \ldots \& \pi_n)$$

$$Qx_1, \ldots, Qx_n(\pi_1 \& \ldots \& \neg\neg\phi \& \ldots \& \pi_n) \leftrightarrow$$
$$Qx_1, \ldots, Qx_n(\pi_1 \& \ldots \& \phi \& \ldots \& \pi_n)$$

The correctness of the quantifier rules follows from the following four formulas, where each left-hand-side rewrites the top half of an inference rule, and the right-hand-side rewrites the bottom half. The formulas are correct because we know that none of the formulas $\pi_1, \ldots, \pi_n$ contains the variable x.

$$Qx_1, \ldots, Qx_n(\pi_1 \& \ldots \& (\forall x)\phi x \& \ldots \& \pi_n)$$
$$\leftrightarrow Qx_1, \ldots, Qx_n(\forall x)(\pi_1 \& \ldots \& \phi x \& \ldots \& \pi_n)$$

$$Qx_1, \ldots, Qx_n(\pi_1 \& \ldots \& \neg(\forall x)\phi x \& \ldots \& \pi_n)$$
$$\leftrightarrow Qx_1, \ldots, Qx_n(\exists x)(\pi_1 \& \ldots \& \neg\phi x \& \ldots \& \pi_n)$$

$$Qx_1, \ldots, Qx_n(\pi_1 \& \ldots \& (\exists x)\phi x \& \ldots \& \pi_n)$$
$$\leftrightarrow Qx_1, \ldots, Qx_n(\exists x)(\pi_1 \& \ldots \& \phi x \& \ldots \& \pi_n)$$

$$Qx_1, \ldots, Qx_n(\pi_1 \& \ldots \& \neg(\exists x)\phi x \& \ldots \& \pi_n)$$
$$\leftrightarrow Qx_1, \ldots, Qx_n(\forall x)(\pi_1 \& \ldots \& \neg\phi x \& \ldots \& \pi_n)$$

The above establishes that the inference rules are truth preserving. We now use this to prove soundness. It is easy to check that if a sequent is closed, it is rewritten as a conjunction that contains both π and $\neg\psi$ where π and ψ unify. The conjunction therefore can never be true. The first sequent in a proof tree for a formula ϕ is rewritten as $\neg\phi$. If a formula ϕ can be proven, then each final sequent will be closed and can therefore never be true. Thus, if ϕ is proven, then the assumption $\neg\psi$ is shown to imply a disjunction of always false conjunctions. Therefore, the assumption that the formula is false leads to a contradiction, and hence the formula is valid. Thus, if $\vdash \psi$, then $\models \psi$.

6.2.4   Completeness

The completeness of the revised proof theory can be proven in the following indirect way. Consider the following complete Hilbert-type proof theory:

Axioms:

$\pi \rightarrow (\psi \rightarrow \pi)$
$(\pi \rightarrow \psi) \rightarrow ((\pi \rightarrow (\psi \rightarrow \rho)) \rightarrow (\pi \rightarrow \rho))$
$\pi \rightarrow (\psi \rightarrow (\pi \& \psi))$
$(\pi \& \psi) \rightarrow \pi$
$(\pi \& \psi) \rightarrow \psi$
$\pi \rightarrow (\pi \vee \psi)$
$\psi \rightarrow (\pi \vee \psi)$
$(\pi \rightarrow \psi) \rightarrow ((\rho \rightarrow \psi) \rightarrow ((\pi \vee \rho) \rightarrow \psi))$
$(\pi \rightarrow \psi) \rightarrow ((\pi \rightarrow \neg\psi) \rightarrow \neg\pi)$
$\neg\neg\pi \rightarrow \pi$
$\pi\alpha \rightarrow (\exists x)\pi x$
$(\forall x)\pi x \rightarrow \pi\alpha$

Inference rules:

$\pi, \pi \rightarrow \psi \vdash \psi$
if $\vdash \pi \rightarrow \psi\alpha$, then $\vdash \pi \rightarrow (\forall x)\psi x$
  provided α does not occur in π
if $\vdash \psi\alpha \rightarrow \pi$, then $\vdash (\exists x)\psi x \rightarrow \pi$
  provided α does not occur in π

We get completeness by proving that everything provable in the above Hilbert type proof theory is also provable in the revised proof theory. The first step is to prove that all the axioms can be proven. This left as an exercise to the reader. The second step involves proving that if the input to an inference rule can be proven, then the output can be proven as well.

We first prove the correctness of modus ponens. The proof is straightforward:

$$\frac{T\pi, T\pi \rightarrow \psi, F\psi}{T\pi, \underset{closed}{F\pi, F\psi} \ \Big| \ \underset{closed}{T\pi, T\psi, F\psi}}$$

The next theorem proves that, if the input to the second of the inference rules is provable, then the output is provable as well.

THEOREM 2 If $\pi \rightarrow \psi\alpha$ is provable, where π does not contain α, then $\pi \rightarrow (\forall x)\psi x$ is provable.

Proof If $\pi \rightarrow \psi\alpha$ is provable, then $F\pi \rightarrow \psi\alpha$ leads to a closed final set of sequents. Because π does not contain α, every closure must be the result of a closure between two sub-formulas of π, or a closure between a sub-formula not containing α of π and $\psi\alpha$, or a closure between two sub-formulas of $\psi\alpha$. In the first case, $F\pi \rightarrow (\forall x)\psi x$ is provable as well, as the same sub-formula of π will give a closure. In the second case, because the sub-formula does not contain α, the sub-formula is independent of the universal quantifier, and will therefore result in a closure as well. In the final case, if the sub-formula contains in the original proof contains α, then applying a quantifier rule will result in two clashing formulas as well; if it does not contain α, then we get the clash independent of the quantifier rule.

The proof of the final inference rule is along the same lines, and is left to the reader.

6.3   Assertion-time inference

The basic idea behind our assertion-time inferencer rests on the observation that retrieving a proposition ϕ from a knowledge base KB amounts to trying to establish whether $KB \vdash \phi$. Assuming that KB is a finite set of formulas, let $\&KB$ stand for the conjunction of the formulas in KB. Then the above query is equivalent to asking $\vdash (\&KB \rightarrow \phi)$. In a tableau proof system, in order to find a proof for this query, one would have to apply the rules to $F(\&KB \rightarrow \phi)$. We apply the rule $F\text{-} \rightarrow$, which results in the sequent $T\&KB, F\phi$. Because $\&KB$ is a conjunction, $T\&KB$ can be reduced to $\{T\psi | \psi \in KB\}$. In order to prove that $KB \vdash \phi$, one would have to prove that the sequents obtained by reducing $\{T\psi | \psi \in KB\} \cup \{F\phi\}$ are closed. At the time at a knowledge base is constructed, it is not known which queries will be asked. Therefore, all one can do is apply the T-rules to the assertions in the knowledge base, store the results and use them whenever a query is asked of the system at retrieval time. The system that we have implemented does exactly this.

Using the proof theory defined in the previous section, each formula is reduced to a final set of sequents. From the final set of sequents the system constructs a set of pairs of what we call *entry* and *proof* formulas. An entry formula is a formula that can be derived from the original formula, provided that the proof formula can be derived from other information in the knowledge base. Entry formulas are always either atomic formulas or negations thereof, or formulas constructed from these by replacing occurrences of one or more constants by universally or existentially quantified variables. If the original formula is itself a formula of this type, then this formula will become the entry formula, while the proof formula will be empty. This reflects the fact that the entry formula can itself already be proved. Entry formulas and proof formulas are stored in the knowledge base together with the original formula on the basis of which they were constructed. One reason for storing the original formula is that it may be necessary for explanation purposes. However, in this chapter, we ignore this.

In order to explain the above ideas more fully, we first discuss the propositional case. We then generalize it to the first-order case and prove the correctness of the various algorithms. In the next section, we will then discuss the actual implementation.

6.3.1 Classical propositional logic

Consider the sentence $(\phi \& \psi) \rightarrow (\pi \vee \chi)$. When this proposition is asserted, the formula is signed with a T, and the T-rules are applied.

$$
\begin{array}{c}
T(\phi \& \psi) \rightarrow (\pi \vee \chi) \\
\hline
\begin{array}{c|c}
F(\phi \& \psi) & T(\pi \vee \chi) \\
\hline
F\phi \mid F\psi & T\pi \mid T\chi
\end{array}
\end{array}
$$

The final set of sequents represents a disjunction of cases under which the sentence would be true. Thus in order for $(\phi \& \psi) \rightarrow (\pi \vee \chi)$ to be true, either ϕ should be false, or ψ should be false, or π should be true, or χ should be true. One can therefore conclude that ϕ is false if ψ is true, π false, and χ false as well. In other words, one can use the above proof tree to build up proof and entry formulas. From the above proof tree, one can construct the following pairs of entry and proof formulas. We used the transformation that in order to prove that π is false, one has to prove that $\neg \pi$ is true.

Entry formula :	Proof formula :
$\neg \phi$	$\psi \& \neg \pi \& \neg \chi$
$\neg \psi$	$\phi \& \neg \pi \& \neg \chi$
π	$\phi \& \psi \& \neg \chi$
χ	$\phi \& \psi \& \neg \chi$

The above illustrated the simplest case because each final sequent in the tree contained only one formula. The following formula illustrates a more complicated case:

$$T(\phi \vee \psi) \rightarrow (\pi \& \chi)$$

$F \phi \vee \psi$	$T \pi \& \chi$
$F \phi, F \psi$	$T \pi, T \chi$

As said before, the final set of sequents again represents a disjunction of cases under which the above formula would be true. However, unlike in the above case, each sequent itself contains more than one formula. Sequents are interpreted as conjunctions. Thus, in order to prove π based on the above tree, one has to prove that it is not the case than both ϕ and ψ are false. Thus, in order to prove π, based on the above proof tree, one has to prove either ϕ or ψ . Using similar arguments one can obtain the following:

Entry formula :	Proof formula :
$\neg \phi$	$\neg \pi \vee \neg \chi$
$\neg \psi$	$\neg \pi \vee \neg \chi$
π	$\phi \vee \psi$
χ	$\phi \vee \psi$

Applying rules to a formula signed T is in fact equivalent to rewriting the formula in disjunctive normal form, i.e. as a disjunction of conjunctions, in which each conjunct is either atomic or a negation of an atomic formula. One can use this fact to formulate the algorithm for building up knowledge bases for the propositional case. Let $\{S_1,,\ldots,S_n\}$ be the final set of sequents, then the following pairs of entry-formulas and proof-formulas can be obtained: let $\phi_i \in S_i$, $0 < n+1$. Then $rew(\phi_i) = \psi$ if $\phi = T\psi$, and $rew(\phi_i) = \neg\psi$ if $\phi = F\psi$. $rew(\phi_i)$ is an entry-formula with as proof formula

$$(\neg rew(\phi_1)\&\ldots\&\neg rew(\phi_{i-1})\&\neg rew(\phi_{i+1})\&\ldots\&\neg rew(\phi_n)),$$

where each $\phi_j \in S_j$, $0 < j < n+1$ and $i \neq j$. Because we are dealing with classical logic, we can eliminate double negations. Thus, the above definition in fact says that in order to find a proof formula for a given entry formula in a sequent, a conjunction has to be formed that has as conjuncts one negated rewritten formula from every other sequent.

6.3.2 Predicate logic

The problem with generalizing the propositional case to full first order predicate calculus concerns the relative scopes of the variables that occur in the final sequents and the negations that are introduced in the process of finding entry formulas and proof formulas. In this section we present the algorithm for constructing entry formulas and proof formulas. Earlier we defined an algorithm for rewriting the final set of sequents called the rewriting algorithm. Applying the inference rules more or less amounts to rewriting the matrix formula in disjunctive normal form. (This is not quite accurate because the rewritten formula is not in prenex normal form, but this detail need not concern us.) Using this fact, we formulate an algorithm for the construction of proof formulas, which we call the *proof formula formation algorithm*. We then prove that the construction of entry and proof formulas is indeed correct, i.e. we show that the entry formula is implied by the proof formula and the rewritten final set of sequents.

In order to construct an entry formula, one deskolemises a single formula from a final sequent in the normal way with the proviso that if the formula was signed with an F, then the formula will have to be negated before it is deskolemised. The construction of the proof formula is more complicated than in the propositional case. The following algorithm specifies the correct way of constructing a proof formula.

Proof formula formation algorithm   Let S be a set of sequents $\{S_1,\ldots,S_n\}$ from which the proof formula is to be constructed, then form a proof formula as follows:

1. For every sequent S_i, $0 < i < n + 1$, take $\phi \in S_i$.

2. If ϕ is of the form $F\psi$, then negate ψ.

3. Deskolemise each resulting formula with exception of the wide scope variables and wide scope skolem terms that also occur in the entry formula, or terms with a wider scope, in the normal way.

4. Negate each formula.

5. Conjoin the formulas.

6. If the formula contains wide scope variables and wide scope skolem terms also contained in the entry formula, or terms with a wider scope, then replace each of these by a free variable, and deskolemise.

If S is a set of sequents from which a proof formula is to be constructed, then *p-rew*(S) denotes a formula obtained by applying the proof formula formation algorithm to S.

There are two remarks to be made about the proof formula formation algorithm. First, step 6. implies that even wide scope skolem constants and terms with wider scope are replaced by universally quantified formulas. Second, the proof formula formation algorithm does not specify one proof formula. Step 1. contains a choice, and different choices lead to different proof formulas.

In order to illustrate the algorithm, we will consider a few cases. As a first example consider:

$$T(\forall x)\big((\phi x \vee \psi x) \to (\chi x \& \pi x)\big)$$
$$T(\phi x \vee \psi x) \to (\chi x \& \pi x)$$
$$F(\phi x^w \vee \psi x^w) \mid T(\chi x^w \& \pi x^w)$$
$$F\phi x^w, F\psi x^w \mid T\chi x^w, T\pi x^w$$

One the basis of this, one can construct the following entry and proof formulas:

Entry formula :   Proof formula :

$(\forall x)\neg\phi x$ $(\forall x)\neg\chi x$

                     $or\,(\forall x)\neg\pi x$

$(\forall x)\neg\psi x$ $(\forall x)\neg\chi x$

                     $or\,(\forall x)\neg\pi x$

$(\forall x)\chi x$ $(\forall x)\neg\neg\phi x$

                     $or\,(\forall x)\neg\neg\psi x$

$(\forall x)\pi x$ $(\forall x)\neg\neg\phi x$

                     $or\,(\forall x)\neg\neg\psi x$

Consider the following example:

$$T(\forall x)(\exists y)((\exists z)(\phi xyz\,\&\,\psi xy)\rightarrow\pi xy)$$
$$T(\exists y)((\exists z)(\phi xyz\,\&\,\psi xy)\rightarrow\pi xy)$$
$$\frac{T(\exists z)(\phi xf(x)z\,\&\,\psi xf(x))\rightarrow\pi xf(x)}{}$$

$$\frac{F(\exists z)(\phi x^w f(x)^w z\,\&\,\psi x^w f(x)^w)}{}\;\Big|\;T\pi x^w f(x)^w$$

$$\frac{F\phi x^w f(x)^w z\,\&\,\psi x^w f(x)^w}{F\phi x^w f(x)^w z\;\Big|\;F\psi x^w f(x)^w}\;\Big|\;T\pi x^w f(x)^w$$

We can construct the following entry and proof formulas on the basis of the above:

Entry formula :   Proof formula :

$(\forall x)(\exists y)(\forall z)\neg\phi xyz$ $(\forall x)\neg(\exists y)\neg\psi xy\,\&\,(\forall x)\neg(\exists y)\pi xy$

$(\forall x)(\exists y)\psi xy$ $(\forall x)\neg(\exists y)(\forall z)\neg\phi xyz\,\&\,(\forall x)\neg(\exists y)\pi xy$

$(\forall x)(\exists y)\pi xy$ $(\forall x)\neg(\exists y)(\forall z)\neg\phi xyz\,\&\,(\forall x)\neg(\exists y)\neg\psi xy$

Finally, consider the following example

$$T(\exists x)(\forall y)(\phi y\rightarrow\psi xy)$$
$$T(\forall y)(\phi y\rightarrow\psi ay)$$
$$\frac{T\phi y\rightarrow\psi ay}{F\phi y_w\;\Big|\;T\psi ay_w}$$

We construct the following entry and proof formulas:

Entry formula :   Proof formula :

$(\exists x)(\forall y)\psi xy$ $(\forall y)\neg\neg\phi y$

$(\forall y)\neg\phi y$ $(\forall x)(\forall y)\neg\psi xy$

The reader can verify that in each example the original formula and the proof formula do indeed imply the entry formula. We will now prove this result formally.

The proof formula formation algorithm for constructing entry and proof formulas is correct if it can be proven that the proof formula and the original formula imply the entry formula. Because of the soundness proof we know that the rewritten formula, i.e. the formula that results from applying the rewriting algorithm to the set of final sequents, is equivalent to the original formula. Therefore, in order to prove the correctness of the algorithm, we have to prove for every entry and proof formula that the proof formula and the rewritten formula imply the entry formula.

In the proof below, we will first consider cases where entire sequents are rewritten as entry and proof formulas. The entry sequent is obtained from a sequent Seq by applying the rewriting algorithm to $\{Seq\}$. The proof sequent is obtained by rewriting the set of final sequents minus the one that gave rise to the entry formula in a similar vein to the proof formation algorithm. First, for all sequents minus the entry sequent, we apply step 1 to 4 of the rewriting algorithm. Note that the disjunction in the formula obtained in this way all occur as disjuncts in the formula resulting from applying the rewriting algorithm to the final set of sequents. We then negate this formula and apply step 6 of the proof formula formation algorithm. If S is a set of sequents, then, we write $pp\text{-}rew(S)$ for the formula thus obtained.

The following illustrates the construction of $pp\text{-}rew(S)$. Suppose that we start with

$$T(\forall x)(\exists y)((\exists z)(\phi xyz \& \psi xy) \to \pi xy \& \chi x).$$

This will eventually lead to the final set of sequents

$$\{\{F\phi x^w f(x)^w z\}, \{F\psi x^w f(x)^w\}, \{T\pi x^w f(x)^w, T\chi x^w\}\}.$$

Assuming that we use the first sequent to construct the entry formula $(\forall x)(\exists y)(\forall z)(\phi xyz)$ we construct the following proof theory from the remaining sequents:

$$\{\{F\psi x^w f(x)^w\}, \{T\pi x^w f(x)^w, T\chi x^w\}\}$$
$$\{\{\neg\psi x^w f(x)^w\}, \{\pi x^w f(x)^w, \chi x^w\}\}$$
$$\{\{\neg\psi x^w f(x)^w\}, \{\pi x^w f(x)^w \& \chi x^w\}\}$$
$$\neg\psi x^w f(x)^w \vee (\pi x^w f(x)^w \& \chi x^w).$$

This formula can be obtained by applying steps 1 to 4 of the rewriting algorithm. Note that once more step 3 is not applicable. The two disjuncts obtained here also occur in formula obtained from rewriting the entire set of final sequents according to the rewriting algorithm. Now we negate the formula, and apply step 6 in the proof formula formation algorithm to give

$$(\forall x)(\forall y)(\neg(\neg\psi xy \vee (\pi xy \& \chi x))).$$

The reader can check that this proof formula and the original formula imply the entry formula.

We first prove that the entry formulas and proof formulas obtained from considering entire sequents are correct, and later generalize this result to the cases where the entry formula is formed from only one formula, and the proof formula is constructed in accordance with the proof formula formation algorithm proper.

THEOREM 3 Let $S = \{S_1, \ldots, S_n\}$ be a sequent, $0 < i < n + 1$, then $rew(S)\&pp\text{-}rew(S\backslash\{S_i\}) \rightarrow rew(\{S_i\})$.

Proof In order to prove that the result, we make use of the proof theory described in section 6.2. We first make four observations about the various formulas.

Let us call the quantifiers that were introduced by rewriting wide scope terms *wide scope quantifiers*. Then the wide scope quantifiers in the entry formula $(rew(\{S_i\}))$ are a *subsequence* of the wide scope quantifiers in the rewritten formula $(rew(S))$ in the sense that the quantifiers that have the variables in the entry formula in their scope occur in the same order in the quantifiers in the rewritten formula, or can be made to occur in the same order without loss of logical equivalence. The latter qualification is necessary because the universal quantifiers in a cluster of universal quantifiers need not occur in the same order in both formulas. However, because they occur in a cluster of universal quantifiers they can be re-ordered to give a logically equivalent formula. A similar argument applies to existential quantifiers. That the sequence of wide scope quantifiers governing the entry formula is not necessarily identical to the sequence of wide scope quantifiers governing the entire formula can be seen from the following simple case.

$$T(\exists x)(\forall y)(\phi xy \vee \psi y)$$
$$T(\forall y)(\phi ay \vee \psi y)$$
$$T\phi ay \vee \psi y$$
$$T\phi a^w y^w \quad | \quad T\psi y^w$$

One possible entry formula would be $(\forall y)\phi y$, whereas the set of final sequents would obviously be rewritten as $(\exists x)(\forall y)(\phi xy \vee \psi y)$

The second observation is that the quantifiers in $rew(S)$ that do not occur in $rew(\{S_i\})$ have in their scope variables that do not occur in $rew(\{S_i\})$.

The third observation is that whenever a universal quantifier in $pp\text{-}rew(S \backslash \{S_i\})$ binds more than one occurrence of a variable, then there is a corresponding quantifier in $rew(S)$ that binds occurrences of variables on corresponding places.

The fourth and final observation is that if

$$rew(\{S_i\}) = Q_1, \ldots, Q_n \phi,$$

where $Q_1, \ldots, Q_n$ are the wide scope quantifiers in S_i, and

$$rew(S \backslash \{S_i\}) = Q'_1, \ldots, Q'_j \neg(\psi_1 \vee \ldots \vee \psi_i),$$

with $Q'_1, \ldots, Q'_j$ the wide scope quantifiers for $pp\text{-}rew(S \backslash \{S_i\})$ then

$$rew(S) = Q''_1, \ldots, Q''_m (\psi_1 \vee \ldots \vee \psi_i \vee \phi).$$

In other words, the formulas that occur in the scope of the wide scope quantifiers in $rew(S_i)$ and $rew(S \backslash \{S_i\})$ occur in the same form in the scope of the wide scope quantifiers in $rew(S)$.

With these four observations in mind, we can now show that the rewritten formula and the proof formula indeed imply the entry formula. We have to prove that

$$(Q''_1, \ldots, Q''_m (\psi_1 \vee \ldots \vee \psi_i \vee \phi) \&$$
$$(\forall x_1), \ldots, (\forall x_j) \neg(\psi_1 \vee \ldots \vee \psi_i)) \rightarrow Q_1, \ldots, Q_n \phi.$$

We use the proof theory defined in section 6.2 to prove that this is indeed correct.

$$F(Q_1'', \ldots, Q_m''(\psi_1 \vee \ldots \vee \psi_i \vee \phi)\&$$
$$(\forall x_1), \ldots, (\forall x_j)\neg(\psi_1 \vee \ldots \vee \psi_i)) \to Q_1, \ldots, Q_n\phi$$

$$TQ_1'', \ldots, Q_m''(\psi_1 \vee \ldots \vee \psi_i \vee \phi)\&$$
$$(\forall x_1), \ldots, (\forall x_j)\neg(\psi_1 \vee \ldots \vee \psi_i), FQ_1, \ldots, Q_n\phi$$

$$TQ_1'', \ldots, Q_m''(\psi_1 \vee \ldots \vee \psi_i \vee \phi),$$
$$T(\forall x_1), \ldots, (\forall x_j)\neg(\psi_1 \vee \ldots \vee \psi_i), FQ_1, \ldots, Q_n\phi.$$

Because the proof formula is in the scope of universal quantifiers, the variables in it are replaced by free variables. Because the wide scope quantifiers in the entry formula are a subsequence of the wide scope quantifiers in the rewritten formula, each variable in $rew(\{S_i\})$ is in the scope of an identical quantifier in the rewritten formula. However, because the rewritten formula is signed T, and the entry formula is signed F, whenever it is replaced by a free variable in one, it is replaced by a skolem term in the other. Applying the propositional rules to the above sequent, leads to a split because the rewritten formula is a disjunction. Each branch in the split closes. In the first i branches we can unify one of the signed formulas that results from applying $T\text{-}\forall$, $T\text{-}\neg$ and $F\text{-}\vee$ to the proof formula, with the signed formula that corresponds to the ith disjunct in $rew(S)$. They unify because the former has free variables in every argument position. The $i+1$th branch closes because the signed formula that results from applying all the quantifier rules to the entry formula unifies with signed formula corresponding to the $i+1$th disjunct in the $rew(S)$. They unify because wherever one has a skolem term, the other has a free variable. The unification for the wide scope variables are compatible as well: the skolem terms in the reduced proof formula are all variables, and whenever a skolem variable occurs in two places in the reduced proof formula, the corresponding places in reduced $rew(S)$ were filled by an application of a quantifier rule to the same quantifier.

The above proves that rewritting whole sequents according to the algorithms means that the formula that results from rewriting one sequent is implied by the original formula and the proof formula that can be formed from the other sequents in the way described above. In order to generalize this to the general case, we have to prove two things: first, the entry formula that can be obtained from rewriting only one formula in the entry sequent is indeed implied by the rewritten entry sequent; second, we have to prove that the proof formula formed from the other sequents is implied by the formula that would be obtained by applying the proof formation algorithm proper to the sequents, i.e. we have to prove that for every set of sequents S, $p\text{-}rew(S) \rightarrow pp\text{-}rew(S)$.

The first generalisation can be proven as follows:

THEOREM 4 Let S be a sequent with a signed formula ϕ as an element. Then, $rew(S) \rightarrow rew(\phi)$.

Proof $rew(\phi)$ is of the form $Q'_1, \ldots, Q'_i \psi$ and $rew(S)$ is of the form $Q_1, \ldots, Q_n(\ldots \& \psi \& \ldots)$. We again observe that $Q'_1, \ldots, Q'_i$ is a subsequence of $Q_1, \ldots, Q_n$. Again using the proof theory of section 6.2, we see

$Frew(S) \rightarrow rew(\phi)$

$TQ_1, \ldots, Q_n(\ldots \& \psi \& \ldots), FQ'_1, \ldots, Q'_i \psi.$

Because $Q'_1, \ldots, Q'_i$ is a subsequence of $Q_1, \ldots, Q_n$, whenever a universal quantifier in $FQ'_1, \ldots, Q'_i \psi$ is reduced and replaced by a skolem term, it is replaced in $TQ_1, \ldots, Q_n(\ldots \& \psi \& \ldots)$ by a free variable, and, conversely, whenever an existential quantifier is reduced in $FQ'_1, \ldots, Q'_i \psi$ and replaced by a free variable, it is replaced by a skolem term in $TQ_1, \ldots, Q_n(\ldots \& \psi \& \ldots)$. Therefore, the formula $T\chi$ that is introduced into the final sequent after applying all the quantifier rules and the rule $T\text{-}\&$ to $TQ_1, \ldots, Q_n(\ldots \& \psi \& \ldots)$, and the formula $F\pi$, which is in the final sequent because of successive applications of the quantifier rules to $FQ'_1, \ldots, Q'_i \psi$ will close the tree. χ and π will unify because every argument in χ that is a free variable corresponds to a skolem term in π, and, every skolem term in χ corresponds to a free variable in π.

The second generalisation that we have to prove is that the proof formula that can be obtained from rewriting the final set of sequents minus the one that gave rise to the entry formula is implied by the proof formula obtained by taking only one conjunct from each final sequent, and rewriting these according to the proof formula formation algorithm.

THEOREM 5 Let $S = \{S_1, \ldots, S_n\}$ be a sequent, then
$p\text{-}rew(S) \to pp\text{-}rew(S)$.

Proof First, note that applying the proof formula formation algorithm to S returns in fact a whole set of formulas. There is a choice of which formula to choose from every S_i. We will prove the result for arbitrary $\phi \in S_i$.

$$p\text{-}rew(S) = Q_1, \ldots, Q_i(\neg\phi_1 \& \ldots \& \neg\phi_n).$$

$$pp\text{-}rew(S) = Q'_1, \ldots, Q'_k \neg(\psi_1 \vee \ldots \vee \psi_n).$$

Note that $Q_1, \ldots, Q_i$ is a subsequence of $Q'_1, \ldots, Q'_k$. Moreover, each ϕ_i is of the form $Q'_1, \ldots, Q'_j \pi$, whereas each ψ_i is of the form $Q'_k, \ldots, Q'_l(\ldots \& \chi \& \ldots)$, where $Q'_k, \ldots, Q'_l$ is a subsequence of $Q'_k, \ldots, Q'_l$, and π and χ are corresponding formulas. The result can now be proven by using the same proof theory. The quantifier rules that reduce the wide scope variables will reduce corresponding arguments in each ϕ_i in complementary ways, i.e. variables in the one correspond to skolem terms in the other. After applying the quantifier rules to the wide scope variables, we end up with the following sequent:

$$T\neg\phi_1 \& \ldots \& \neg\phi_n, F\neg(\psi_1 \vee \ldots \vee \psi_n).$$

Applying T-&, $T\neg$ n times, and $F\neg$ gives

$$F\phi_1, \ldots, F\phi_n, T\psi_1 \vee \ldots \vee \psi_n.$$

Applying T-$\vee$ now leads to n sequents

$$F\phi_1, \ldots, F\phi_n, T\psi_i.$$

We prove that every sequent closes because ϕ_i and ψ_i can be rewritten as $Q'_1, \ldots, Q'_j \pi$ and $Q'_k, \ldots, Q'_l(\ldots \& \chi \& \ldots)$, where χ

and π are corresponding formulas. We can now apply the quantifier rules to each of these formulas. Again, because $Q'_1, \ldots, Q'_j$ is a subsequence of $Q'_k, \ldots, Q'_l$, every time a quantifier is reduced and a free variable is introduced in π, a skolem term is introduced in χ, and every time a skolem term is introduced in π, a free variable is introduced in χ. Therefore, when all the quantifier rules have been applied, and T-& has been applied, the sequent is closed. The substitutions obtained from the different final sequents for the wide scope variables are compatible, because the wide scope quantifiers in $p\text{-}rew(S)$ are a subsequence of the wide scope quantifiers in $pp\text{-}rew(S)$, and every wide-scope variable in the final set of sequents obtained from $p\text{-}rew(S)$ corresponds to the same wide-scope skolem-term in the final set of sequents obtained from $pp\text{-}rew(S)$, while every wide-scope skolem-term corresponds to the same wide-scope variable. We thus obtain the desired result.

6.4   Implementation

The system described above has been implemented in Kyoto Common Lisp on a SUN. It has not been used to build serious expert systems with and we therefore cannot report on its behaviour on large knowledge bases. On a few toy examples that we used, the system performed satisfactorily. Because the system uses a different proof theory from Socrates, it has not been possible to integrate the two. It is therefore not possible to get any reasonable idea about the efficiency gains that would result from using of assertion-time inference. However, because a large number of inferences which would otherwise have to be drawn at retrieval time, are already drawn at assertion time, one would also expect a considerable speed-up in realistically sized knowledge bases. In this section, we will discuss the present implementation and point to some of its shortcomings. We also briefly mention a few extensions to the system.

In section 6.3 of this chapter we proved the correctness of the various algorithms such as the rewriting algorithm and the proof formula formation algorithm. We can thus be assured that the behaviour of the system is logically correct. However, in the implementation, we usually do not apply the algorithms on the formulas that are stored in the knowledge base. The reason is implementational efficiency. If we were to apply the algorithms, then, whenever a formula was successfully matched against an entry formula, we would have to undo the effect of the proof formation algorithm by applying inference rules to the proof formulas. In practice then, we store the entry formulas in their un-rewritten form, while proof formulas are stored by simply storing all the other final sequents. Whenever a formula has been successfully matched against an entry formula, the interpreter will use a signed formula in each sequent and try to derive a contradiction from it.

The knowledge base uses a very simple indexing mechanism. We use two hash-tables: one for entry formulas signed with a T, and one for entry formulas signed with an F. Because we do not rewrite entry formulas, they do not contain any connectives or quantifiers. We can therefore simply hash on the predicate of the formula. We store with each predicate a set of triples where each triple consists of the arguments in the original entry formula, the set of other final sequents, and the original formula. The following is a simple illustration of this. Consider the following knowledge base, which has been constructed by asserting both $(\forall x)((\psi x \vee \phi x) \rightarrow \pi x)$ and ϕa. Then we construct the following two hash-tables.

Hash table for entry formulas signed T

Key :	Value :
π	$(((x^w) \, \{\{F\psi x^w, F\phi x^w\}\} \, (\forall x)((\psi x \vee \phi x) \rightarrow \pi x))$
ϕ	$(((a) \, \text{nil} \, \phi a))$

Hash table for entry formula signed F

Key :	Value :
ϕ	$(((x^w) \, \{\{T\pi x^w\}\} \, (\forall x)((\psi x \vee \phi x) \rightarrow \pi x))$
ψ	$(((x^w) \, \{\{T\pi x^w\}\} \, (\forall x)((\psi x \vee \phi x) \rightarrow \pi x))$

In order to see how this knowledge base might be used, suppose the system is asked to derive $(\exists x)\pi x$. $F(\exists x)\pi x$ yields $F\pi y$. The system now has to attempt to derive a contradiction, and therefore has to try to match πy against a formula stored in the hash-table for entry formulas signed with a T. It derives the information stored with π and tries to match the arguments of the query (y) with the arguments in each of the triples stored in the hash-table. Clearly, there is only one triple for π, and x^w and y unify with substitution $\{y/x^w\}$ so that this triple can be used.

The reason for using unification rather than a more stringent equality test can be illustrated in the following example. Rewriting the entry and proof formulas once again, suppose that the knowledge base contains:

Entry formula :   Proof formula :
$(\forall x)\phi x$ $(\forall y)\psi y$

Because $(\forall x)\phi x$ implies ϕa for any constant a, and $(\exists x)\phi x$, we would like the above proof formula also to be used when the goal to be proved is ϕa or $(\exists x)\phi x$. Thus, the goal merely needs to be a logical consequence of the entry formula and need not be logically equivalent. Because the information is stored in the hash-table for entry formulas signed with a T in the following form:

Key :   Value :
f $(((x)\ \{\{\psi y\}\}\ (\forall x)(\phi x) \vee (\forall y)(\psi y)$

using unification will give the desired effect.

There is a complication that arises from this. Suppose that we asserted $(\forall x)(\phi x \vee \neg \psi x)$. The goal ϕ a for any constant a could then also be proven if one could prove $\neg \psi a$, and similarly in order to prove $(\exists x)\phi x$ it would have been sufficient to prove $(\exists x)\neg \psi x$. Thus, in certain cases the substitution that results from matching the goal with the entry formula, could also be substituted into the proof formula to give a weaker proof formula. Not surprisingly, it turns out that the only variables for which this is possible are the wide scope variables. It is therefore important that in the entry and the proof formula, the wide scope variables remain recognizable. Because we do not apply the rewriting and the proof formula formation algorithm to the propositions stored in the knowledge base, the present implementation also allows us to do this.

Returning to our original example then, we have unified y with x^w and we apply this unification to the set of sequents stored with π. This gives the following set of sequents: $\{\{F\psi y, F\phi y\}\}$. The interpreter will now try to derive a contradiction for each sequent. In the above example there is only one sequent. The interpreter will first try to derive a contradiction from the first signed formula in the sequent $F\psi y$. However, there is no entry for ψ in the hash-table for entry formulas signed with a

T, and the attempt to find closure for $F\psi y$, therefore fails immediately. The second signed formula is then tried, and the goal thus becomes to find closure with $F\phi y$. There is an entry for ϕ in the hash-table for T-signed entry formulas, and y unifies with a. Because the proof formula associated with ϕa is empty, we therefore obtain closure immediately and know that we can derive $(\exists x)\pi x$ from the knowledge base with the unification $\{x/a\}$.

The control regime that is used by the current interpreter is rather simple-minded. Whenever a query is received, it will simply try to match it against the first element of the set of triples stored with a predicate. At assertion-time we order the triples so that entry-formulas with more instantiated arguments are tried first. The heuristic is that more specific knowledge should be used before more general knowledge. This however is a rough and ready heuristic. Moreover it is hard-wired. The advantages of using explicit representation of control knowledge were made clear in chapter 1. It would therefore be worthwhile to use explicit meta-level reasoning when making this choice. Meta-level reasoning can also be used to decide which sequent in a set of sequents stored in a proof formula to work on first (a choice incidentally that did not have to be made in the example that we discussed above). Also, once one has decided on a sequent, meta-level reasoning can be used to decide which signed formula in the sequent to work on first. As illustrated in the above example, in the present implementation we just try the first signed formula first.

Two more aspects are worth mentioning. First, although we have only described an assertion-time inference system for first-order predicate calculus, we have also used the technique in an implementation of a knowledge base based on modal logic. This is described in chapter 8. Second, we mentioned that one reason for storing the original formulas in the knowledge base was for use in explanation. [Reic88] describes another possible use. He interfaces the assertion-time inference system to a McAllester-type Reason Maintenance System which uses the original formulas that the user has asserted. Before, a particular pair of entry and proof formulas is used in the possible derivation of a query, the interpreter first checks in the Reason Maintenance System if the formula that led to its inclusion in the knowledge base is indeed believed. Only if it is will the entry and proof formulas be used.

6.5   Related work

The work reported here is, at least in spirit, related to the work done
on partial or symbolic evaluation in the logic programming community
(see e.g. [Bjor87] and references therein, and chapter 5). In partial
evaluation, one partially specifies the input of a program and the partial
evaluator will then specialise the logic program. As a consequence, the
program will run faster for these inputs. The cost is that one looses
generality. In particular, the program will no longer run on the more
general cases.

Our program does not suffer from this problem. It does not loose
any generality: everything that can be derived without assertion-time
inference can also be derived when one uses assertion-time inference. Of
course, as a result, the knowledge base constructed by our system are
less efficient than partially evaluated logic programs.

Another system that also seems to use some form of assertion-time
inference is KRYPTON [Brac85]. KRYPTON is a hybrid knowledge representation language. It distinguishes between a *TBox*, in which one stores
definitions of concepts, and an *ABox*, which contains contingent information about the domain. The *TBox* uses a frame-based knowledge representation language, whereas the *ABox* is logic-based. KRYPTON uses
a version of a connection graph theorem prover for the *ABox* suitably
modified to take into account the definitional information in the *TBox*.
Connection graph theorem provers were developed by [Kowa75], [Stic82]
and [Bibe82a]. Basically a connection graph is a set of well-formed formulas and a set of links between the literals in these formulas. The links
can be thought of as markers that identify two literals that can in principle be used in resolution, although the resolution rule is not actually
applied. Whenever a new formula is added to a connection graph, the
theorem prover will construct for each literal in the formula the set of
links to other literals already in the graph. Thus, adding a new formula
amounts to trying to determine against which other formulas already
in the knowledge base the proposition could in principle be resolved.
Clearly, this is very similar in spirit to the approach of assertion-time
inference described in this chapter.

6.6   Conclusion

In this chapter, we described a logic-based system that does assertion time inferencing. The system uses a semantic tableau style proof theory, and uses the tableaus to create pairs of entry formulas and proof formulas, where the proof formula is a formula to be proved in order to prove the entry formula. We proved the correctness of the various algorithms that are used in this process.

7 A Comparison of First Order and Modal Logics of Time

Han Reichgelt

7.1 Introduction

There is a need for temporal reasoners in Artificial Intelligence. First, planning systems have to be able to reason about time, especially in applications where one action may interact with the effect of another. Second, since natural languages often have complicated tense systems, an adequate natural language system will need to be able to reason about time as well. Third, in certain expert systems applications, the system has to be able to reason explicitly about time. A clear example is a monitoring systems, such as VM [Faga80]. [Shoh85] gives many more examples of areas in AI where temporal reasoning is necessary.

Various researchers have argued for the advantages of using logic for knowledge representation (e.g. [Haye77]; [Moor84]). Given the need for temporal reasoners, and the advantages of logic, it seems only natural to turn to temporal logics. However, there are many different temporal logics and it is often not clear which one to choose. In this chapter, I compare three different "styles" of temporal logic, namely modal temporal logic, the method of temporal arguments, and reified temporal logic.

The comparison of the various logics of time can be generalized to other concepts for which there are both modal and first order analyses. An obvious example is the logic of knowledge and belief. Thus, although I will ostensibly compare different temporal logics, at least certain aspects of the comparison are more general.

The outline of the chapter is as follows: first, I discuss some requirements that an adequate temporal logic has to meet. Second, I discuss a modal temporal logic. Third, I turn my attention to the method of temporal methods. Fourth, I concentrate on reified temporal logic. It is important to stress here that I will define model theories for each of the temporal logics. I will use fairly standard logical techniques in all cases. So, this chapter will not contribute much to the study of logic. In a lot of the papers in the AI literature, however, model theories are omitted and as a consequence some of the problems with the proposed formalisms remain hidden.

7.2   Requirements on a temporal logic

In this section I discuss some requirements that an adequate temporal logic should meet. The temporal logics proposed in this chapter have all been defined with these requirements in mind. The list is similar to a list of ten requirements on a theory of change proposed by [Shoh85].

The first and second requirement follow from the fact that we are looking at temporal logics in the context of AI. The temporal logics are ultimately intended as knowledge representation languages. It should therefore be possible to build an inference engine that can automatically draw the inferences that are licensed by the logic in an *efficient* manner.

A second requirement is that the language of the logic be *sufficiently expressive*. We are interested in the representation of temporal knowledge. We therefore need a language which is first expressive enough to allow us to represent whatever piece of temporal knowledge we would like to represent, and second allows us to do in a reasonably natural way.

Obviously, there is a trade-off between these first two requirements. More expressive representation languages are more difficult to implement efficiently and languages for which there are efficient implementations are often not expressive enough. Since it is hard to determine in a general way if a given formalism is expressive enough, the discussion will be focussed on two pieces of temporal knowledge, namely iterated modalities and time dependent expressions.

The first type of temporal knowledge, repeated temporal expressions, is illustrated by the following sentence:

Yesterday, John still had not arrived.   (7.1)

A possible context in which this sentence could be used is the following. Speaker and hearer are expecting John. The hearer has asked the speaker whether the speaker knows if John has arrived. The speaker answers that yesterday, John still had not arrived. In other words, the speaker answers that yesterday John's arrival was still in the future. Using some quasi-logical notation, 7.1 can be translated as

$$AT(yesterday)(FUTURE(arrives(john)))$$ (7.2)

where $AT(yesterday)$ and $FUTURE$ are propositional operators.

Although this sentence might seem rather far-fetched, one can think of various settings in which representations of this type are relevant. Suppose that a medical expert system is written to determine precisely the moment at which the patient contracted an infection. Suppose moreover that there is only indirect evidence. For example, it is known that the patient was tested three months ago and seemed all right then. The system can then conclude that the patient contracted the infection in the period between three months ago and now. One way to represent this in a standard temporal logic requires iterated modalities. The knowledge in question is something like:

$$PAST(infected(pat1))\&$$
$$AT(3\text{-}months\text{-}ago)(FUTURE(infected(pat1)))$$

(7.3)

A second problem that an adequate temporal logic should be able to deal with is the existence of time dependent expressions, expressions whose reference changes over time. Examples in English include *Miss America* and *the Prime Minister of Great Britain*. Clearly, what individual these expressions refer to depends on the point of time at which they are intended to be interpreted.

Again, the examples might seem far-fetched but one can think of settings in which they naturally occur. In a dialogue system used as a front-end to a medical expert system such as MYCIN for example, one might want to include rules such as "first ask all questions which are relevant to the culture currently under consideration". Clearly, the expression *culture currently under consideration* in this rule is an example of a time dependent expression.

As a digression, note that sentences that contain both a time dependent expression and an explicit time operator are ambiguous. Thus, 7.4 is true at the time of writing under one reading but not under another. The reason is that the expression *the Prime Minister of Great Britain* can refer either to the individual who is currently Prime Minister or to the individual who was Prime Minister in 1953.

In 1953, the Prime Minister of Great Britain was female.   (7.4)

This suggests that the definite description *the Prime Minister of Great Britain* should be analysed as containing an explicit quantifier, as indeed is proposed by [Russ05]. So, 7.4 could either be analysed as 7.5 or as 7.6 where $(\exists!x)(p(x))$ is to be read as "there is exactly one x with the property p".

$$(\exists!x)(Prime\text{-}Minister(x)\&IN(1953)(female(x))) \tag{7.5}$$

$$IN(1953)((\exists!x)(Prime\text{-}Minister(x)\&female(x))) \tag{7.6}$$

A completely adequate temporal logic should be able to represent both readings. However, in this chapter I will ignore this problem. Whether we adopt the simple-minded analysis taken here, or the more complicated Russellian analysis, in both cases we have to deal with time dependent expressions. Under the simple-minded case, the time dependent expression is the constant *the Prime-Minister of Great Britain*, under the Russellian analysis it is the 1-place predicate *Prime-Minister of Great Britain*.

A third criterion for an adequate temporal logic is the consequence of the fact that temporal knowledge can both be *precise and imprecise*. Often, temporal knowledge is imprecise in the sense that one knows that something happened at some time in the past, or will happen at some time in the future, without knowing at which precise point in time the event took place or will take place [Alle82]. The representation must allow for this kind of imprecision. Conversely, sometimes temporal knowledge is precise in the sense that one knows exactly at what time something happened, and the formalism should make it possible to represent this too.

A fourth requirement on a temporal logic is that it should be possible to *combine it with any type of other logic*, such as logics for knowledge and belief or modal logics with necessity and possibility operators. After all, one might want to use the temporal logic in an application where one also wants to reason about other people's beliefs or about the necessity and possibility of certain propositions. As a special case, it should be possible to combine a temporal logic with a logic of knowledge and belief in such a way that the following two English sentences can be distinguished:

John knows now if Jim will come in the future.   (7.7)

John will know in the future if Jim comes now.   (7.8)

It would be an obvious advantage if combining the temporal logic with another modal logic could be done incrementally and in such a way that the original temporal logic, and the original other modal logic, would remain as recognizable sub-systems. It would for example mean that knowledge bases written in one logic could be used in the richer logic without the need for detailed rewriting.

A fifth and final criterion is that an adequate temporal logic should allow for *changing ontologies*. Things come and go and a temporal logic should be able to cope with that. Changes in the world not only concern the properties of individuals, or the relationships between individuals, they also concern the existence of individuals. If a temporal logic is to be used to reason about domains where the set of existing individuals can change, then the temporal logic should be able to deal with this.

Some authors (e.g. [Alle82]) have argued that a further requirement on an adequate temporal representation is that it should be able to deal with persistence. That is, it should cope with the fact that most things remain true as time goes by. The problem of persistence is of course identical to the frame-problem (see [Brow87] for various papers concerning this problem). [Shoh85] distinguishes between two kinds of frame-problem, the inter-frame and the intra-frame problem. The inter-frame problem is Allen's persistence: in a theory of change, one should specify what does change as the result of an action, and what remains the same. The intra-frame problem arises when one allows concurrent actions: the result of an action no longer depends on whether that action was performed, but also on what other actions were performed during the same interval. Thus, if a block is pushed to the left, then it will only be to the left of its original position if it was not pushed to the right as well during the same interval. The problem that both frame-problems pose for a theory of change is of course that the set of axioms becomes very large. For the inter-frame problem, one would have to specify exactly what does not change as the result of a certain action, while for the intra-frame problem, one would have to specify which other actions cannot occur simultaneously in order for the original action to have its expected effect. Obviously, the sets of axioms will then become so large that it is no longer feasible to implement a temporal theorem prover.

The frame problem is of course a special case of default reasoning. There have been various attempts at devising logics for default reasoning. Recently, [Hank87] attempted to formulate a simple instance of the inter-frame problem in various default and non-monotonic logics,

and they found that given their formalisation none of the available logics yielded the required results. Although their work has come under
attack (e.g. [Haug87b]; and various papers in [Brow87]), it seems to
me that their paper has at least shown that naive formalisations of the
frame problem in default logics are problematic. Whether the stronger
conclusion that there is no satisfactory logic for default reasoning holds
remains to be seen. In the meantime, I will ignore the various frame
problems in this chapter. I suspect that, if someone develops an adequate extension to one logic to deal with default reasoning (see e.g.
[Shoh87] for one attempt), then it should be possible to extend this
technique to other logics as well. I therefore surmise that it is unlikely
that different temporal logics can be distinguished on the basis of their
ability to deal with the frame problems.

Concluding then, I listed five requirements that an adequate temporal
logic should meet. First, it should have an efficient implementation. Second, it should enable its user to represent the knowledge naturally. In
particular, it should be able to cope with repeated temporal expressions
and with time varying expressions. Third, it should allow for the expression of imprecise temporal knowledge, while also making the expression
of precise temporal knowledge possible. Fourth, it should be possible to
embed the temporal logic into any other type of logic, preferably in an
incremental way. Finally, it should be able to cope with the problem of
changing ontologies.

7.3   A modal temporal logic

In this section I introduce a modal temporal logic. Its main purpose is
to investigate if and how such a logic would satisfy the five requirements.
I am therefore not going into the mathematical properties of the logic
in question. Interested readers are referred to [Resc71].

7.3.1   A modal temporal language, TM

In this section, I define the temporal modal language TM. In certain
respects, TM is slightly out of the ordinary. Unlike the more standard
temporal modal languages, it is possible to refer to particular points
in time in TM. Thus, while most standard temporal modal languages
only have P (meaning "sometime in the Past"), F ("sometime in the

Future"), H ("Has always been the case") and G ("is always Going to be the case"), TM allows operators referring to specific points in time. The following defines the language TM.

Definition 1 The vocabulary of TM is the union of

1. the set of constants $C = \{a_1, a_2, \ldots\}$

2. the set of variables $V = \{v_1, v_2, \ldots\}$

3. for at least one $n > 0$, the set of n-ary predicate symbols $P^n = \{p_1^n, p_2^n, \ldots\}$

4. the set of time constants $TC = \{t_0, t_1, \ldots\}$

The set of operators, OP, is defined as

1. F, P are operators

2. if $t \in TC$, then $AT(t)$ is an operator.

The set of well-formed expressions of TM, wff^{TM}, is defined as

1. if $i_1, \ldots, i_n \in C \cup V$ and $p \in P^n$ then $p(i_1, \ldots, i_n) \in wff^{TM}$

2. if $p, q \in wff^{TM}$, then $(p \to q), (\neg p) \in wff^{TM}$

3. if $p \in wff^{TM}$ and $x \in V$ then $(\forall x)(p) \in wff^{TM}$

4. if $p \in wff^{TM}$ and $O \in OP$, then $(Op) \in wff^{TM}$

The connectives $\vee$, $\&$ and $\leftrightarrow$ and the existential quantifier $\exists$ can be defined in terms of $\to$, $\neg$ and $\forall$ in the usual way. Also, the operators H and G can be defined in terms of P and F as

$$Hp := \neg P \neg p$$
$$Gp := \neg F \neg p$$

Brackets are omitted wherever this can be done without ambiguity. It is important to point out that it is not possible to quantify over time constants. Their only role is to function as arguments to the operator scheme AT.

7.3.2 TM-structures

In this section, I define the notion of a TM-structure. TM-structures are used in the next section to define an interpretation for the language TM.

Definition 2 A TM-structure is a quintuple $(I, T, <, n, ind)$ where

- I and T are disjoint non-empty sets,
- $<$ is a partial order relation on T,
- $n \in T$,
- ind is a function from T into the power set of I, i.e. a function which assigns to every $t \in T$ an $I' \subseteq I$.

In the above definition, I and T are the sets of possible individuals and temporal states respectively. The requirements that both sets be non-empty and that the two sets be disjoint are obvious.

There are no constraints on T. In particular, I have not specified whether T is a set of points, or a set of intervals. There are different ways of viewing time, and one of the basic choices is whether one wants to regard points in time or stretches of time as basic (Cf part I of [Bent82]). In this chapter, I will not go into this question. A TM-structure is compatible with either choice. For the purposes of this chapter, which is to compare various styles of temporal logic, the choice is irrelevant. Following Allen's work ([Alle84] and [Alle82]), there is a growing consensus that intervals are to be preferred to points. For some counter-arguments, see [Shoh86]. In the remainder of the chapter, I will use points in time as this makes the subsequent discussion simpler. However, the reader should keep in mind that nothing hinges on this.

The second element in a TM-structure is the partial order relation $<$ on T. The intuitive meaning of this relation is the earlier-than relationship. It should be clear from this why $<$ is (at least) a partial ordering.

The intuitive meaning of n is the present time. n plays the special role that all formulas are interpreted with respect to it. Again there are no additional requirements on n. In order to make the above definition of a TM-structure more in accordance with our intuitions about time, one probably has to add some conditions on the behaviour of n with respect to $<$. In particular, even if one does not want to insist that there is exactly one future, but rather that there are many different possible future courses of events, there is still only one past (Cf [McDe82b]).

Thus, the restriction of the $<$-relation to the points in time before n has to be a total ordering. There are probably many other requirements one could think of, but I will not go into this question here.

The final element in a TM-structure is the function *ind*. It is a function from temporal states to sets of individuals. Intuitively, it assigns to every point in time the set of individuals existing at that point in time. This function enables modal temporal logics to cope with the problem of changing ontologies. Thus, while I is the set of possible individuals, the function *ind* assigns to every point in time the set of possible individuals that actually exist at that point. Again, there are many additional requirements that might be put on the function *ind*, depending on one's view of individuals. For example, is the same individual allowed to exist at a given time, then to disappear out of existence at a later time, and to come into existence again at some time after that? If this is not allowed, then one has to add some requirements to the definition of *ind*.

7.3.3   Interpretations for TM

In this section, I use TM-structures to provide interpretations for the language TM. The following defines the notion of an interpretation for TM.

Definition 3 A TM-interpretation is a pair (S, f) where S is a TM-structure, $S = (I, T, <, n, ind)$, and f is a function from the set of basic expressions of TM, except the variables, to objects constructed by set-theoretical means out of I and T such that

- if $c \in C$, then $f(c) \in \bigcap_{t \in T} ind(t)$.
- if $p \in P^n$ then $f(p)$ is a function from T into the power set of I^n such that for every $t \in T$, $f(p)(t) \subseteq ind(t)^n$.
- if $t \in TC$, then $f(t) \in T$.

The first clause of the definition ensures that the denotation of a constant exists at every point in time. Thus, in TM constants always denote entities which exist at every point in time. Moreover, the individual denoted by a constant is always the same. The technical reason behind this will become clear later on. The second clause assigns interpretations to predicates. The extra clause is there to ensure that the individuals which stand in some relationship to each other or have some property at a point in time, actually exist at that point. The third clause is straightforward.

The following definition is of the central notion of a TM-sentence being true in a TM-interpretation. I first define the notion of a sentence being true in a TM-interpretation under a value assignment g. A value assignment is a function from the set of variables of TM into the set D of domain individuals.

Definition 4 Let p be a TM-sentence, let $M = ((I, T, <, n, ind), f)$ be a TM-interpretation, let g be a value assignment. Then p is true in M under g, symbolically $M \models_g p$, iff

- if p is of the form $q(k_1, \ldots, k_n)$, then $M \models_g p$, if $\langle h(k_1), \ldots, h(k_n) \rangle \in f(q)(n)$, where $h(k_i) = f(k_i)$ if $k_i \in C$, and $h(k_i) = g(k_i)$ if $k_i \in V$.

- if p is of the form $(p1 \rightarrow p2)$, then $M \models_g p$, if $M \not\models_g p1$, or $M \models_g p2$.

- if p is of the form $(\neg p1)$, then $M \models_g p$, if $M \not\models_g p1$.

- if p is of the form $(\forall x)(q)$, then $M \models_g p$, if for all value assignments h, such that $h(y) = g(y)$ for all variables y except possibly x, $M \models_h q$.

- if p is of the form Pq, then $M \models_g p$, if there is some M' exactly like M except that $n' < n$, and $M' \models_g p$.

- if p is of the form Fq, then $M \models_g p$, if there is some M' exactly like M except that $n < n'$, and $M' \models_g p$.

- if p is of the form $AT(t)q$, then $M \models_g p$, if there is some M', exactly like M except that $n' = f(t)$, and $M' \models_g p$.

The above definition are relative to a value assignment. The following definition generalizes it to truth of a proposition as such.

Definition 5 A sentence p is true in a TM-interpretation M, $M \models p$, if for all value assignments g, $M \models_g p$.

7.3.4   TM and the criteria

In section 7.2 I listed five criteria for an adequate temporal logic. In this section I examine TM with respect to them.

The first criterion concerns efficiency of implementation. Although there recently have been some attempts at providing efficient theorem provers for modal logic (see chapter 8) general first order modal theorem provers are slower than theorem provers for first order predicate calculus. A comparison of a resolution based modal theorem prover with a similar first order theorem prover will illustrate this. In a first order theorem prover the formulas p and $(\neg q)$ may be resolved against each other iff p and q unify. The intuitive motivation is that it is impossible for a formula to be both true and false. However, in the modal case the intuitive motivation applies only if the formula would have to be both true and false *in the same world*. Thus, in addition to checking whether the formulas unify, one also has to ensure that they unify in the same world, and an additional test is needed.

The second criterion concerns the naturalness of expression. Although it is probably to a large extent a matter of taste which formalism is easier to use, TM seems to provide a natural way of expressing temporal knowledge, especially when compared to the first order formalisms developed below. In particular, there are no problems with repeated temporal expressions, or time dependent expressions.

Note that individual constants are treated as time independent. They always have the same individual as their interpretation and they exist at every point in time. In Kripke's terminology [Krip72], they are "rigid designators". There is a technical reason behind this treatment of constants: if one does not insist on constants being rigid designators, then the rule of universal elimination, from $(\forall x)(p(x))$ conclude $p(c)$ for some constant c, is not valid. If c were not a rigid designator, and denoted an object that existed only at some points in time, then the rule of universal elimination would fail because c might not have a denotation in the world in which the universal quantifier was evaluated, thus making $p(c)$ false, even though $(\forall x)(p(x))$ might be true. Given this treatment of constants, one has to follow Russell and analyse the time dependent definite description *The Prime-Minister of Great Britain* as involving an existential quantifier.

The third criterion is based on the fact that sometimes temporal knowledge is precise, whereas at others it is not. TM allows for both possibilities. The operator AT can be used to express precise knowledge, whereas the operators P and F can be used for imprecise knowledge. In this respect, TM is superior to standard modal temporal logics, which lack the ability to express precise knowledge because P and F are the only available temporal operators.

The fourth criterion is that it should be possible to combine a temporal logic with any other type of logic. For TM this is straightforward. The definition of the language of such a combined logic can simply be obtained by adding to the syntactic rules that define the language TM, some rules for the operators in the other logic. The structures for the extended language can be obtained by including in the definition of TM-structures an accessibility relation for the new modal concept. In order to get the semantics for the extended language one adds some clauses to the definition of truth in a model corresponding to the newly introduced operators, and making use of the new accessibility relation.

The final criterion is the problem of changing ontologies. TM copes with this problem without any difficulty because of the function *ind* in a TM-structure. *ind* assigns sets of existing individuals to each point in time. Because quantification is always over the individuals that exist at the time at which the proposition is evaluated, TM's quantificational machinery also gives the right results.

Concluding then, TM does very well on what one might call the logical criteria of adequacy, such as the ones having to do with expressiveness of the language and the ease of combining TM with any other logics. It probably fares less well on the computational criterion.

7.4   First order temporal logics

In a first order temporal logic, there are two possibilities. The first option is to complicate the object-level language; the second to reason in the meta-language of a modal language. Following [Haug87a], I will call the former strategy the *method of temporal arguments*. The basic idea is to complicate the first order language and add to the predicates extra arguments that refer to points in time (or intervals). The second strategy, which I will call the *reified approach*, is to reason in the meta-language of a modal language such as TM, which is itself first order. [Moor85a] uses this technique for epistemic logics. I first discuss the method of temporal arguments.

7.4.1 The method of temporal arguments

The basic ideas, the language TA. In the method of temporal arguments, one starts out with the standard language of first order logic and complicates it by adding an extra argument to every predicate. The extra argument refers to the time at which the atomic proposition formed with it holds. The method of temporal arguments is of course very similar to the situation calculus of [McCa69], where propositions hold in particular states. Because the model theory for a language of this type is very close to the model theory for standard first order languages, I will not explicitly define it. Rather I consider some examples. The language will be called TA.

In TA, it is convenient to move to a sorted first order logic. There are good reasons for moving to a sorted language anyway. First, it is often more natural to express in sort hierarchies what [Clan83b] calls "structural knowledge", knowledge about the classes of objects which are relevant in a given domain. Second, [Cohn85] shows that many efficiency gains can be achieved by using a sorted logic in which structural knowledge is expressed in a sort hierarchy rather than in logical axioms. Using a sorted logic then, we have two sorts of individual in any model for TA, namely individuals of sort i, normal individuals, and individuals of sort t, points in time.

To illustrate TA, consider the two-place predicate *loves*. In TA, this predicate is complicated to a three-place predicate $loves(x, y, t)$ which is interpreted as x *loves* y *at time* t. The syntax of TA is obvious: assuming a sorted first order logic, every predicate which was n-place in the original language becomes an $n + 1$-place relation in TA, where the first n elements are of sort i and the last argument is of sort t.

In order to be able to do temporal reasoning in TA, one needs to introduce an explicit ordering relation $<_{TA}$. $t_1 <_{TA} t_2$ is to be read as t_1 is earlier than t_2. In order to be able to express that something was the case at some unspecified time in the past, one also has to add to the language a special time-constant, t_0, referring to the present time. One can then express the proposition that Harry loved Mary at some time in the past as follows, where the notation $(\exists x{:}s)$ means that the variable x is of sort s.

$$(\exists t{:}t)((t <_{TA} t_0) \& (loves(h, m, t))$$

Clearly, in order to make sure that $<_{TA}$ is the correct earlier-than relation, one has to add a few axioms to the standard first order axioms. In this respect, the situation is similar to the case in which equality is added to first order logic. In order to make sure that the equality predicate is interpreted in the right way, one adds the three axioms to the standard axioms stating that the equality relation is reflexive, transitive and symmetric. The ordering relation $<_{TA}$ can be treated in a similar vein.

TA and the criteria.   Judged by the criteria of section 7.2, TA suffers from some shortcomings. On the first criterion, efficiency, it does reasonably well. TA is a first order logic. One can use the standard efficient techniques for implementing first order logic. There is a slight complication because of the special status of the predicate $<_{TA}$. If one uses a standard implementation for first order logic, or a subset thereof, such as for example Prolog, then $<_{TA}$ is just like any other predicate. But if it is used a lot, then this may be a source of inefficiency. It might therefore be worthwhile to try to build the axioms about $<_{TA}$ into the theorem prover directly, just as the axioms about the logical connectives have been built in, and just as the equality axioms have been built into Prolog. Whereas this is no doubt possible, it is not entirely trivial.

On the criterion of ease and naturalness of expression however, TA does less well. Although expressing 7.9 as 7.10 is still reasonably natural, it is less natural than $P(loves(h, m))$.

In the past, Harry loved Mary.   (7.9)

$(\exists t{:}t)\big((t <_{TA} t_0)\,\&\,loves(h, m, t)\big)$ (7.10)

The situation becomes worse however for repeated temporal expressions. For example, a sentence like 7.11, which in TM would be analysed as 7.12, would now have to be written as 7.13.

Harry will have loved Mary.   (7.11)

$F(P(loves(h, m)))$ (7.12)

$(\exists t'{:}t)\big((t' <_{TA} t_0)\,\&\,(\exists t{:}t)((t <_{TA} t')\,\&\,loves(h, m, t))\big)$ (7.13)

There is a way out of the problem of unnaturalness of expression. We can use three levels of representation, as in TAG [Jack87b]. At the first level, TAG has a user language in which the user interacts with the system. The main objective of the user language is to make human interaction with the system as easy as possible. At the second level, there is the logical representation into which the user language is transformed. Its main objective is ease of processing. The third level is the internal representation in which formulas are stored in the machine. The internal representation may (but need not) be different from the logical representation. It is especially useful for storing extra-logical information with propositions, such as justifications. In TAG, the user language is the Polish notation for first order predicate calculus. The logical representations into which this is translated, are list structures, which are easily processed in TAG's implementation language LISP. Finally, the internal representation language is a frame-like language with each proposition corresponding to a frame with some logical and non-logical slots. In TAG's case these are used to reason about the user's beliefs and make a more natural dialogue with the user possible. Using this idea of three levels in the present context, TM could be the user-language, with TA as the logical representation language. Whether TA is also used as the internal language, is an implementational question that need not concern us here.

It must be said that using TM as the user-language, because of the naturalness of expression, gives some overhead, especially in a system where there is a lot of interaction with the user. After all, translating from TA into TM and the other way around will cost something. There thus is some danger that the computational gain that one gets out of using TA is lost because one is translating in and out of it quite often. It has to be said, however, that this loss in efficiency is probably of a different order of magnitude compared to the computational gain out of using a first order inference engine. Another qualification is that the TA-translations of TM formulas can themselves be fairly complicated, and the first order theorem prover, although faster in itself than a modal theorem prover, might loose some of its efficiency advantage because it uses longer and more complicated formulas. This qualification certainly applies to the language TR discussed below.

In order to formulate the translation algorithm, let us first look at the translation of sentences without a temporal operator, such as 7.14.

$$loves(Harry, Mary) \qquad\qquad (7.14)$$

The problem is that the predicate *loves* which was a two-place predicate in TM becomes a three-place predicate in TA because of the additional time argument. So, one has to add an additional time argument, and it seems most intuitive to let the additional time argument be the time constant t_0, which refers to the present time. This would reflect the intuition that 7.14 seems equivalent to 7.15. So, whenever one translates a sentence that is not embedded under a temporal operator, the constant t_0 is added as the extra constant.

Harry loves Mary now.   (7.15)

The rest of the translation algorithm relies on the intuition that the temporal operator changes the time at which the proposition in their scope is evaluated. The tense operators P and F change it to a point in time which is specified relative to the present time of evaluation, whereas the AT operators change it into an absolutely specified time. So, the translation of 7.16 is 7.17 of 7.18, 7.19, and of 7.20, 7.21, where $Sub(t, t_0, p)$ is a formula obtained from p by replacing all occurrences of t_0 in p by occurrences of t and $trans(p)$ is the translation of p.

Pp (7.16)

$(\exists t{:}t)\big((t <_{TA} t_0)\,\&\,Sub(t, t_0, trans(p))\big)$ (7.17)

     where t is the first variable not occurring in $trans(p)$

Fp (7.18)

$(\exists t{:}t)\big((t_0 <_{TA} t)\,\&\,Sub(t, t_0, trans(p))\big)$ (7.19)

     where t is the first variable not occurring in $trans(p)$

$AT(t_n)p$ (7.20)

$Sub(t_n, t_0, trans(p))$ (7.21)

It is straightforward to extend the translation algorithm to cope with quantified formulas, negated formulas and implications. A quantified formula is translated by placing the same quantifier in front of the translated matrix sentence, where variables are translated as themselves. Negated formulas are translated by putting a negation sign in front of the translation of the negated formula, and implications are similarly translated by placing an implication sign between the translated antecedent and the translated consequent.

In order to illustrate the sketched translation algorithm, and in order to show that the algorithm gives the right result for sentences with multiple temporal operators, I will translate the following two TM sentences into TA.

$$PFloves(harry, mary) \qquad\qquad (7.22)$$

$$PAT(t_1)loves(harry, mary) \qquad\qquad (7.23)$$

The translation of 7.22 is as follows:

$trans(PFloves(harry, mary))$
$(\exists t{:}t)((t <_{TA} t_0)\&Sub(t, t_0, trans(Floves(harry, mary))))$
$(\exists t{:}t)((t <_{TA} t_0)\&Sub(t, t_0, (\exists t'{:}t)((t_0 <_{TA} t'\&$
$\qquad\qquad\qquad Sub(t', t_0, trans(loves(harry, mary))))))$
$(\exists t{:}t)((t <_{TA} t_0)\&(\exists t'{:}t)((t <_{TA} t')\&$
$\qquad\qquad\qquad Sub(t', t_0, trans(loves(harry, mary)))))$
$(\exists t{:}t)((t <_{TA} t_0)\&(\exists t'{:}t)((t <_{TA} t')\&$
$\qquad\qquad\qquad Sub(t', t_0, loves(harry, mary, t_0))))$
$(\exists t{:}t)((t <_{TA} t_0)\&(\exists t'{:}t)((t <_{TA} t')\&loves(harry, mary, t')))$

The translation of 7.23 is as follows:

$trans(PAT(t_1)loves(harry, mary))$
$(\exists t{:}t)((t <_{TA} t_0)\&Sub(t, t_0, trans(AT(t_1)loves(harry, mary))))$
$(\exists t{:}t)((t <_{TA} t_0)\&Sub(t, t_0,$
$\qquad\qquad\qquad Sub(t_1, t_0, trans(loves(harry, mary)))))$
$(\exists t{:}t)((t <_{TA} t_0)\&Sub(t, t_0, Sub(t_1, t_0, loves(harry, mary, t_0))))$
$(\exists t{:}t)((t <_{TA} t_0)\&Sub(t, t_0, loves(harry, mary, t_1)))$
$(\exists t{:}t)((t <_{TA} t_0)\&loves(harry, mary, t_1))$

For a full implementation of the above ideas, one also has to define a translation algorithm from TA into TM. After all, if users communicate with the system in TM, then they will also expect the system to communicate with them in that language. It is not difficult to formulate such a translation algorithm and I leave it as an exercise for the reader. However, as I will show below, there might be some complications.

Apart from the problem of the iterated modalities, there is also the problem of time dependent expressions. It is clear that predicates are time dependent. After all, the sets of objects in the extension of predicates also contain a point in time. Thus, the set of individuals having a certain property, or standing in certain relationships to each other, varies with time. Of course, every predicate is assigned one extension once and for all in a model, but because there is the additional time argument, the set of individuals having a property at a given time need not be the same as the set of individuals having the property at a different time. It is in this (conceptual) sense that predicates are time dependent. It is however not possible for constants to be time dependent. Once a constant has been assigned a value, this value remains the same. All constants are rigid designators. Therefore, in TA, as in TM, one has to take the Russellian analysis of time dependent constants as hidden definite descriptions.

TA has an important expressive advantage over TM. The reader will recall that although TM has time-constants, it is not possible to quantify over them. Quantification over points in time can only be achieved through using the modal operators. As a result, one cannot express knowledge such whenever a loaded gun is fired, it will be smoking immediately afterwards. In TA, this can be expressed because time-points appear as arguments to the predicates, and therefore can be quantified over. Thus, we could express the above piece of knowledge:

$$(\forall t{:}t)(\forall x{:}i)((gun(x,t)\&loaded(x,t)) \rightarrow smokes(x,(+t))) \qquad (7.24)$$

where we assume that $+$ is a function which returns for every point in time the immediately following point in time.

By having both explicit time constants and time variables TA also meets the criterion of allowing for both precise and imprecise information. Thus, it also meets the third and fourth criterion laid down in section 7.2.

There are some problems, however, when it comes to incrementally combining TA with another logic. In TM this posed no problems, but in TA it does. In order to combine TA with another modal logic one has to change every n-place predicate in the original language into an $n + 2$-place predicate with one time argument and one additional argument corresponding to the new modal operators. Thus, if one wants an epistemic logic, then one has to add a belief-worlds argument. This of course implies that one has to adapt the translation algorithm. Clearly, this cannot be done incrementally and the old logic does not remain as an integral subpart of the new logic.

The final criterion is the problem of changing ontologies. In this respect, TA does not do well. The set of individuals is determined once and for all and does not change from one point in time to the next, as it does in TM. This is not only undesirable on conceptual grounds but also leads to a serious logical difficulty, to which I will turn now.

In first order languages, provided there are no intervening quantifiers of another sort, the order in which quantifiers of the same sort occur is irrelevant. Thus, if Qx and Qy are both universal or both existential quantifiers, then the formulas $(Qx)(Qy)(p)$ and $(Qy)(Qx)(p)$ are equivalent. The result of translating 7.25 into TA, using the translation algorithm described above, is 7.26, which of course is equivalent to 7.27.

$$P(\exists x{:}i)(p(x)) \tag{7.25}$$

$$(\exists t{:}t)((t < t_0)\,\&\,(\exists x{:}i)(p(x, t))) \tag{7.26}$$

$$(\exists t{:}t)(\exists x{:}i)((t < t_0)\,\&\,p(x, t)) \tag{7.27}$$

Similarly, the translation of 7.28 is equivalent to 7.29.

$$(\exists x{:}i)(P(p(x))) \tag{7.28}$$

$$(\exists x{:}i)(\exists t{:}t)((t < t_0)\,\&\,p(x, t)) \tag{7.29}$$

But because the order of the quantifiers in (7.29) can be changed, the following equivalence holds:

$$P(\exists x)(p(x)) \leftrightarrow (\exists x)(P(p(x))) \tag{7.30}$$

Clearly, from an intuitive point of view this is not correct. For example, one would want to make a distinction between the following two sentences:

In the past some people suffered from scurvy. $\tag{7.31}$

Some people (existing today) suffered from scurvy $\tag{7.32}$
 in the past.

Similar arguments can be given to show that given the translation algorithm, the following equivalences hold.

$$F(\exists x)(p(x)) \leftrightarrow (\exists x)(F(p(x))) \tag{7.33}$$

$$AT(t)(\exists x)(p(x)) \leftrightarrow AT(t)(\exists x)(p(x)) \qquad (7.34)$$

$$G(\forall x)(p(x)) \leftrightarrow (\forall x)(G(p(x))) \qquad (7.35)$$

$$H(\forall x)(p(x)) \leftrightarrow (\forall x)(H(p(x))) \qquad (7.36)$$

In TM these equivalences do not hold. It may be instructive to see why for example 7.31 does not hold in TM. Let us first analyse the truth conditions of the first sub-formula. The formula $F(\exists x)(p(x))$ is true in a TM-interpretation if at some point in time t later than the present time, $(\exists x)(p(x))$ is true. Thus at t, there is some individual with the property p. On the other hand, $(\exists x)(F(p(x)))$ is true if there is some individual at the present point in time such that this individual has the property p at some future time. Obviously, $(\exists x)(F(p(x)))$ implies $F(\exists x)(p(x))$. However, $F(\exists x)(p(x))$ does not imply $(\exists x)(F(p(x)))$. After all, the individual which has the property p at some future time, may not exist at the present time. Therefore, one cannot infer the existence of an individual in the present world that will have the property p at some future time from the fact that one knows that at some future time some individual will exist with the property p.

Thus, there seem to be certain formulas that one is forced to accept as equivalent in TA even though this is counter-intuitive. Fortunately there is way out. The solution is quite natural once it is realised that the problem does not arise in TM because quantification is over the set of individuals existing at the point in time at which the formula is evaluated, and this set may change from one point in time to the next. In TA the set of individuals does not change. This suggest that if one could find a way in TA to ensure that this were not the case, then there would be some hope of solving the present problem.

[Scot70] offers some advice to logicians working in the framework of modal logic and struggling with similar problems. Scott recommends to include an *exist* predicate in the language. The same set of individuals can then be used at all points in time and one can drop the function *ind* from the definition of a TM-interpretation. Quantification is over the entire set of individuals and is not restricted to individuals existing at the world with respect to which the (quantified) formula is evaluated. To get around the obvious objection that this means that one cannot deal with the problem of changing ontologies, Scott introduced the *exist* predicate, which is a time dependent predicate as all other predicates.

So, although all individuals are present at all points in time or possible worlds, the predicate *exist* is true of only a subset at a given point in time. If one then wants to restrict quantification to individuals existing at a given world, then one has to use the predicate *exist*.

One can follow Scott's advice to avoid the problems surrounding TA, and introduce the predicate *exist*. However, if one does, then one also has to change the translation algorithm. After all, if TM is the "interface" language, then the TM-sentences have to be translated into equivalent TA-sentences. But in TM, sentences always quantify over the individuals existing at a given point in time, and the corresponding TA-sentences should also quantify over individuals existing at a given point in time. Therefore, in the translation for quantified sentences, one has to add a clause making sure that sentences quantify over existing individuals. Thus, sentences 7.37 and 7.38, which under the old translation algorithm were translated as 7.39 and 7.40 will now be translated as 7.41 and 7.42.

$$F(\exists x)(p(x)) \tag{7.37}$$

$$(\exists x)(F(p(x))) \tag{7.38}$$

$$(\exists t{:}t)(\exists x{:}i)((t_0 <_{TA} t)\&p(x,t)) \tag{7.39}$$

$$(\exists x{:}i)(\exists t{:}t)((t_0 <_{TA} t)\&p(x,t)) \tag{7.40}$$

$$(\exists t{:}t)(\exists x{:}i)((t_0 <_{TA} t)\&exist(x,t)\&p(x,t)) \tag{7.41}$$

$$(\exists t{:}t)(\exists x{:}i)(exist(x,t_0)\&(t_0 <_{TA} t)\&p(x,t)) \tag{7.42}$$

It is clear that under this new translation algorithm the unwanted equivalences no longer hold. The cost of course is a more complicated translation algorithm and a more complicated formula as the translation.

As an aside, another consequence of the above solution is that the translation algorithm from TA into TM becomes more complicated. Rather than translate "from the outside in", one first has to re-write the formula into some normal form to make sure that quantifiers ranging over "normal" individuals actually stand as near their corresponding "exist-clause" as possible. Only then can one start the original translation algorithm from TA into TM. Thus, sentence 7.43 will first have to be transformed into sentence 7.42 before it can be translated back.

$$(\exists x)(\exists t{:}t)(exist(x,t_0)\&(t_0 <_{TA} t)\&p(x,t)) \tag{7.43}$$

Although there is no doubt that Scott's advice is sound from a purely logical point of view, it seems to me to be less acceptable from an intuitive point of view. There is a sense in which one can regard it as moving some information from the meta-language into the object-language. For TM, the function *ind* in the definition of a TM-structure ensures that quantification is not always over the same set of individuals. If one follows Scott's advice, then the role of the function *ind* is taken over by the object-language predicate *exist*. It seems to me more elegant to treat the problem of changing ontologies as part of the definition of a structure rather than by introducing an extra predicate into the object-language.

Conclusion about TA.   TA is preferable to TM on computational grounds. One can use first order proof procedures. However, on logical grounds TA fares badly in comparison with TM. First, the ease of expression in TA is low; it soon becomes very unnatural to express temporal knowledge in the language of TA. I sketched one way of getting around this problem, but there is a danger that by doing this some of the efficiency gains are lost. Second, it is impossible to combine TA with another modal logic in an incremental manner. Third, and most serious, TA forces certain equivalences that one would like to be able to avoid in certain applications. I sketched a solution for this problem but this solution implies a complication of the translation algorithm and of the resulting formulas. Again, this will undo some of the efficiency gains that one obtains from using a first order theorem prover.

7.4.2 Reified temporal logic

The second strategy for a first order temporal logic involves moving into the meta-language. I am using the term "meta-language", in the logician's sense as a language in which one can talk about the (logical) object language in which one is primarily interested. The term "meta-knowledge" (and related terms such as "meta-language", and "meta-level") has also become generally used in the context of expert systems, where meta-knowledge is defined as knowledge that the system has about its domain knowledge. I am *not* using the terms in this sense. What I am describing here is a meta-language in the logicians' sense of the word, which can be used as the object-language in some reasoning system that may or may not have an explicit meta-level in the AI-people's sense of the word.

In section 7.2 I defined the modal temporal logic TM. The language in which the model theory for TM was formulated, TM's meta-language, was a first order language. The technique discussed in this section for dealing with temporal logic is based on this observation. The basic idea is to formalise TM's meta-language using a sorted first order logic, and to reason in this new logic. The obvious advantages are that one stays in a first order theory, while getting the full power of a modal language. [McDe82b] presents his temporal system as an attempt of doing just this.

The work of [Alle84], and [Kowa86] can be also interpreted in this way. In each of their systems, there is a two-place truth-predicate, whose intended meaning is that its first argument is true during the interval denoted by its second argument. In each of the systems mentioned the predicate has a different name. Allen uses the predicates *HOLDS* and *OCCUR*, whereas McDermott uses the predicates *T*, *TT* and *OCC*. I will follow Allen and use the predicate *HOLDS*.

None of the systems of Allen, McDermott or Kowalski and Sergot have been given a model theory. Thus, although the systems are claimed to be logics, no full semantics is defined for any of them, although there is a semantics for Allan's interval algebra [Ladk87]. McDermott defines a semantics for the propositional case, but unfortunately does not generalize it to the first order case. [Shoh86] defines a semantics for his reified temporal logic. Unfortunately, his system is not rich enough. In particular, it cannot cope with the problem of a changing ontology. I will return to Shoham's system below. In this section, I define a semantics for a reified temporal logic which avoids the problems with Shoham's system.

The outline of this section is as follows. First, I define the language TR. Then I define a model theory for TR. Finally, I discuss TR with regard to the criteria mentioned above. Because TR is basically a formalisation of the model theory for TM, a lot of the discussion might look more obscure than it actually is. Whenever the formalism seems to be completely *ad hoc*, readers are advised to keep the model theory for TM in mind.

The language TR. Since TR is a meta-language for the modal language TM, one needs two types of expression. On the one hand, one should be able to talk about expressions of TM. On the other hand, one needs to be able to talk about the entities to which the expressions of TM refer. Thus, TR is most conveniently defined as a many sorted first

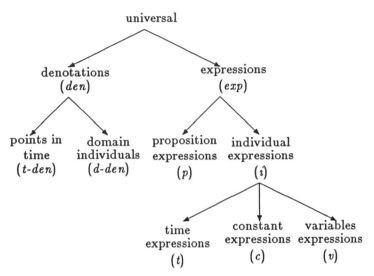

Figure 7.1
Sort hierarchy for TR

order language. The sortal structure of TR is as follows. The two main sorts are *exp* and *den*, expressions and denotations respectively. Each of them has some sub-sorts. The sub-sorts of *exp* are *p* and *i*, proposition expressions and individual expression. There are three sorts of individual expression, *t*, *c* and *v*, time-constants, individual constants and variables. Note that variables of TM are treated as TR-constants. This reflects the fact that at the meta-level, object-level variables are regarded as just another type of expression, more or less on a par with object-level constants. The sub-sorts of *den* are *t-den*, points in time, and *d-den*, domain individuals. The sort hierarchy can be represented as in figure 7.1.

For every one of the above sorts, TR will contain both constants and variables. There might be some confusion here because there are both TR-constants and TR-variables corresponding to TM-variables. The confusion should disappear once it is realised that TR-variables are in fact what logicians call *meta-variables*, variables in the meta-language which stand for an arbitrary expression in the object-language.

One can partially construct the vocabulary of TR out of the vocabulary of TM. For each time constant in TM, there is a constant of sort *t* in TR.

Each individual constant in TM corresponds to a TR-constant of sort c, and each TM-variable to a TR-constant of sort v. Each n-ary function symbol in TM is also an n-ary function symbol in TR whose arguments and whose value are all of sort i. Finally, each n-ary predicate symbol in TM becomes an n-ary function symbol in TR with arguments of sort i, and value of sort p. The last clause reflects the fact that predicates in TM take individual expressions to make sentences. Thus, there is a TR-function symbol corresponding to each TM-predicate taking TR-expressions of sort c or v denoting TM-terms, to give a TR-expression of sort p denoting a TM-proposition.

In addition to the above TR contains the following special function symbols. There are three two-place function symbols with as arguments and values expressions of sort p, *AND*, *IF* and *OR*. There are also three one-place function symbols, *NOT*, *PAST* and *FUTURE*, whose argument and value are both of sort p as well. TR has two two-place function symbols *FORALL* and *THEREIS*, whose first argument is of sort v, whose second argument is of sort p, and whose value is of sort p as well. Finally, there is a two-place function symbol *AT*, taking as arguments a expression of sort t and an expression of sort p, to give an expression of sort p as result. Clearly, these special function symbols are the counterparts in TR of the logical connectives, quantifiers and operators of TM.

Given the above set of constants and function symbols, the set of terms of TR, $TERM^{TR}$, is defined in the usual way.

TR has five predicate symbols *HOLDS*, $<_{TR}$, E, *T-DEN*, and *DEN*. *HOLDS* is a two-place predicate. Its first argument is of sort p, while it second argument is of sort t-den. Its intuitive reading is that the first argument is true at the time denoted by the second argument. Thus, *HOLDS* is the counterpart in TR of the double turn-style ($\models$) for the modal language TM. $<_{TR}$ is also a two-place predicate, both of whose arguments are of sort $t - den$. Intuitively, $<_{TR}$ stands for the ordering relation on times. E is a two-place predicate whose arguments are of sort $d - den$ and $t - den$ respectively. Intuitively, E holds between a domain individual and a point in time if the individual exists at that point in time. E thus is the TR-predicate corresponding to the function ind in a TM-structure. *T-DEN* is a two-place predicate whose first argument is a time-expression and whose second argument is a point in time. *T-DEN* is the counterpart of that part of an interpretation function which assigns a point in time to time constants. *DEN* is a three-place relation whose first argument is of sort c, whose second argument is of sort d and whose third argument is of sort t. The intuitive reading of *DEN* is that the expression denoted by the first argument refers to the (real) individual denoted by the second argument at the time denoted by the third argument.

TR contains the logical connectives $\neg$ and $\rightarrow$ and the universal quantifier $\forall$.

Given the above set of predicates, connectives and quantifier, and given the definition of $TERM^{TR}$, the set of well-formed formulas of TR, WFF^{TR}, is defined in the usual way.

TR-structures.   TR is a complicated first order language. This is reflected in the definition of the notion of a TR-structure. Because TR is a formal meta-language for TM, TR-structures contain counterparts of TM-expressions themselves, as well as of denotations of TM-expressions. Given these preliminaries, the following definition of a TR-structure, although complicated, should be comprehensible.

Definition 6 A TR-structure is a $\langle C_d, V_d, TC_d, P_d, I_d, T_d \rangle$ where C_d, V_d, TC_d, P_d, I_d, T_d, T_d are non-empty and mutually disjoint sets. The set T_d contains a distinguished element t_0.

The set C_d is the set of denotations of constants of sort c, and is corresponds to the set of TM-constants. Similarly, the sets V_d, TC_d and P_d are the counterparts of the TM-variables, TM-time-constants and TM-sentences. The sets I_d and T_d are the sets of real individuals and points in time respectively, and are used to construct entities that correspond to TM-denotations.

TR-interpretations.   In this section, I first define the notion of a TR-interpretation. Then, I will define the notion of truth in a TR-interpretation. The definition of a TR-interpretation given below is not entirely satisfactory. In order to reflect all the intuitions accurately, the definition would have to be complicated considerably. I ignore these complications in this section but I return to them in the next section.

Definition 7 A TR-interpretation is an ordered pair $\langle M, f \rangle$ where $M = \langle C_d, V_d, TC_d, P_d, I_d, T_d \rangle$ is a TR-structure and f is an interpretation function such that

- if c is a constant of sort τ, then $f(c) \in M(\tau)$, where $M(c) = C_d$, $M(v) = V_d$, $M(t) = TC_d$, $M(p) = P_d$, $M(i\text{-}den) = I_d$, and $M(t\text{-}den) = T_d$.

- if m is an n-place function symbol with arguments of sorts $\tau_1, \ldots, \tau_n$ and value of sort τ, then $f(m)$ is a function from $M(\tau_1) \times, \ldots, \times M(\tau_n)$ into $M(\tau)$.

- if$P$ is an n-place predicate whose arguments are of sorts $\tau_1, \ldots, \tau_n$, then $f(P)$ is an element of the n-ary cartesian product of the sets corresponding to each τ_i.

A TR-value-assignment g is a function which assigns to each variable of sort τ an element of $M(\tau)$. The notion of truth in a TR-interpretation with respect to a TR-value-assignment is defined as:

Definition 8 Let S be a TR-interpretation, $\langle M, f \rangle$, let g be a TR-value-assignment, then a TR-proposition p is true in S under g, $S \models_g p$, if the following hold:

if p is of the form $pred(arg_1, \ldots, arg_n)$,
then $S \models_g p$ if $\langle h(arg_1), \ldots, h(arg_n) \rangle \in f(pred)$ where $h(arg_i) = g(arg_i)$ if arg_i is a variable and $arg_i = f(arg_i)$ otherwise.

In addition to these clauses, there are the normal clauses for conjunctions, disjunctions, negations, implications and universally and existentially quantified formulas.

The notion of truth in a TR-interpretation can now be defined.

Definition 9 A TR-proposition p is true in a TR-structure S if $S \models_g p$ for all TR-value-assignments g.

Some complications. The above system, baroque as it is, does not capture all the intuitions. There are various additional constraints that have to be put on the interpretations of the TR-predicates. Rather than define these directly in the definition of a TR-interpretation, I will, for the sake of clarity, define them as meaning postulates. One can then define the notion of an *preferred* TR-interpretation as a TR-interpretation in which the meaning postulates are true. Of course, we are primarily interested in the preferred TR-interpretations, and in the remainder of this chapter, whenever I use the term "TR-interpretation", I will mean "preferred TR-interpretation".

The first meaning postulates concern the relationships between names for individuals and individuals. First, I assume that every term denotes an existing individual at every point in time, and, second, I assume that for every individual that exists at a given point in time, there is a name for that individual.

$$(\forall c{:}c)(\forall t{:}t\text{-}den)(\exists d{:}d\text{-}den)(DEN(c,d,t)\,\&\,E(d,t)) \qquad (7.44)$$

$$(\forall d{:}d\text{-}den)(\forall t{:}t\text{-}den)(E(d,t) \leftrightarrow (\exists c{:}c)(DEN(c,d,t))) \qquad (7.45)$$

Note that because of 7.44 constant expressions are not treated as rigid designators. If one wanted to treat constants as rigid designators, then 7.44 would have to be replaced by 7.46:

$$(\forall c{:}c)(\exists d{:}d\text{-}den)(\forall t{:}t\text{-}den)(DEN(c,d,t)\,\&\,E(d,t)) \qquad (7.46)$$

However, given 7.45 and the desire to have changing ontologies, this would lead to problems. After all, intuitively, 7.45 says that every individual existing at a point in time is denoted by some constant at that point in time, whereas 7.46 says that an individual always has the same name and exists at every point in time. It follows from these two that if an individual exists at one point in time, then it exists at all points in time. Thus, treating constants as rigid designators and assuming that an existing individual always has a name are not compatible with the desire to have changing ontologies. As we shall see below, we cannot drop the assumption that an individual always has a name as this would lead to problems in the treatment of the quantifiers. The best way to deal with this problem would be to add a sub-sort r of c, standing for the rigid designator constants, and restrict 7.46 to the rigid designator constant. In this chapter, then, I will use 7.44 and 7.45 as meaning postulates. Note that given these two meaning postulates it is possible that the set of individuals denoted by some individual constant at a given point in time is different from the set of individuals denoted by some individual constant at another point in time.

More meaning postulates have to be introduced because of the interaction between the *HOLDS*-predicate and the function symbols, *AND*, *OR*, *NOT*, and *IF*. One would like the following sentences to be valid. After all, to take the first one, if a proposition $(p\&q)$ is true at time t, then p is true at t, as is q.

$$(\forall t{:}t\text{-}den)(\forall p{:}p)(\forall q{:}p)(HOLDS(AND(p,q),t) \leftrightarrow \tag{7.47}$$
$$(HOLDS(p,t)\&HOLDS(q,t)))$$
$$(\forall t{:}t\text{-}den)(\forall p{:}p)(\forall q{:}p)(HOLDS(OR(p,q),t) \leftrightarrow \tag{7.48}$$
$$(HOLDS(p,t) \vee HOLDS(q,t)))$$
$$(\forall t{:}t\text{-}den)(\forall p{:}p)(\forall q{:}p)(HOLDS(IF(p,q),t) \leftrightarrow \tag{7.49}$$
$$(HOLDS(p,t) \rightarrow HOLDS(q,t)))$$
$$(\forall t{:}t\text{-}den)(\forall p{:}p)(HOLDS(NOT(p),q) \leftrightarrow \neg HOLDS(p,t)) \tag{7.50}$$

More meaning postulates arise because of the interaction of *HOLDS* and the function symbols, *THEREIS* and *FORALL*. In order to formulate these criteria, the three-place function symbol *SUBST* has to be introduced. The first argument to *SUBST* is of sort v, the second argument of sort c, and the third argument of sort p. Its value is of sort p as well. The intuitive interpretation of *SUBST(v,c,p)* is the proposition obtained from the proposition denoted by p be replacing all occurrences of the variable denoted by v by occurrences of the constant denoted by c. Given this function symbol, one can now formulate two more meaning postulates.

$$(\forall p{:}p)(\forall t{:}t\text{-}den)(\forall v{:}v)(HOLDS(ALL(v,p),t) \rightarrow \tag{7.51}$$
$$(\forall i{:}i\text{-}den)(\forall c{:}c)(DEN(c,i,t) \rightarrow$$
$$HOLDS(SUBST(c,v,p),t)))$$
$$(\forall p{:}p)(\forall t{:}t\text{-}den)(\forall v{:}v)(HOLDS(THEREIS(v,p),t) \rightarrow \tag{7.52}$$
$$(\exists i{:}i\text{-}den)(\exists c{:}c)(DEN(c,i,t)\&$$
$$HOLDS(SUBST(c,v,p),t)))$$

The reader will have noticed that the above encodes a substitutional account of quantification: in order to determine whether a universally quantified sentence holds, one replaces the variable by a name in the language. If each such sentence is true, then the universally quantified sentence is true as well. Note, first, that this is the only account of quantification that is possible in the reified language defined here, and, second, that given this account, we have to make the assumption that every individual existing at some point in time has a name. This leads to yet another meaning postulate:

$$(\forall d{:}d\text{-}den)(\forall t{:}t\text{-}den)(E(d,t) \rightarrow (\exists c{:}c)(DEN(c,d,t))) \tag{7.53}$$

The last meaning postulates follow from the interaction between the function symbols *PAST*, *FUTURE* and *AT*, and the predicate *HOLDS*. In particular, the following three formulas should be valid:

$$(\forall t{:}t\text{-}den)(\forall p{:}p)(HOLDS(PAST(p),t) \rightarrow \tag{7.54}$$
$$(\exists t'{:}t\text{-}den)((t' < t)\,\&\,HOLDS(p,t')))$$

$$(\forall t{:}t\text{-}den)(\forall p{:}p)(HOLDS(FUTURE(p),t) \rightarrow \tag{7.55}$$
$$(\exists t'{:}t\text{-}den)((t < t')\,\&\,HOLDS(p,t')))$$

$$(\forall t{:}t\text{-}den)(\forall t'{:}t\text{-}den)(\forall p{:}p)(\forall t\text{-}exp{:}t) \tag{7.56}$$
$$((HOLDS(AT(t{:}exp,p),t))\,\&\,T\text{-}DENOTES(t\text{-}exp,t')) \rightarrow$$
$$HOLDS(p,t'))$$

The intuitions behind the above formulas are again straightforward. We want the function symbols *PAST*, *FUTURE* and *AT* to behave as their counterparts in TM.

TR and the criteria.   TR is a first order language, be it a complicated one, and therefore the notion of inference in TR should be efficiently implementable. However, because TR is so complicated, and because one has to add quite a few additional axioms governing the behaviour of *HOLDS*, the situation might not be as positive as for TA. The main argument for preferring first order theorem provers to modal ones is the fact that in modal theorem provers a basic resolution step is more expensive. However, when it comes to comparing TR and TM, this loss in efficiency for TM might well be offset by two factors. First, TR is too complicated to function as a user-language. Therefore, one has to include a translation algorithm from TM into TR and vice versa. It is relatively straightforward to write such a translation algorithm. Translating TM-connectives, TM-operators and TM-quantifiers into the corresponding TR-function symbols, all one has to do is form a new sentences saying that the TR-term corresponding to the proposition *HOLDS* at time t_0. The axioms and inference rules governing the behaviour of *HOLDS* ensure that the function symbols will be transformed correctly into the corresponding TR-quantifiers and TR-connectives, etc. The translation algorithm from TR into TM is more complicated but will not pose any unsurmountable difficulties either. However, the translation algorithm might lose TR some of its computational advantage.

A second factor that adversely affects the efficiency of TR is that fact that the TR-translations of TM formulas are themselves very complicated. The search space for TR formulas will therefore be much larger than for the corresponding TM-formulas. It might be possible for TR to regain some of its computational advantages, for example by building the axioms for the *HOLDS* predicate into the theorem prover, but at the moment it is an open question as to which theorem prover is more efficient.

Turning to the other criteria, TR has both variables referring to points in time and constants denoting specific points in time, and one can therefore express both precise and imprecise temporal knowledge in TR. Also, as TA, it allows arbitrary quantification over points in time. As far as incremental combination of TR with other modal logics is concerned, the situation is akin to the situation with TA. In TA, one had to add an argument to every predicate. The situation in TR is alike. Thus, if one were to combine TR with some epistemic logic, then one would have to add a belief-world argument to both *HOLDS* and *DENOTES*. Also, for every modality, one has to add some accessibility predicate to the language. The result is that incremental combination of TR with another modal logic is not possible. Finally, as said before, TR can cope with the problem of changing ontologies.

An important advantage of TR. Although TR might not fare better than TA on the criteria in section 7.2, TR has an important expressive advantage over TM and TA. The advantage, which is pointed out by [Shoh86],[1] is a direct consequence of the fact that one can quantify over propositions. In TM and in TA, it is impossible to express general temporal knowledge such as *effects cannot precede their causes*. Because one cannot talk about effects and causes in general, one can at most make the above statements about specific causes and effects.

In TR, one can in principle talk about causes and effects in general. TR

---

[1]Shoham makes a similar distinction between three ways of doing temporal logic to the one drawn here. Shoham rejects the methods of temporal arguments because it does not allow one to say anything general about time. However, the same argument also applies against the modal approaches.

contains constants and variables of sort p, denoting expressions which in turn are naturally interpreted as denoting events, etc. Because one can quantify over expressions of sort p, TR gives one the power to talk about propositions and their denotations in general. Note that in the model theory of the present system there are no entities of sort *event*, and there is no TR-predicate *P-DEN* which relates propositions to appropriate denotations in a way similar to the way in which *T-DEN* relates time-expressions to points in time, and *DEN* relates individual expressions to domain individuals. Obviously, for the above proposals to work in an intuitive way, such a predicate would have to be introduced together with the required complication of the model theory. One can interpret Allen's work as a partial specification of the necessary complications in the underlying ontology. Note that this would also entail that TR can no longer be regarded as purely a formalisation of the metalanguage of TM. After all, TM does not contain any expressions referring to events. But, even without further complications the present language is rich enough to allow one to express general temporal knowledge. For example, assuming a two-place predicate *CAUSES*, both of whose arguments are of sort p,[2] then one can express the above general temporal knowledge as:

$$(\forall p{:}p)(\forall q{:}q)(CAUSES(p,q) \rightarrow$$
$$(\forall t{:}t\text{-}den)(\forall t'{:}t\text{-}den)(HOLDS(p,t)\,\&\,HOLDS(p,t')$$
$$\rightarrow \neg(t' < t)))$$

In order to be able to write down this piece of general temporal knowledge, one has to be able to quantify over propositions. Since this is possible neither in TA nor in TM, this is a definite advantage of TR over either. It must be said however that, if one wants to use TR to express this type of knowledge, then one cannot use TM as the language in which the user interacts with the system.

A comparison with Shoham's formalism. [Shoh86] proposes a formalism which is also intended as a precise formal system for reified temporal logic. Rather than discuss Shoham's formalism in detail, I will point out the major differences between his system and the present system, and the main weaknesses of his system. I will call Shoham's system SL.

---

[2] This shows that the predicate *P-DEN* should really be introduced. It is counterintuitive to regard *CAUSES* as a predicate involving two propositions.

First, it has to be admitted that SL looks far more elegant than TR, but, as I argue below, SL achieves this at the expense of less expressive power. Sometimes, elegance has to be sacrificed for expressiveness.

Atomic propositions in SL are triples $\langle t_1, t_2, p \rangle$ where t_1 and t_2 are points in time and p is an atomic proposition of classical first order predicate calculus. The intuitive reading is that p is true between t_1 and t_2. More complex propositions can be constructed from these atomic propositions in the normal way, where quantifiers can range both over the points in time t_1 and t_2 and over terms occurring in p.

A first criticism concerns the expressiveness of the language SL. First, SL cannot cope with iterated modalities, although it might be possible to write a translation algorithm from TM into SL that can deal with this problem. Second, SL cannot cope with the problem of changing ontologies. Quantifiers always have the temporal formulas inside their scope, and it seems impossible to express the difference between *something has the property p between t_1 and t_2* and *between t_1 and t_2 something has the property p*. In order to get around this problem, Shoham would have to introduce the *exist* predicate of TA.

A second criticism is that it is not clear in what sense SL is a reified temporal logic. It seems to me that it is more appropriate to regard SL as a hybrid of a modal approach and the method of temporal arguments. The third argument in an SL proposition is an atomic proposition of first-order predicate calculus and not a name of a proposition. Therefore, one is not allowed to quantify over it, and I find it therefore somewhat puzzling that Shoham presents his system as a reified temporal logic. Because SL propositions are formed from first-order propositions, SL has certain things in common with a modal language. On the other hand, SL contains explicit time arguments in formulas and allows quantification over them. SL has this in common with the method of temporal arguments.

Concluding then, it seems to me that SL is not a reified temporal logic. It is best regarded as a hybrid of a modal language and a language based on the method of temporal arguments. SL is not a particularly expressive language, and it is not obvious that it can cope with the problem of iterated modalities, or with the problem of changing ontologies. Also, it is not clear to me how SL could express the proposition *effects cannot precede their causes*.

7.5   Conclusion

The overall conclusion which I draw from the above considerations is as follows. If one restricts oneself to purely logical considerations, then modal treatments of temporal logics are superior to first order treatments. First, they have a natural semantics. Contrast for example the semantics for TM with that of TR. Second, modal treatments allow for the incremental combination of temporal logics with other modal logics, such as the logic of knowledge and belief. Third, the language of TM is much more natural than the language of either TA or TR. I sketched however a way of getting around this problem by using TM as the user language and translating it into either TA or TR.

From the computational point of view, first order treatments seem preferable. It has to be kept in mind however that some of the computational gains are lost because of the need of translating the first order languages into more "user-friendly" logical languages, and because the resulting formulas are very complicated. The main objections against first order treatments, however, is the fact that they do not allow for incremental combination of different modal logics.

Finally, reified temporal logic has one important advantage over both modal treatments and the method of temporal arguments. Because it allows quantification over propositions, it allows the natural expression of general temporal knowledge of the type *effects never precede their causes*. It would be impossible to express similar knowledge in either of the other formalisms.

8 A General Proof Method for Modal Predicate Logic

Peter Jackson
Han Reichgelt

8.1 Introduction

We present a sequent based proof method for modal predicate logic that is both general and natural. The inference rules are identical for all modal logics; different logics differ only in the conditions under which two formulas in sequents can be resolved against each other. The conditions for a particular modal logic are closely related to the restrictions on the accessibility relation in the Kripke semantics for that logic.

Part of the motivation for this work is the desire to provide efficient proof methods that are sufficiently flexible to support experimentation with different logics of knowledge and belief [Jack87a]. The emphasis is on the design of modal meta-interpreters which endow a knowledge base management system with varying degrees of introspection capability [Jack88a] (see also [Jack88c]). Another motivation is an interest in temporal logic, and in particular a comparison of a modal temporal logic with other possible approaches, such as a reified approach ([Shoh86] and chapter 7 of this volume).

The outline of the chapter is as follows. First we provide a proof method for modal predicate logics in which both the Barcan formula and its converse hold. Thus, both $(\forall x)Lp \rightarrow L(\forall x)p$ and $L(\forall x)p \rightarrow (\forall x)Lp$ are valid formulas. From a model-theoretic point of view, this means that the set of individuals existing in one possible world is always identical to the set of individuals existing in another possible world. We present a proof method for modal logics of this kind and prove its completeness and soundness. Next we generalize the proof method to modal predicate logics in which neither the Barcan formula nor its converse holds, where it is possible that the set of individuals is not identical between worlds. Finally, we show that by some simple modifications the proof method can be generalized to logics in which the Barcan formula holds while its converse does not, and to logics in which the Barcan formula does not hold while its converse does.

The proof method has been implemented and we discuss some implementational details. Finally, we discuss some related work. This chapter expands on and corrects earlier work reported in [Jack87c], [Jack88b].

8.2 Proof theory for logics with the Barcan formula

In this section we define a proof theory for logics in which both the Barcan formula (BF) and its converse (FB) hold.

8.2.1 Syntax

Our logical language is defined in the normal way. We use only the connectives $\rightarrow$ and $\neg$, the universal quantifier $\forall$ and the necessity operator L. The other connectives, the existential quantifier $\exists$ and the possibility operator M are introduced as abbreviations. We use the following meta-variables: p, q and r denote predicates (including 0-ary predicates, i.e. formulas). S, T and U are used to denote sets of formulas, while u, v and w denote possible worlds.

The proof theory that we present is sequent based. A *sequent* is an expression $S \leftarrow T$ where S and T are (possible empty) sets of formulas. If S and T are both empty, then we call the sequent *empty*. The informal reading of $S \leftarrow T$ is that if all the formulas in T are true, then at least one of the formulas in S is true. This is equivalent to saying that at least one of the formulas in T is false or at least one of the formulas in S is true. Thus, formulas in T have an implicit negative polarity, while formulas in S have positive polarity. Consequently, we shall often speak of formulas in sequents as if they were explicitly signed. Note incidentally that the empty sequent is always false.

In sequent based proof theories for classical predicate logic, two formulas p and q are *complementary* if they have opposite truth values in all interpretations, in other words, if $p \leftrightarrow \neg q$ is valid. For modal logic the notion of complementarity needs to be complicated. Propositions may change their truth value when we move from one world to another, and we are not allowed to unify across worlds, so to speak. Therefore, in addition to ensuring that the formulas are complementary, we need to ensure that they are complementary *in the same world*. In the present proof method, we introduce the notion of a *world-index*. With each sentence we associate a world-index, which represents the world in which the sentence is true or false. If p is a formula, and i an index, then we shall write the indexed formulas as $|p|_i$. The meaning and utility of this notation will become clearer when we define the internal structure of the world indices and give the rules that govern their deployment. However, before we can do so, we first remind the reader of the standard semantics for modal predicate logic.

8.2.2 Kripke models

A standard model for modal predicate logic is a triple consisting of a Kripke structure $\langle W, R, aw \rangle$, a set of individuals I and a valuation function V. W is a (non-empty) set of worlds, $R \subseteq W^2$ (the accessibility relation), $aw \in W$ (the actual world), and V is a valuation function which, for every expression e in the language (with the exception of individual variables), and every world $w \in W$, assigns a denotation to e in w. For all constants c in the language, $V(w, c) \in I$, while for all k-place predicates p, $V(w, p) \subseteq I^k$. A ground atomic formula $p(c_1, \ldots, c_n)$ is then true at world w just in case $\langle V(w, c_1), \ldots, V(w, c_n) \rangle \in V(w, p)$. Let $p(a/x)$ is the result of uniformly substituting a for x in p. Then, a universally quantified sentence $(\forall x)p$ is true at world w if and only if $V'(w, p(a/x)) = true$ for each V' such that $V'(w, e) = V(w, e)$ for all expressions e except possibly some individual constant a not appearing in p.

Finally, $V(w, Lp)$ is true if for all w', such that wRw', $V(w', p) = true$. Because we are dealing with systems in with both BF and FB hold, the set of individuals is identical for all worlds $w \in W$. When we generalize the proof method to systems of modal predicate logic in which neither BF nor FB hold, we shall see that the basic notion of a Kripke model will need to be complicated.

A system of modal logic can be specified semantically in terms of the properties of the accessibility relation, R, that hold in all standard models of the system [Chel80]. The conditions under which one world is accessible from another differ between modal logics. It is well-known that there is a close relationship between the axioms of a given modal logic, and the properties of the accessibility relation. The following are some examples: if $Lp \rightarrow Mp$ is an axiom, then the accessibility relation is serial, i.e. for every possible world w, there is a possible world w' such that wRw'. If $Lp \rightarrow p$ is an axiom, then the accessibility relation is reflexive, i.e. for every possible world w, wRw. Note that reflexivity implies seriality. If $p \rightarrow LMp$ is an axiom, then the accessibility relation

is symmetric, i.e. for all possible worlds w and w', wRw' implies $w'Rw$.
If $Lp \to LLp$ is an axiom, then the accessibility relation is transitive, i.e.
for all possible worlds w, w' and w'', if wRw' and $w'Rw''$, then wRw''.
Finally, if $Mp \to LMp$ is an axiom, then the accessibility relation is
euclidean, i.e. for all possible worlds w, w' and w'', if wRw' and wRw'',
then $w'Rw''$. A modal logic can be specified syntactically by a set of
axioms or semantically by giving the properties of the accessibility relation. For example, in S4 the accessibility relation has to be transitive
and reflexive.

We make use of this correspondence between axioms and properties of
the accessibility relation in the definition of a special form of unification
which we call *modal unification* or *m-unification*. The conditions under
which two indexed formulas m-unify are relative to the accessibility relation R. Changing the properties of the accessibility relation therefore
influences which indexed formulas can unify. Before we can define the
notion of m-unification, we first need to define the notion of a world
index more precisely.

8.2.3   World indices

As said before, the world index associated with a formula denotes the
world at which a formula is true or false. The following defines this
notion more precisely:

Definition 1 A *world-index* is a (non-empty) sequence of world symbols, $s_1\!:\ldots\!:s_n$, where each $s_i \in S = N \cup X \cup Sk$, where

N is the set of numerals $\{0, 1, 2, \ldots\}$

X is the set of world variables $\{w_1, w_2, \ldots\}$

Sk is the set $\{f_j(x_1, \ldots, x_j) \mid f_j \in F_j \text{ and } x_1, \ldots, x_j \in X \cup Var\}$,
  where F_j is the set of j-place skolem functions, and Var is the set
  of individual variables in the language

A world-symbol in which no world variable occurs is called *ground*, as
is a world-index all of whose world-symbols are ground. If $s_1\!:\ldots\!:s_n$ is a
world-index, then we call s_1 the *end symbol* and s_n the *start symbol*. We
write $end(s_1\!:\ldots\!:s_n)$ and $start(s_1\!:\ldots\!:s_n)$ respectively. If $s_1\!:s_2\!:\ldots\!:s_n$ is
a world-index, then s_2 is called the *parent symbol* of s_1 in $s_1\!:s_2\!:\ldots\!:s_n$,
written $parent(s_1\!:s_2\!:\ldots\!:s_n)$. We call $s_2\!:\ldots\!:s_n$ the *parent index*, and
write $parent\text{-}index(s_1\!:s_2\!:\ldots\!:s_n)$. Note that not every world-index has

a parent-symbol or a parent-index, and that indices are read from right to left.

Intuitively, world-symbols in N represent specific possible worlds in some Kripke model. World-symbols in X act like variables. When occurring in a world index, they represent any possible world accessible from the world denoted by their parent symbols. Finally, world-symbols in Sk represent possible worlds the choice of which depends on some earlier possible world, or on the choice of some individual. The order in which worlds occur in a world-index corresponds to the accessibility relation in a Kripke model. Thus, the world-index $f(w){:}w{:}0$ describes a world $f(w)$ that is accessible from world w, which is itself accessible from world 0. However, whereas w represents *any* world accessible from 0, $f(w)$ represents a particular world accessible from w whose identity depends on the specific world chosen as the instantiation of w. Clearly, if the accessibility relation has other properties, then one can use the world-index to establish other pairs of accessible worlds. For example, if we insist that $f(w){:}w{:}0$ is a world-index in a Kripke model in which the accessibility relation is transitive, then one can also conclude that $f(w)$ is accessible from 0, for all w accessible from 0.

8.2.4 World-unification

In order for two formulas to unify, their indices need to denote the same world. Here we define an algorithm for determining this, called the *world unification algorithm.*

Definition 2 Two world-indices i and j *w-unify* with unification σ under accessibility relation R iff

1. $start(i) = start(j) = 0$, and

2. (a) if $end(i)$ and $end(j)$ are ground,
       and $end(i) = end(j)$,
       then i and j w-unify with $\sigma = \emptyset$.

   (b) if $end(i)$ is ground and $end(j)$ is a world variable
       and the accessibility relation is serial
       and there is a unification θ such that
       $\langle parent(end(j))\theta, end(i)\rangle \in R$
       then i and j w-unify with $\sigma = \{end(i)/end(j)\}\theta$
       where $\{end(i)/end(j)\}\theta$ is the composition of the substitutions $\{end(i)/end(j)\}$ and θ.

(c) if $end(i)$ and $end(j)$ are world variables
and the accessibility relation is serial, and

   i. if there is a substitution θ such that
     either $\langle parent(end(j))\theta, end(i)\rangle \in R$
     or $\langle parent(end(i))\theta, end(j)\rangle \in R$,
    then i and j w-unify with $\sigma = \{end(i)/end(j)\}\theta$.

  ii. if $parent\text{-}index(i)$ w-unifies with $parent\text{-}index(j)$ with
    unification θ,
    then i and j w-unify with $\sigma = \{end(i)/end(j)\}\theta$.

By insisting on part 1, we ensure that R defines a connected graph on W, the set of possible worlds. By convention, we let the numeral 0 stand for the actual world, and this will be the start symbol of all world-indices considered in this chapter.

Part 2 distinguishes between three cases, depending on whether the end symbols are ground or not. The first case 2a arises when both end symbols are ground. The world-indices w-unify if and only if their end symbols are identical. In other words, we assume that possible worlds have unique names. The proof theory defined below indeed ensures this.

The second case 2b arises when one world symbol is ground and the other is not, i.e. we are dealing with a specific world n and an arbitrary world w. In order for these two worlds to be identifiable, we insist that n is accessible from the parent world of w. Clearly, if w represents any world accessible from $parent(w)$ and n is accessible from $parent(w)$, then we can take n as an instantiation of w.

A complication arises when the accessibility relation is not serial, and the ground world symbol contains a world variable. If the accessibility relation is not serial, then there is no guarantee that for every world there is an accessible possible world. Consider the world-index $f(w){:}w{:}0$. For every world w accessible from 0, $f(w)$ denotes a world accessible from it. However, if the accessibility relation is not serial, then we cannot guarantee that there is a world w accessible from 0, and if there is not, then $f(w)$ need not exist either. We will return to this point in section 8.2.7 when we discuss some examples.

The third case 2c arises when neither end symbol is ground. In this case, we are dealing with two arbitrary worlds accessible from their respective parent symbols. Therefore, if one of the worlds is accessible from the parent of the other, or the parents can be shown to be identical (by a recursive application of w-unification), then the two arbitrary worlds can be assumed to be identical. However, as before, the argument applies only if we can assume that world variables always have a non-empty denotation. Thus we insist that R be serial.

Conditions 2(c)i and 2(c)ii are not identical, and neither of them implies the other (see examples 6 and 7 in section 8.2.7).

8.2.5 M-unification

As said before, our proof theory relies on a special notion of unification, called *m-unification*. In the previous section, we defined the world unification algorithm that can be used to determine whether two world-indices denote the same world under the accessibility relation R. In this section, we use the definition of w-unification to define the notion of m-unification.

Definition 3 Two indexed formulas $|p|_i$ and $|q|_j$ *m-unify* with substitution σ iff

1. the formulas p and q unify with unification θ, *and*

2. the world-indices i and j w-unify, with unification η, *and*

3. σ is the unifying composition of θ and η.

Let $\theta = \{a_1/x_1, \ldots, a_n/x_n\}$ and $\eta = \{b_1/y_1, \ldots, b_m/y_m\}$. The unifying composition can be obtained by taking the most general unifier of $(x_1, \ldots, x_n, y_1, \ldots, y_m)$ and $(a_1, \ldots, a_n, b_1, \ldots, b_m)$. For example, the unifying composition of $\{f(x)/v, 1/w\}$ and $\{g(w)/x, h(v, w)/y\}$ is the substitution $\{g(1)/x, h(f(g(1)), 1)/y, f(g(1))/v, 1/w\}$. For more examples of unifying compositions of two substitutions the reader is referred to [Nils82, pp. 207-209].

8.2.6 Proof theory

In this section we define the full proof theory.

Let S, T, S', T' be sets of indexed formulas, and $S\sigma$ be the result of applying substitution σ to every indexed formula in S, where if $|p|_i$ is an indexed formula, then the result of applying σ to it is defined as $|p\sigma|_{i\sigma}$. Let i and j be arbitrary world-indices. Let p and q be any propositions, and let $p(a/x)$ be the result of uniformly substituting a for x in p. Then we have the following inference rules.

R1. If $S, |p|_i \leftarrow T$ and $S' \leftarrow |q|_j, T'$,
    and $|p|_i$ and $|q|_j$ m-unify with unification σ,
    then $S\sigma \cup S'\sigma \leftarrow T\sigma \cup T'\sigma$.

R2. If $S, |(p \rightarrow q)|_i \leftarrow T$ then $S, |q|_i \leftarrow |p|_i, T$

R3. If $S \leftarrow |(p \rightarrow q)|_i, T$ then $S \leftarrow |q|_i, T$

R4. If $S \leftarrow |(p \rightarrow q)|_i, T$ then $S, |p|_i \leftarrow T$

R5. If $S, |\neg p|_i \leftarrow T$ then $S \leftarrow |p|_i, T$

R6. If $S \leftarrow |\neg p|_i, T$ then $S, |p|_i \leftarrow T$

R7. If $S \leftarrow |Lp|_i, T$ then $S \leftarrow |p|_{n:i}, T$, where

    1. n is a new world-constant if i is a ground world-index and p does not contain any free variables;

    2. otherwise, n is $f(w_1, \ldots, w_k, x_1, \ldots, x_m)$, where f is a skolem function of world variables $w_1, \ldots, w_k$ in i and free individual variables $x_1, \ldots, x_m$ in $|p|_i$.

R8. If $S, |Lp|_i \leftarrow T$ then $S, |p|_{w:i} \leftarrow T$, where w is a new world variable.

R9. If $S \leftarrow |(\forall x)p|_i, T$ then $S \leftarrow |p(a/x)|_i, T$, where

    1. a is a new individual constant if p contains no free individual variables and i is a ground world-index;

    2. otherwise a is $f(w_1, \ldots, w_k, x_1, \ldots, x_m)$ where f is a skolem function of world variables $w_1, \ldots, w_k$ in i and free individual variables $x_1, \ldots, x_m$ in $|p|_i$.

R10. If $S, |(\forall x)p|_i \leftarrow T$ then $S, |p(y/x)|_i \leftarrow T$,
    where y is a new individual variable.

A proof of a formula p is defined as a finite sequence of sequents $\Sigma_0, \ldots, \Sigma_n$ where Σ_0 is the sequent $\leftarrow |p|_0$, Σ_n is the empty sequent, and every sequent apart from Σ_0 has been obtained from one or more previous sequents by an application of an inference rule. Given the intuitive interpretation of sequents that we gave before, one can see that a proof consists of attempting to construct a countermodel for the formula in question by assuming that it is false in some arbitrary Kripke-model. Every successful proof discovers a contradiction in the putative countermodel.

In the set of inference rules specified above, R1 corresponds to the resolution rule, while R2-R6 correspond to the truth tables for classical propositional logic. R8 states that if Lp is true at world w, then p is true at any world accessible from w, while R10 says that if $(\forall x)p$ is true, then any individual has the property p. The intuitions behind R7 and R9 are similar to those behind the elimination of existential quantifiers in skolemisation. When we skolemise in R9, we need to take into account not only the free variables in the formula p, but also the world variables in the index i associated with p. This can be illustrated when we consider the sequent $\leftarrow |(\forall x)p(x)|_{w:0}$. Intuitively this means that $(\forall x)p(x)$ is false in all worlds w accessible from 0. So, for each such world there is an individual that makes $p(x)$ false. Clearly, the choice of individual depends on the world: individual a may provide the counterexample to $p(x)$ in world 1 accessible from 0, while individual b may provide the counterexample in world 2. The skolem term therefore needs to take into account the free variables both in the formula and in the index. A similar argument can obviously also be applied to justify R7 from an intuitive point of view.

8.2.7 Examples

In this section, we give a number of examples that clarify the proof method and illustrate the need for some of its less obvious aspects.

Example 1 We first show how the S4 axiom can be proven if the accessibility relation is transitive.

1		$\leftarrow$	$|Lp \rightarrow LLp|_0$	
2	$|Lp|_0$	$\leftarrow$		$R4, 1.$
3	$|p|_{w:0}$	$\leftarrow$		$R8, 2.$
4		$\leftarrow$	$|LLp|_0$	$R3, 1.$
5		$\leftarrow$	$|Lp|_{1:0}$	$R7, 4.$
6		$\leftarrow$	$|p|_{2:1:0}$	$R7, 5.$
7		$\leftarrow$		$R1, 3, 6, \{w/2\}$

In order to show that the above proof is correct, we show that $|p|_{w:0}$ m-unifies with $|p|_{2:1:0}$. We represent this situation in a *world diagram* as follows:

Because we are in S4, the accessibility relation between worlds is reflexive and transitive. Obviously, p and p unify with the empty unification. The world-indices $w{:}0$ and $2{:}1{:}0$ w-unify if the accessibility relation is transitive. 2 is accessible from 1 and 1 is accessible from 0. Therefore, if the accessibility relation is transitive, 2 is accessible from 0 which is the parent of w. Condition 2b in the definition of w-unification therefore applies. Note that if the accessibility relation was not transitive, the above proof would fail.

Example 2 As another illustration, we discuss the formula $L(\exists x)p(x) \to (\exists y)Lp(y)$. This formula should not be provable because for each world there might be a different individual with the property p, making the antecedent true and the consequent false. In the proof we make use of the following derived inference rules that can be obtained by rewriting $(\exists x)p$ as $\neg(\forall x)\neg p$. Again, S and T are sets of formulas with associated world-indices.

DR1. If $S, |(\exists x)p|_i \leftarrow T$ then $S, |p(a/x)|_i \leftarrow T$, where

1. a is a new individual constant if p does not contain any free individual variables other than x and i is a ground world-index;

2. otherwise, a is $f(w_1, \ldots, w_k, x_1, \ldots, x_m)$ where f is a skolem function of world variables $w_1, \ldots, w_k$ in i and free individual variables $x_1, \ldots, x_m$ in $|p|_i$.

DR2. If $S \leftarrow |(\exists x)p|_i, T$ then $S, |p(y/x)|_i \leftarrow T$ where y is a new individual variable.

1		$\leftarrow$ $\;|L(\exists x)p(x) \to (\exists y)Lp(y)|_0$	
2	$|L(\exists x)p(x)|_0$	$\leftarrow$	$R4,1$
3	$|(\exists x)p(x)|_{w:0}$	$\leftarrow$	$R8,2$
4	$|p(f(w))|_{w:0}$	$\leftarrow$	$DR1,3$
5		$\leftarrow$ $\;|(\exists y)Lp(y)|_0$	$R3,1$
6		$\leftarrow$ $\;|Lp(y)|_0$	$DR2,5$
7		$\leftarrow$ $\;|p(y)|_{g(y):0}$	$R7,6$

The empty clause cannot be derived because although $p(f(w))$ and $p(y)$ unify with unification $\{f(w)/y\}$, and w:0 and $g(y)$:0 w-unify with unification $\{g(y)/w\}$, we cannot form the unifying composition: (y, w) and $(f(w), g(y))$ do not unify because of the occurs check (see e.g.[Gene87, p. 69]).

Example 3 The next three examples illustrate the restrictions in clauses 2b and 2c of the definition of w-unification. We use the following two derived inference rules. Both can be derived by rewriting Lp as $\neg M \neg p$.

DR3. If $S \leftarrow T, |Mp|_i$, then $S \leftarrow T, |p|_{w:i}$,

  where w is a new world variable.

DR4. If $S|Mp|_i \leftarrow T$ then $S|p|_{n:i} \leftarrow T$, where

  1. n is a new world-constant if i is a ground world-index and p does not contain any free variables;

  2. otherwise, n is $f(w_1, \ldots, w_k, x_1, \ldots, x_m)$, where f is a skolem function of world variables $w_1, \ldots, w_k$ in i and free individual variables $x_1, \ldots, x_m$ in $|p_i$.

First consider proposition $Lp \rightarrow Mp$ which should not be provable if the accessibility relation is not serial. The following is an attempt at proving this proposition:

$$
\begin{array}{llll}
1 & & \leftarrow \quad |Lp \rightarrow Mp|_0 & \\
2 & |Lp|_0 \leftarrow & & R4, 1 \\
3 & |p|_{w:0} \leftarrow & & R8, 2 \\
4 & & \leftarrow \quad |Mp|_0 & R3, 1 \\
5 & & \leftarrow \quad |p|_{w':0} & DR3, 4
\end{array}
$$

If the accessibility relation is not serial, then 3 and 5 cannot be resolved against each other since there are no worlds for w and w' to range over, and the empty sequent is not derivable.

Example 4 The need for the seriality qualification in the definition of w-unification can be illustrated by considering $LMp \rightarrow Mp$. Again this proposition should not be provable if the accessibility relation is not serial.

1		$\leftarrow$	$|LMp \to Mp|_0$	
2	$|LMp|_0$	$\leftarrow$		$R4, 1$
3	$|Mp|_{w:0}$	$\leftarrow$		$R8, 2$
4	$|p|_{f(w):w:0}$	$\leftarrow$		$DR4, 3$
5		$\leftarrow$	$|Mp|_0$	$R3, 1$
6		$\leftarrow$	$|p|_{w':0}$	$DR3, 5$

The reader can check that 4 and 6 cannot be resolved against each other if the accessibility relation is not serial, even if it is symmetric and transitive.

Example 5 The next example is a proof of the T-theorem $Lp \to LMp$

1		$\leftarrow$	$|Lp \to LMp|_0$	
2	$|Lp|_0$	$\leftarrow$		$R4, 1$
3	$|p|_{w:0}$	$\leftarrow$		$R8, 2$
4		$\leftarrow$	$|LMp|_0$	$R3, 1$
5		$\leftarrow$	$|Mp|_{1:0}$	$R7, 4$
6		$\leftarrow$	$|p|_{v:1:0}$	$DR3, 5$

In order to derive the empty sequent, we have to w-unify $w:0$ and $v:1:0$. In T the accessibility relation is reflexive (and hence serial). We can therefore apply clause 2(c)i. There is a unification, namely $\{1/w\}$, such that $\langle 1, w\theta \rangle \in R$, as $w\theta = 1$. Hence, the two world-indices w-unify with the unification $\{1/v, 1/w\}$.

Example 6 The following two examples show that the two conditions in 2c are not identical and that neither implies the other. In this example and the next it is assumed that the accessibility relation is serial. First consider the formula $LLp \to MMp$. Clearly, this formula is provable if the accessibility relation is serial.

1		$\leftarrow$	$|LLp \to MMp|_0$	
2	$|LLp|_0$	$\leftarrow$		$R4, 1$
3	$|Lp|_{w:0}$	$\leftarrow$		$R8, 2$
4	$|p|_{w':w:0}$	$\leftarrow$		$R8, 3$
5		$\leftarrow$	$|MMp|_0$	$R3, 1$
6		$\leftarrow$	$|Mp|_{v:0}$	$DR3, 5$
7		$\leftarrow$	$|p|_{v':v:0}$	$DR3, 6$
8		$\leftarrow$		$R1, 4, 7$

Lines 4 and 7 can be resolved against each other. p and p obviously unify, and their respective world-indices w-unify: consider the following world diagram

Although neither v' is accessible from w, nor w' is accessible from v, condition 2(c)ii applies, and the two world-indices w-unify.

Example 7 Consider the formula $MLp \rightarrow LMp$. Assume that, as well as serial, the accessibility relation is transitive and symmetric. Then this formula should be provable. The following is a proof:

1		$\leftarrow$	$|MLp \rightarrow LMp|_0$	
2	$|MLp|_0$	$\leftarrow$		$R4, 1$
3	$|Lp|_{1:0}$	$\leftarrow$		$DR4, 2$
4	$|p|_{w:1:0}$	$\leftarrow$		$R8, 3$
5		$\leftarrow$	$|LMp|_0$	$R3, 1$
6		$\leftarrow$	$|Mp|_{2:0}$	$R7, 5$
7		$\leftarrow$	$|p|_{v:2:0}$	$DR3, 5$
8		$\leftarrow$		$R1, 4, 7$

Lines 4 and 7 can be resolved against each other. p and p obviously unify, and the respective world-indices world-unify:

Because the accessibility relation is transitive and symmetric, v is accessible from 1 and we can w-unify the world-indices under condition 2(c)i. Note that condition 2(c)ii is not applicable.

Example 8 Consider the proof of the Barcan formula (BF) in the weakest normal system, K.

$$
\begin{array}{llll}
1 & & \leftarrow & |(\forall x)Lp(x) \rightarrow L(\forall x)p(x)|_0 \\
2 & |(\forall x)Lp(x)|_0 & \leftarrow & & R4,1. \\
3 & |Lp(y)|_0 & \leftarrow & & R10,2. \\
4 & |p(y)|_{w:0} & \leftarrow & & R8,3. \\
5 & & \leftarrow & |L(\forall x)p(x)|_0 & R3,1. \\
6 & & \leftarrow & |(\forall x)p(x)|_{1:0} & R7,5. \\
7 & & \leftarrow & |p(a)|_{1:0} & R9,6. \\
8 & & \leftarrow & & R1,4,7, \\
& & & & \{1/w, a/y\}.
\end{array}
$$

Example 9 The proof of the converse of the Barcan formula (FB) is also straightforward in K:

$$
\begin{array}{llll}
1 & & \leftarrow & |L(\forall x)p(x) \rightarrow (\forall x)Lp(x)|_0 \\
2 & |L(\forall x)p(x)|_0 & \leftarrow & & R4,1. \\
3 & |(\forall x)p(x)|_{w:0} & \leftarrow & & R8,2. \\
4 & |p(y)|_{w:0} & \leftarrow & & R10,3. \\
5 & & \leftarrow & |(\forall x)Lp(x)|_0 & R3,1. \\
6 & & \leftarrow & |Lp(a)|_0 & R9,5. \\
7 & & \leftarrow & |p(a)|_{1:0} & R7,6. \\
8 & & \leftarrow & & R1,4,7, \\
& & & & \{1/w, a/y\}
\end{array}
$$

The above examples should give the reader some feeling for what is involved in trying to find proofs. In the next two sections, we show w-unification is correct and that the proof theory is sound. (We do not have a full completeness proof at the present time)

8.2.8   Soundness of w-unification

Before we establish that the proof theory is sound, we show the soundness of the w-unification algorithm. We establish that if two world-indices w-unify, then they denote the same world. We first define the notion of a denotation of a world-index.

Definition 4 If i is a world-index then the *denotation* of i, $\delta_K(i)$ in a Kripke structure $K = \langle W, R, aw \rangle$, is defined as follows:

1. (a) $\delta_K(0) = \{aw\}$

    (b) if $end(i)$ is a world-constant not identical to 0, then
    $$\delta_K(i) \in \{w \mid \langle w', w \rangle \in R \text{ and } Rw' \in \delta_K(parent\text{-}index(i))\}$$

2. if $end(i)$ is a skolemised world symbol, then
$$\delta_K(i) = \bigcup_{w' \in \delta_K(parent\text{-}index(i))} \{\{w\} \mid w \in \{w'' \mid \langle w', w'' \rangle \in R\}\}$$

3. if $end(i)$ is a free world variable, then
$$\delta_K(i) = \bigcup_{w' \in \delta_K(parent\text{-}index(i))} \{w \mid \langle w', w \rangle \in R\}$$

Making the denotation of a world-index with a world constant as its end-symbol a singleton set instead of a possible world, simplifies the presentation.

Earlier we said that by convention 0 stood for the actual world. Clause 1a in the above definition reflects this. If the end-symbol of a world-index is a world-constant, then all the other symbols in the world-index have to be world-constants as well. (If there had been a free variable in the world-index, then, given the way the proof theory works, the end-symbol would have been a skolemised world variable.) In this case, we make the index stand for some accessible from the world denoted by the parent-index (clause 1b). The interpretation of a world-index whose end-symbol is a skolemised world symbol is a set of worlds, such that for every world denoted by its parent-symbol, there is a accessible world. The interpretation of a world symbol with a world variable as its end-symbol is the entire set of worlds accessible from its parent index.

In order to clarify the definition we give a few examples. $\delta_K(0) = \{aw\}$ is a singleton set with as element the actual world in some Kripke model. $\delta_K(1{:}0)$ is a singleton set with as element a world accessible from the world denoted by the parent-index $\delta_K(0)$, i.e. a world accessible from the actual world. $\delta_K(w{:}0)$ is the set of all worlds which are accessible from the actual world. Clearly, if the accessibility relation is not serial, then $\delta_K(w{:}0)$ may be empty. The denotation of $\delta_K(f(w){:}w{:}0)$ is a set of worlds such that for every world w' in $\delta_K(w{:}0)$, there is a world w'' in $\delta_K(f(w){:}w{:}0)$ such that $w'Rw''$.

We now use this definition to define the notion of two world-indices denoting the same world.

Definition 5 Two world-indices i and j *denote the same world* in a Kripke structure K iff $\delta_K(i) \cap \delta_K(j) \neq \emptyset$.

We can now prove that if two world-indices w-unify, they do indeed denote the same world for all Kripke structures.

THEOREM 1 If two world-indices, i and j w-unify then for every Kripke structure $K = \langle W, R, aw \rangle$ where R meets the same restrictions as those applied in the w-unification algorithm, i and j denote the same world for K.

Proof The proof is by case analysis on the definition of w-unification.

1. If $end(i)$ and $end(j)$ are ground, then i and j w-unify if $end(i) = end(j)$. But if $end(i) = end(j)$, then for all Kripke structures K, $\delta_K(i) = \delta_K(j)$. Since $\delta_K(i) \neq \emptyset$, $\delta_K(i) \cap \delta_K(j) \neq \emptyset$, and hence i and j denote the same world in K.

2. If $end(i)$ is ground and $end(j)$ is not, and either the accessibility relation is serial, or $end(i)$ is a world-constant, then i and j w-unify if $end(i)$ is accessible from parent-symbol of $end(j)$. First recall that $\delta_K(j)$ for some Kripke structure K is $\bigcup_{w' \in \delta_K(parent\text{-}index(j))} \{w \mid \langle w', w \rangle \in R\}$.

   We distinguish two cases, corresponding to the two conditions in the relevant clause in the definition of w-unification. If $end(i)$ is a world-constant, then $\delta_K(i) = \{w\}$ for some $w \in W$. We know by hypothesis that w is accessible from $parent(j)\theta$ for some unification θ. Since $\delta_K(j\theta) \subseteq \delta_K(j)$ for all world-indices i and unifications θ, there is for all Kripke structures K some world $w' \in parent\text{-}index(j)$, $\langle w', w \rangle \in R$. Hence, $w \in \delta_K(j)$, and hence i and j denote the same world for any Kripke model K.

   Second, assume that the accessibility relation is serial. Then, if $end(i)$ is a world constant, then the proof is as before. Otherwise, if $end(i)$ is a skolemised world term, then, because $end(i)$ is accessible from $parent(end(j))\theta$ for some substitution θ for all Kripke structures K, $\delta_K(i) \subseteq \delta_K(j\theta) \subseteq \delta_K(j)$. Because the accessibility relation is serial, we know that $\delta_K(i) \neq \emptyset$. Therefore, $\delta_K(i) \cap \delta_K(j) \neq \emptyset$, and i and j denote the same world.

3. If $end(i)$ and $end(j)$ are both free world variables, then we have two possibilities. First, i and j w-unify if the accessibility relation is serial and there is a unification θ such that either $end(i)$ is accessible from $parent(end(j\theta))$, or vice versa. The proof in this case is identical to the second part of the proof for the previous case.

Second, i and j w-unify if the accessibility relation is serial, and *parent-index*(i) w-unifies with *parent-index*(j). The proof for the second case is by induction. If *parent-index*(i) and *parent-index*(j) denote the same world, then i and j denote the same world as well. This is easily checked. This argument may appear circular as both *parent*(i) and *parent*(j) may themselves be free world variables. However, at some stage at least one of the end-symbols of the parent-indices will be ground. After all, the starting symbols of both world-indices are identical and equal to 0.

8.2.9 Soundness of proof theory

In this section we establish that our proof system is sound. In order to do so, we make the intuitive interpretation of sequents more precise, and show that under this interpretation, if a formula is provable, then it is valid as well. We first give a definition for the notion of an indexed formula being true in a Kripke model.

In the definition of the notion of an indexed formula being true in a Kripke model, we make use of the notion of a value assignment. As usual, a value assignment g is a function from the set of individual variables into the set of individuals associated with a Kripke model. (The valuation function V in a Kripke model only assigns interpretations to the non-logical constants in the language.) The symbol $\models$ will be used with a variety of meanings. However, in every case, context will disambiguate.

Definition 6 Let $K = \langle \langle W, R, aw \rangle, I, V \rangle$ be a Kripke model, let $|p|_i$ be an indexed formula, then $|p|_i$ is true in K (symbolically, $K \models |p|_i$) iff for all value assignments g and all $w \in \delta_K(i)$, $w \models_g p$.

We now generalize this notion to the notion of a sequent being true in a Kripke model.

Definition 7 Let $S \leftarrow T$ be a sequent with $S = \{|p|_i, \ldots, |p'|_{i'}\}$, and $T = \{|q|_j, \ldots, |q'|_{j'}\}$ let $K = \langle \langle W, R, aw \rangle, I, V \rangle$ be a Kripke model, then $S \leftarrow T$ is true in K (symbolically, $K \models S \leftarrow T$) iff for all value assignments g and all $w \in \delta_K(i), \ldots, w' \in \delta_K(i')$, $v \in \delta_K(j), \ldots, v' \in \delta_K(j')$ if $v \models_g q$, and $\ldots$ and $v' \models_g q'$, then $w \models_g p$, or $\ldots$ or $w' \models_g p'$.

We will show that, given this definition, the proof theory is indeed sound. The proof will be by induction on the various inference rules that we presented earlier. The only rule that poses any real difficulty is the resolution rule; the proofs for the other inference rules are all straightforward.

Before we prove the correctness of the resolution rule, we observe that if two world-indices i and j w-unify with substitution σ, then $\delta_K(i\sigma) = \delta_K(j\sigma)$ for all Kripke models K. The proof is by induction over the definitions of w-unification and $\delta_K(i)$. Also, if σ is a substitution, then for every index i and for every Kripke model K, $\delta_K(i\sigma) \subseteq \delta_K(i)$. The proof is by induction over the definition of $\delta_K(i)$.

We first prove a simple lemma:

LEMMA 1 Let p be an indexed formula, and σ a substitution, then for all Kripke models K, $K \models p \to p\sigma$.

Proof Suppose p is of the form $|r|_i$. First, observe that for every (non-indexed) formula r, r entails $r\sigma$: if r is true for all value assignments, then it is certainly true for the value assignments which assign to the free variables in r the values of the bindings of these variables in σ. Also, $\delta_K(i\sigma) \subseteq \delta_K(i)$. Thus, if r is true in all worlds in $\delta_K(i)$, then r is also true in all worlds in $\delta_K(i\sigma)$. Hence, if $K \models |r|_i$, then $K \models |r\sigma|_{i\sigma}$.

We now prove that if a sequent is true in a Kripke model K, then the sequent obtained from applying a unification to each indexed formula in the sequent is also true in K.

LEMMA 2 For all Kripke models K, if $K \models S \leftarrow T$, then $K \models S\sigma \leftarrow T\sigma$.

Proof Suppose that $K \models S \leftarrow T$, and suppose that not $K \models S\sigma \leftarrow T\sigma$. If the latter is true, then there is a Kripke model K and a value assignment, and a set of worlds such that for each different world-index i in the indexed formulas in $S \cup T$ there is a world $w \in \delta_K(i)$, such that every formula in $S\sigma$ is false in the world corresponding to its world-index while all the formulas in $T\sigma$ are true in the worlds corresponding to their world-indices. Let $q\sigma_{j\sigma}$ be a formula in $T\sigma$. Suppose that $q\sigma$ is true under some assignment g in some world $w \in \delta_K(j\sigma)$. Then there is an assignment g' such that q is true as well in w, namely the assignment which is just like g except that it assigns to the free variables in q that have been replaced by constants in $q\sigma$, the values that are assigned to these constants in w by the interpretation function V. Moreover since $\delta_K(j\sigma) \subseteq \delta_K(j)$, $w \in \delta_K(j)$. Clearly, a similar argument can be applied to all the formulas in $T\sigma$. However, because $K \models S \leftarrow T$ in all these worlds at least one indexed formula p in S is true as well. The previous lemma then implies that $p\sigma$ must be true in that world as well. We thus obtain a contradiction, and derive the result.

We now prove that if two indexed formulas p and q m-unify with unification σ, then the formulas obtained from applying σ to p and q are equivalent in all Kripke models.

LEMMA 3 If two indexed formulas p and q m-unify with unification σ then for all Kripke models K, $K \models p\sigma \leftrightarrow q\sigma$.

Proof First, suppose that the indexed formulas $|p|_i$ and $|q|_j$ m-unify, but that there is some Kripke model K such that not $K \models |p\sigma|_{i\sigma} \leftrightarrow |q\sigma|_{j\sigma}$. Since $|p|_i$ and $|q|_j$ m-unify with substitution σ, i and j w-unify with unification σ as well, so that $i\sigma = j\sigma$. Thus, in K, there is a value assignment g and a world $w \in \delta_K(j\sigma)$, such that $q\sigma$ is false while $p\sigma$ is true in w (or vice versa). But p and q unify with unification σ as well so that always $p\sigma \leftrightarrow q\sigma$. We therefore obtain a contradiction, and derive the result.

We can now finally prove the correctness of the resolution rule:

LEMMA 4 For all Kripke models K, if $K \models S, |p|_i \leftarrow T$ and $K \models S' \leftarrow |p'|_j, T'$ and $|p|_i$ and $|p'|_j$ m-unify with unification σ, then $K \models S\sigma \cup S'\sigma \leftarrow T\sigma \cup T'\sigma$.

Proof The proof is a matter of some simple propositional reasoning. For all Kripke models K, $K \models S, p_i \leftarrow T$ implies $K \models S\sigma, p\sigma_{i\sigma} \leftarrow T\sigma$, while $K \models S' \leftarrow p'_j, T'$ implies $K \models S'\sigma \leftarrow p'\sigma_{j\sigma}, T'\sigma$. Also, for all Kripke models, if p'_j and p_i m-unify with substitution σ then $K \models p\sigma_{i\sigma} \leftrightarrow p'\sigma_{j\sigma}$. Hence, if the instantiated sequents are true in a Kripke model K, then $S\sigma \cup S'\sigma \leftarrow T\sigma \cup T'\sigma$ is true in K as well.

The correctness of inference rules R2 to R6 can be proved more or less directly from the truth tables of the connectives and this is left as an exercise for the reader. The correctness of the remaining rules can also be proved in a straightforward manner. We observe that the correctness of R7 can be proved because Lp is false in some w if there is an accessible possible world w' in which p is false. Similarly, if Lp is true in a world w, then p is true in all accessible worlds w'. The reader can check that the way in which we defined $\delta_K(i)$ ensures that the above conditions are fulfilled. Finally, the correctness of R9 and R10 can be proved on the basis of some simple quantificational reasoning.

The soundness of the proof theory can now be established in a completely straightforward manner. The first sequent in a successful proof of a formula p is $\leftarrow p_0$. $K \models \leftarrow p_0$ for a Kripke model $K = \langle\langle W, R, aw \rangle, I, V\rangle$ just in case $V(p, aw) = false$. Since the inference rules are truth preserving, we know that if the input sequent to some inference rule holds in some Kripke model K, then the output sequent holds as well. The final sequent in a successful proof is the empty sequent (which is always false). Therefore, for every Kripke model, the assumption that p is false in the actual world leads to a contradiction, and hence p is true in the actual world. Hence, for all Kripke models p is true, and hence p is valid:

THEOREM 2 If $\vdash p$, then $\models p$.

8.2.10   Concerning completeness

It turns out that the proof theory as currently formulated is *not* complete. The problems attach to the non-serial case, ie. logics where $Lp \rightarrow Mp$ is not a theorem. Thus the systems affected are K, KB, K4, K5, K45 and KB4.

The main problem is that, when performing w-unification, we must entertain the possibility that, if R is not serial, a world variable may have an empty denotation. Hence, when unifying two world indices whose end symbols each contain variables, it is possible that each end symbol denotes an empty set of worlds, so that the intersection of their denotations is empty. If this is indeed the case, then we cannot claim to have found a world in which some atom has opposite truth values.

There are some rather subtle cases that have to be considered here, but the following example is critical, and will help to give the reader some feel for the problem. Consider the formula $(Lp \& Mp) \rightarrow MLp$. This is a theorem of K4, so we should be able to prove it without seriality. If we apply our inference rules, then we end up with the following sequents:

$$
\begin{aligned}
&\qquad\qquad\ \leftarrow \quad |p|_{f(w):w:0}\\
&|p|_{v:0} \quad \leftarrow\\
&|p|_{1:0} \quad \leftarrow
\end{aligned}
$$

$f(w){:}w{:}0$ and $v{:}0$ do not w-unify, because R is not serial. Yet we know that there is a world 1 accessible from 0, and that there is a world $f(1)$ accessible from 1, so we ought to be able to w-unify $f(1){:}1{:}0$ and $1{:}0$ as a prelude to generating the empty sequent. This is clearly an area for further work.

8.3 Proof theory without the Barcan formula or its converse

In this section, we relinquish the Baracan formula (BF), $(\forall x)Lp \rightarrow L(\forall x)p$, and its converse (FB), $L(\forall x)p \rightarrow (\forall x)Lp$. The reader will recall that our motivation for doing this is that, if BF and FB are theorems of a modal logic, then the set of individuals must remain constant as we pass from one possible world to another. This can sometimes be constraining, e.g. if we want to hypothesize the existence of individuals that may not exist in the real world.

Given the close correspondence between our proof method and the underlying model theory, we will first consider the consequences of this on the semantics of modal predicate logic. We need to complicate our notation, and we introduce the notion of a term-index. We then present the revised proof theory and sketch a soundness proof.

8.3.1 Kripke models again

As said in the previous section, a Kripke model for a modal logic in which BF and FB hold is a structure $\langle\langle W, R, aw\rangle, I, V\rangle$, where W is a set of worlds, R is an accessibility relation, aw is a world in W, I is a universe of individuals, and V is a valuation function which, for every expression e in the language and every world $w \in W$, assigns a denotation to e in w. If BF and FB hold, then I is common to all worlds.

If BF and FB do not hold, then the assumption of a common set of individuals has to be given up. As a consequence, we need to add to the standard Kripke model a function ϕ from W into 2^I such that $\phi(w) \neq \emptyset$ for any $w \in W$. Thus, a Kripke model becomes a structure of the form $\langle\langle W, R, aw\rangle, \phi, I, V\rangle$. I is now intuitively interpreted as the set of possible individuals. ϕ then assigns to each $w \in W$ a subset of I, which can be regarded as the set of individuals that actually exist at w. For any constant c, $V(w, c) \in \phi(w)$, while for each k-place predicate p and $V(w, p) \subseteq |\phi(w)|^k$. A universally quantified sentence $(\forall x)p$ is true at world w, if and only if, for each V', such that for all expressions e except possibly some constant a not appearing in p, $V'(w, e) = V(w, e)$, $V'(w, p(a/x)) = true$. The definition of $V(w, Lp)$ is as before.

This treatment follows [Krip63] in all essentials. Informally, it interprets "everything has p in w" as as "everything in (the universe of) w has p". Note that unlike [Krip72] and [Hugh68, p. 172]) we do not treat constants as rigid designators which always have the same denotation in all possible worlds.

8.3.2   Term-indices

In order to represent the more complicated semantics, we need to complicate our notation. When we moved from non-modal predicate calculus to modal predicate calculus, we attached world-indices to formulas to indicate in which world the formula had a particular truth-value. We now use a similar ploy, and introduce the notion of a *term-index*. A term-index is attached to a term to indicate in which world the terms were introduced.

Syntactically, term-indices are identical to world-indices. Thus, in our more complicated notation, formulas have world-indices attached to them, while terms in them have term-indices associated with them. The intuitive reading of an indexed formula like $|p(a^{1:0})|_{1:0}$ is that the individual denoted by a in world 1 has the property p in world 1 accessible from 0. Similarly, the intuitive reading of $|p(a^0)|_{1:0}$ is that the individual i denoted by a in world 0 has the property p in world 1 accessible from 0. If $i \notin \phi(1)$, and hence does not exist at 1, then $|p(a^0)|_{1:0}$ is obviously false.

8.3.3   Modal term unification

In the proof theory for modal logics in which both BF and FB held, we defined the notion of m-unification. For logics in which neither BF nor FB holds we need a more complicated definition of unification, which we call *modal term-unification*, or *mt-unification*. In order to define this notion, we first define the notion of *term unification* (or *t-unification*).

Definition 8 Two indexed terms, a^i and b^j, *t-unify* with substitution σ iff

1. the terms a and b unify with unification θ,

2. the indices i and j w-unify, with unification η,

3. σ is the unifying composition of θ and η.

By insisting that the term-indices associated with the indexed terms w-unify, we ensure that the term-indices denote the same world. Therefore, the two terms can be assumed to denote individuals both existing in the same world.

The revised proof theory uses the notion of t-unification in the definition of mt-unification.

Definition 9 Two indexed formulas $|p|_i$ and $|q|_j$ *mt-unify* with substitution σ iff

1. $|p|_i$ and $|q|_j$ m-unify with substitution θ ,

2. corresponding indexed terms in p and q t-unify with substitution η ,

3. σ is the unifying composition of θ and η.

The following are some examples of mt-unification. The formulas $|p(x^{w:0})|_{w:0}$ and $|p(x^{1:0})|_{1:0}$ mt-unify with substitution $\{1/w\}$, but $|p(a^{w:0})|_{w:0}$ and $|p(x^0)|_{1:0}$ do not. To see why the latter fails, assume that the accessibility relation is reflexive. Then $a^{w:0}$ and x^0 t-unify with the substitution $\{a/x, 0/w\}$. (If the accessibility relation were not reflexive, then the indexed terms would not t-unify.) Also, the world-indices $w:0$ and $1:0$ w-unify with substitution $\{1/w\}$. However, the unifying composition of the two is the failing substitution. From a semantic point of view, the denotation of a in world 1 may not exist in world 0, and would not be in the range of x.

8.3.4 Revised proof theory

The inference rules for modal logics without the Barcan formula are slightly different from those for modal logics with the Barcan formula. First we need to change the resolution rule to take into account the new definition of unification:

R1′. If $S_1, |p|_i \leftarrow T_1$ and $S_2 \leftarrow |p'|_j, T_2$, and $|p|_i$ and $|p'|_j$ mt-unify with unification σ, then $S_1\sigma \cup S_2\sigma \leftarrow T_1\sigma \cup T_2\sigma$.

We also need to modify the rules dealing with quantifiers (R9 and R10), so that term-indices are appropriately introduced:

R9′. If $S \leftarrow |(\forall x)p|_i, T$ then $S \leftarrow |p(a^i/x)|_i, T$, where

1. a is a new individual constant if p contains no free individual variables and i is a ground world-index;

2. a is $f(w_1, \ldots, w_k, x_k, \ldots, x_m)$ where f is a skolem function of world variables $w_1, \ldots, w_k$ in i and free individual variables $x_k, \ldots, x_m$ in $|p|_i$.

R10′. If $S, |(\forall x)p|_i \leftarrow T$ then $S, |p(y^i/x)|_i \leftarrow T$, where y is a new individual variable.

Also, the definition of a proof slightly changes. The first sequence in a proof of a formula p is $\leftarrow |p'|_0$, where p' is obtained from p by associating the term-index 0 with every constant in p. The rest of the definition remains the same.

8.3.5 Examples

We will now illustrate these inference rules by showing that neither BF nor FB can be proven.

Example 10 We first show that BF cannot be proven.

1		$\leftarrow$	$|(\forall x)Lp(x) \to L(\forall x)p(x)|_0$
2	$|(\forall x)Lp(x)|_0$	$\leftarrow$	$R4, 1.$
3	$|Lp(y^0)|_0$	$\leftarrow$	$R10', 2.$
4	$|p(y^0)|_{w:0}$	$\leftarrow$	$R8, 3.$
5		$\leftarrow$	$|L(\forall x)p(x)|_0$	$R3, 1.$
6		$\leftarrow$	$|(\forall x)p(x)|_{1:0}$	$R7, 5.$
7		$\leftarrow$	$|p(a^{1:0})|_{1:0}$	$R9', 6.$

We cannot derive the empty sequent from 4 and 7, because the term-indices of a and x do not w-unify. Semantically, the individuals denoted by y in world 0 may not exist in world 1.

Example 11 We now show the failure of FB.

1		$\leftarrow$	$|L(\forall x)p(x) \rightarrow (\forall x)Lp(x)|_0$	
2	$|L(\forall x)p(x)|_0$	$\leftarrow$		$R4, 1.$
3	$|(\forall x)p(x)|_{w:0}$	$\leftarrow$		$R8, 2.$
4	$|p(y^{w:0})|_{w:0}$	$\leftarrow$		$R10', 3.$
5		$\leftarrow$	$|(\forall x)Lp(x)|_0$	$R3, 1.$
6		$\leftarrow$	$|Lp(a^0)|_0$	$R9', 5.$
7		$\leftarrow$	$|p(a^0)|_{1:0}$	$R7, 6.$

Again, we cannot apply the resolution rule to 4 and 7. Even if we allowed the accessibility relation to be reflexive, so that w:0 and 0 w-unified with $\{w/0\}$, we still could not mt-unify $|p(y^{w:0})|_{w:0}$ and $|p(a^0)|_{1:0}$ because in order to w-unify the indices w would have to be bound to 1, and the two unifications are now incompatible. The semantic motivation is similar to the previous case. The individual denoted by y in world 1 (world 1 because the world-indices associated with the two formula in question w-unify with $\{w/1\}$) need not exist in world 0.

Example 12 As a final example we show the importance of the accessibility relation on the notion of mt-unification. Suppose that the accessibility relation is reflexive, so that $Lp \rightarrow p$ is an axiom. Then $L(\forall x)p(x) \rightarrow p(a)$ is derivable:

1.		$\leftarrow$	$|L(\forall x)p(x) \rightarrow p(a^0)|_0$	
2.	$|L(\forall x)p(x)|_0$	$\leftarrow$		$R4, 1.$
3.	$|(\forall x)p(x)|_{w:0}$	$\leftarrow$		$R8, 2.$
4.	$|p(x^{w:0})|_{w:0}$	$\leftarrow$		$R9', 3.$
5.		$\leftarrow$	$|p(a^0)|_0$	$R3, 1.$
6.		$\leftarrow$		$R1', 4, 5\{1/w, a/x\}.$

The reader can check that the requirement that the accessibility relation be reflexive is crucial. Without it neither the world-indices, nor the term-indices, would have w-unified.

8.3.6 Soundness

Soundness is proved as before. Again, the only inference rule whose correctness is difficult to prove is the revised resolution rule $R1'$. In this section, we establish that if two formulas mt-unify, then they are equivalent. In order to do so, we first define an interpretation for indexed terms, and for formulas which contain indexed terms.

Definition 10 If a^i is an indexed term, then the denotation of a^i in some Kripke model $K\langle\langle W, R, aw\rangle, \phi, I, V\rangle den_K(a^i)$, is defined as follows.

1. If a is ground, then $den_K(a^i) = \bigcup_{w \in \delta_K(i)}\{V(w, a)\}$

2. if a is not ground, then $den_K(a^i) = \bigcup_{w \in \delta_K(i)} \phi(w)$

We can now define the notion of two indexed terms denoting the same individual:

Definition 11 The indexed terms a^i and b^j *denote the same individual* in a Kripke model K iff $den_K(a^i) \cap den_K(b^j) \neq \emptyset$

We can now prove that, if two indexed terms t-unify, then they have the same denotation for all Kripke models.

LEMMA 5   Let a^i and b^j be indexed terms. If a^i and b^j t-unify, then for all Kripke models, a^i and b^j denote the same individual.

Proof If i and j w-unify, then for every Kripke model there are some worlds which are denoted both by i and j. Let w be such a world in a Kripke model K. a and b unify. Then there are three possibilities. First, a and b are both ground and identical. Then a and b both denote $V(w, a)$ in w. Second, a is ground and b is an individual variable. Then because $V(w, a) \in \phi(w)$ and b denotes $\phi(w)$ in w, $V(w, a) \in den_K(a^i) \cap den_K(b^j)$. Third, both a and b are free variables. Then $V(w, a) = V(w, b) = \phi(w)$. In each case, a^i and b^j denote the same individual.

We now establish the correctness of the mt-unification algorithm.

LEMMA 6   If two formulas p_i and q_j mt-unify, with unification σ, then for all Kripke models, $K \models p_i\sigma \leftrightarrow q_j\sigma$.

Proof Ignoring indices on the terms, if p and q unify with unification σ, then $p\sigma$ and $q\sigma$ are equivalent. $|p\sigma|_{i\sigma}$ and $|q\sigma|_{j\sigma}$ can therefore only fail to be equivalent if one of the following three conditions holds: first, if corresponding indexed terms do not denote the same individual; second, if the indices i and j do not denote the same world, third, if a world in which a pair of indexed terms denote the same individual is not a world denoted by i and j.

By the previous lemma, we know that corresponding indexed terms denote the same individual in some world w. Also i and j w-unify, and hence by theorem 1 denote the same world. Because the t-unification and the w-unification are compatible, we know moreover that w is denoted by both i and j. Hence, none of the conditions hold, and $|p\sigma|_{i\sigma}$ and $|q\sigma|_{j\sigma}$ are equivalent.

Once we have established the correctness of mt-unification, the soundness proof now follows the soundness proof for the case in which BF and FB were valid.

8.4 Proof theories with either the Barcan formula or its converse

In the two previous sections we discussed proof theories for logics in which either both BF and FB or neither held. In this section, we will discuss two simple changes to the proof theory presented in the previous section which will make either BF or its converse valid.

8.4.1 Proof theory with FB but without BF

Because of the close connection between our proof method and the semantics for modal logic, we first turn to the Kripke models for modal logics in which FB is valid and BF is not. We first prove a simple lemma.

LEMMA 7 For every Kripke model $\langle\langle W, R, aw\rangle, \phi, I, V\rangle$, for all $w, w' \in W$, if wRw', then $\phi(w) \subseteq \phi(w')$ iff FB is valid.

Proof
$\rightarrow$ Suppose that $\phi(w) \subseteq \phi(w')$ for all w' such that wRw'. Suppose moreover that $V(w, FB) = false$. Then, clearly $V(w, L(\forall x)p) = true$ but $V(w, (\forall x)Lp) = false$. $V(w, (\forall x)Lp) = false$ implies that there is some w' accessible from w and some constant a with $V(w, a) \in \phi(w)$ such that if this individual exists in $\phi(w')$ then it does not have the property p. We know that wRw', and hence by hypothesis $V(w, a) \in \phi(w')$, and hence there is an individual in $\phi(w')$ which does not have the property p. But this contradicts the truth of the antecedent of FB. Hence we obtain a contradiction, and we conclude that FB is true.

← We construct a Kripke model in which the left hand side of the lemma does not hold, and then show that FB is false in this model, and hence cannot be valid. $W = \{w_0, w_1\}$ with $0R1$. $I = \{a, b\}$. $\phi(w_0) = \{a, b\}$, $\phi(w_1) = \{a\}$. w_0 is the actual world. So, although w_0Rw_1, $\phi(w_0) \not\subseteq \phi(w_1)$. Then, FB is not valid in this Kripke model. We will show that FB is false in the actual world w_0. Let $p(x)$ be the property of being equal to a. Then, in the above model, $L(\forall x)p(x)$ in w_0 while not $(\forall x)Lp(x)$ in w_0. Hence, if there is a Kripke model which violates the conditions in the left hand side, then FB is not valid.

Thus, if FB holds, then whenever we move from a world w into an accessible possible world w', all the individuals existing in w will exist at w' as well. In other words, the universes of individuals increase monotonically with the accessibility relation. If we replace R7 in the proof theories presented in the previous sections by R7', then we ensure that this is indeed the case. After all, the newly introduced constant a guarantees the existence of some individual in the world denoted by w. When we then move from world w to world w', we are guaranteed that this individual exists in w' as well. (In section 8.4.3, we shall see that a slight complication is necessary, but it will make the presentation considerably easier if we ignore this complication for the present.)

R7'. If $S \leftarrow L|p|_i, T$ then $S \leftarrow |p(n{:}i/i)|_{n{:}i}, T$,

1. n is a new world-constant if i is a ground world-index and p does not contain any free variables;

2. n is $f(w_1, \ldots, w_k, x_k, \ldots, x_m)$, where f is a skolem function of world variables $w_1, \ldots, w_k$ in i and free individual variables $x_k, \ldots, x_m$ in $|p|_i$;

3. $p(n{:}i/i)$ is the result of replacing every occurrence of i in p by $n{:}i$.

We will illustrate the revised proof method by showing that FB is now derivable while BF is not. We start with the derivation of FB.

1		$\leftarrow$	$|L(\forall x)p(x) \rightarrow (\forall x)Lp(x)|_0$	
2	$|L(\forall x)p(x)|_0$	$\leftarrow$		$R4, 1.$
3	$|(\forall x)p(x)|_{w:0}$	$\leftarrow$		$R8', 2.$
4	$|p(y^{w:0})|_{w:0}$	$\leftarrow$		$R10', 3.$
5		$\leftarrow$	$|(\forall x)Lp(x)|_0$	$R3, 1.$
6		$\leftarrow$	$|Lp(a^0)|_0$	$R9', 5.$
7		$\leftarrow$	$|p(a^{1:0})|_{1:0}$	$R7', 6.$
8		$\leftarrow$		$R1', 4, 7\{1/w\}$

We now show that BF is still not derivable:

1		$\leftarrow$	$|(\forall x)Lp(x) \rightarrow L(\forall x)p(x)|_0$	
2	$|(\forall x)Lp(x)|_0$	$\leftarrow$		$R4, 1.$
3	$|Lp(y^0)|_0$	$\leftarrow$		$R10', 2.$
4	$|p(y^0)|_{w:0}$	$\leftarrow$		$R8, 3.$
5		$\leftarrow$	$|L(\forall x)p(x)|_0$	$R3, 1.$
6		$\leftarrow$	$|(\forall x)p(x)|_{1:0}$	$R7', 5.$
7		$\leftarrow$	$|p(a^{1:0})|_{1:0}$	$R9', 6.$

We cannot derive the empty sequent from 4 and 7, because the term-indices of a and y do not w-unify.

8.4.2 Proof theory with BF but without FB

In the previous section, we established that FB was valid if the set of individuals increased monotonically with the accessibility relation. BF is valid if the set of individuals decreases monotonically.

LEMMA 8 For every Kripke model $\langle\langle W, R, aw\rangle, I, V\rangle$ for all w, $w' \in W$, if wRw', then $\phi(w') \subseteq \phi(w)$ iff BF is valid.

Proof

$\rightarrow$ Suppose that $\phi(w') \subseteq \phi(w)$ for all w' such that wRw'. Suppose moreover that $V(w, BF) = false$. Then, clearly $V(w, (\forall x)Lp) = true$ but $V(w, L(\forall x)p) = false$. $V(w, L(\forall x)p) = false$ implies that there is some w' accessible from w and some constant a with $V(w, a) \in \phi(w')$ such that if this individual exists in $\phi(w)$ then it does not have the property p. We know that $w'Rw$, and hence by hypothesis $V(w', a) \in \phi(w)$, and hence there is an individual in $\phi(w)$ for which there is an accessible world in which it does not have the property p. But this contradicts the truth of the antecedent of BF. Hence we obtain a contradiction, and we conclude that BF is true.

← We construct a Kripke model in which the left hand side of the lemma does not hold, and then we show that BF is false in this model, and hence not valid. $W = \{w_0, w_1\}$ with $0R1$. $I = \{a, b\}$. $\phi(w_0) = \{a\}$, $\phi(w_1) = \{a, b\}$. w_0 is the actual world. So, although $w_0 R w_1$, $\phi(w_1) \not\subseteq \phi(w_0)$. Then, BF is not valid in this Kripke model. We will show that BF is false in w_0. Let $p(x)$ be the property of being equal to a. Then, in the above model, $(\forall x)Lp(x)$ in w_0 while not $L(\forall x)p(x)$ in w_0. Hence, if there is a Kripke model which violates the conditions in the left hand side, then BF is not valid.

We can construct a proof theory for logics in which BF holds but not FB, by replacing R8 in the proof theories presented in the previous sections by R8′. If there is a free variable which ranges over all the individuals existing in w, then because the individuals existing in an accessible possible world w' are a subset of those existing in w, we can replace this free variable by one ranges over the individuals in w'. (Again, we will show in the next section that a slight complication is necessary. For ease of presentation, we ignore this here.)

R8′. If $S, |Lp|_i \leftarrow T$ then $S, |p(w{:}i/i)|_{w:i} \leftarrow T$, where

1. w is a new world variable,

2. $p(w{:}i/i)$ is the result of replacing every occurrence of i in p by $w{:}i$.

Again we illustrate the rule by showing that BF can be derived but that FB cannot. We first derive BF:

1		←	$\|(\forall x)Lp(x) \rightarrow L(\forall x)p(x)\|_0$	
2	$\|(\forall x)Lp(x)\|_0$	←		$R4, 1.$
3	$\|Lp(y^0)\|_0$	←		$R10', 2.$
4	$\|p(y^{w:0})\|_{w:0}$	←		$R8', 3.$
5		←	$\|L(\forall x)p(x)\|_0$	$R3, 1.$
6		←	$\|(\forall x)p(x)\|_{1:0}$	$R7, 5.$
7		←	$\|p(a^{1:0})\|_{1:0}$	$R9', 6.$
8		←		$R1', 4, 7\{1/w\}$

FB cannot be derived in the thus revised proof theory:

1		$\leftarrow$	$|L(\forall x)p(x) \rightarrow (\forall x)Lp(x)|_0$	
2	$|L(\forall x)p(x)|_0$	$\leftarrow$		$R4, 1.$
3	$|(\forall x)p(x)|_{w:0}$	$\leftarrow$		$R8', 2.$
4	$|p(y^{w:0})|_{w:0}$	$\leftarrow$		$R10', 3.$
5		$\leftarrow$	$|(\forall x)Lp(x)|_0$	$R3, 1.$
6		$\leftarrow$	$|Lp(a^0)|_0$	$R9', 5.$
7		$\leftarrow$	$|p(a^0)|_{1:0}$	$R7, 6.$

8.4.3   Correction: BF, FB and symmetry

The inference rules that we have presented for logics in which one of FB and FB but not the other holds are not quite correct. We first observe that if the accessibility relation is symmetric, then if BF is valid, then so is FB. It is not hard to see why this is the case. Suppose that the accessibility relation is symmetric, and that BF holds. Suppose that wRw'. Then $\phi(w) \subseteq \phi(w')$. Because of symmetry, wRw' implies $w'Rw$. Hence, also $\phi(w') \subseteq \phi(w)$. But, if this is the case, then FB is valid. So, if the accessibility relation is symmetric, then if BF is valid, then so is FB. Clearly, by a similar argument, if the accessibility relation is symmetric, then if FB is valid, then so is BF.

It is a relatively straightforward matter to correct the proof theory presented in the previous two sections. We will outline the modification for the proof theory presented in section 8.4.1. We showed that by a simple change to inference rule R7, we could obtain a proof theory for a logic in which FB but not BF was valid. In order to account for the above observation, we need to make slight modifications to both R7' and R8. Rather than never updating term-indices (in R8) or updating term-indices only when they do not occur on free individual variables, we now update the other term-indices as well, provided that the world denoted by the world-index which was introduced by an application of the inference rule is accessible from the world denoted by the old term-index. Thus, under this new proposal, the revised inference rule R8'' would be:

R8''. If $S, |Lp|_i \leftarrow T$ then $S, |p(w:i/i)|_{w:i} \leftarrow T$, where

1. w is a new world variable,

2. $p(w:i/i)$ is the result of replacing every occurrence of i in p by $w:i$ if $end(i)$ is accessible from w, and is p otherwise.

The reader can now check that BF is indeed valid in this revised proof theory:

$$
\begin{array}{llll}
1 & & \leftarrow \quad |(\forall x)Lp(x) \to L(\forall x)p(x)|_0 & \\
2 & |(\forall x)Lp(x)|_0 & \leftarrow & R4,1. \\
3 & |Lp(y^0)|_0 & \leftarrow & R10',2. \\
4 & |p(y^{w:0})|_{w:0} & \leftarrow & R8'',3. \\
5 & & \leftarrow \quad |L(\forall x)p(x)|_0 & R3,1. \\
6 & & \leftarrow \quad |(\forall x)p(x)|_{1:0} & R7',5. \\
7 & & \leftarrow \quad |p(a^{1:0})|_{1:0} & R9',6. \\
8 & & \leftarrow & R1',4,7\{1/w\} \\
\end{array}
$$

Although the above is the correct way of generalizing the proof theory, it is easy to check that the condition in R8'' which allows one to uniformly replace i by $w{:}i$ only holds if the accessibility relation is symmetric. Thus, if the accessibility relation is symmetric, then in any proof theory in which R7' and R8'' are used, one can always uniformly substitute term-indices as one moves from one world to another. As a consequence, one might as well do away with term-indices altogether, and simply use the proof method presented in section 8.2 of this chapter. Clearly, a similar argument applies if the accessibility relation is symmetric, and the proof theory uses R8' and a suitably modified R7''.

8.5   Implementation

The proof method that we discussed in section 8.2 has been implemented in about 1000 lines of code in Kyoto Common Lisp, and runs on a Sun-3. In this section, we will describe the present implementation and point to some of its shortcomings. The system can be used both as a straightforward theorem prover and for determining whether a query follows from a knowledge base containing modal propositions. We will first describe its use as a theorem prover. The appendix contains an annotated run of the theorem prover.

8.5.1   Representing sequents and formulas

The implementation follows the proof theory as presented above more or less directly, and we have not yet made any serious attempts at making the theorem prover as efficient as possible.

The system makes use of sequents consisting of indexed propositions. Indexed propositions are stored as structures with a syntax field and an index field. The syntax field represents the syntactic form of the proposition while the index field contains the associated world-index. The system uses, as most theorem provers implemented in Lisp, Cambridge-Polish notation. Although the actual theorem prover only contains inference rules for the connectives $\rightarrow$, $\neg$, $\forall$ and L, we have interfaced the system to a simple parser which will rewrite the other connectives in terms of the primitive connectives. One can use the full syntactic variety of modal predicate logic.

Sequents are stored as structures with four fields: a name field, a left hand side field, a right hand side field, and a justification field. The name field contains an arbitrarily generated name, while the justification field contains a list of names of other sequents plus the inference rules that were used (if the sequent was derived from other sequents) or the single atom *premise* (which is used if the sequent is the top sequent in a proof). For the purposes of the justification slot, the rewrite rules that the parser uses are treated as inference rules as well.

Whenever the system is trying to prove a formula it will store the old sequents, i.e. sequents to which inference rules have been applied, in a separate data-structure. This data-structure is used when the system has been successful in its attempts to prove a formula. Depending on the value of a user-definable flag, the system will print out a proof-trace "upside down" so to speak, starting with the empty sequent and tracing its derivation from the formula to be proved. The justification field in a sequent stores the names of the sequents that were used in its derivation, and this information is obviously necessary when the system is printing out a proof-trace.

Apart from the name and a justification field, a representation of a sequent also contains left hand and right hand side fields. The information stored in a side field is itself a structure consisting of a set of unreduced formulas and a set of reduced formulas. Reduced formulas are indexed atomic formulas, whereas unreduced formulas are indexed non-atomic formulas. This distinction between reduced and unreduced formulas is necessary because of the control regime. Because trying to unify two formulas can be a relatively expensive operation (see below), the system tries to minimise the number of unification attempts. In particular, it will never try to unify non-atomic propositions. Thus, the system will keep applying inference rules R2 to R10 as long as the sequents that it is currently working on contain unreduced formulas. Slightly expanding the terminology, we will call a sequent reduced if neither of its sides contains any unreduced formulas. If there are unreduced formulas in either the left hand or the right hand side, then we call the sequent unreduced as well. The overall control regime then amounts to reducing all unreduced sequents by means of inference rules R2-R10, and using the resolution rule R1 only when there are no more unreduced sequents left.

8.5.2   Searching for a proof

Initially then, the system is faced with only one unreduced sequent. The left hand field is empty. The right hand field contains only one unreduced formula, namely the formula that the system is trying to prove. The index associated with this formula is 0. The system then applies inference rules (apart from the resolution rule) to this unreduced formula. Clearly, because of rules R3 and R4, which are both applicable to implications on left hand sides of sequents, this may result in more than one unreduced sequent. The old sequent is pushed on the data-structure representing the proof trace while the system now applies the inference rules (again apart from the resolution rule), to the first of the remaining unreduced sequents. Every time an inference rule is applied to a unreduced sequent, it is added to the data-structure representing the proof trace. If a sequent contains no longer any unreduced formulas, then it is pushed onto the set of reduced sequents. When there are no unreduced sequents left, the system constructs all possible resolvents of the set of reduced sequents, until either no more sequents can be resolved against each other, or until the empty sequent has been derived.

The user can attach properties to the accessibility relation. The system then uses these properties when it is trying to w-unify indices against each other. The accessibility relation can be declared to be serial, reflexive, symmetric, transitive or euclidean. In order to make the w-unification algorithm more efficient, the routine that is used for setting restrictions on the accessibility relation contains information about certain relations between properties of the accessibility relation. For example, if the accessibility relation is declared to be reflexive, then the system will automatically declare it to be serial as well. Similarly, if the accessibility relation has already been declared to be serial, symmetric and transitive, then the system uses the fact that the accessibility relation is already reflexive and euclidean. As a consequence, if the user declares the accessibility relation to be reflexive or euclidean in addition to being transitive, symmetric and serial, then the system informs the user that the accessibility relation already has this property and will not change the restrictions on the accessibility relation. For ease of use, the system also allows the user to declare the accessibility relation to be as in T, S4 or S5.

The implementation of the w-unification algorithm follows the definition in section 8.2 more or less directly. If the end-symbols of both indices are ground, then a simple equality test will be sufficient to determine whether two indices w-unify. If at least one is a variable, then, if the accessibility relation is not serial, we simply fail. If the accessibility relation is serial, we store with every world-symbol that occurs in one of the indices, a list of worlds that are accessible from it. Initially, this list is constructed purely on the basis of the indices that the system is trying to w-unify. The system then loops through a list of restrictions on the accessibility relation and adds further accessible worlds to each world, until either the world indices w-unify, or until the data structure that associates with each world symbol the worlds accessible from it, does not change any more. In the latter case, the world-indices do not w-unify.

8.5.3 Assertion-time inferencing

Although we have presented the system as a theorem prover for modal predicate logic, our main motivation for developing the system is an interest in the use of modal logic as a knowledge representation language. We have therefore also used the proof method to implement a modal knowledge representation system. We used (and extended) the technique of assertion-time inference as presented in chapter 6 to this end.

The technique of assertion-time inference is based on the observation that trying to determine whether a query p follows from a knowledge base amounts to trying to establish whether $KB \vdash p$, where KB can be treated as a conjunction of all the propositions in the knowledge base. Clearly, one would like a knowledge base query system to be as efficient as possible at retrieval time, when the system is trying to derive a query from the knowledge base, even if this means a slight loss of speed at assertion-time when the knowledge base is being built. When a knowledge base is constructed, one clearly does not know which queries are going to be asked of the system. However, one can, given the proof theory that the system is using, apply as many inference rules as possible to the propositions that make up the knowledge base, and store these inferences.

Determining whether $KB \vdash p$ in our (sequent-based) system amounts to trying to derive the empty sequent from $\leftarrow (KB \rightarrow p)$. Applying inference rules R3 and R4 to this sequent yields the sequents $KB \leftarrow$ and $\leftarrow p$. p is the query and is therefore not known at assertion-time. Therefore, we cannot apply any other inference rules to p. However, KB is a conjunction, and by rewriting $q \mathbin{\&} r$ as $\neg(q \rightarrow \neg r)$, the reader can establish that from $q \mathbin{\&} r \leftarrow$ one can derive both $q \leftarrow$ and $r \leftarrow$. Thus, whenever a new proposition q is asserted into the knowledge base, one can form the sequent $q \leftarrow$. Because we only apply the resolution rule to reduced formulas, we can reduce this sequent at assertion-time and store the reduced sequents that result from this in the knowledge base. Although it would in principle be possible to resolve sequents stored in the knowledge base at assertion time as well, we have decided against this. We believe that this extension would lead to an unacceptable overhead at assertion time. Although one is prepared to put up with some efficiency loss at assertion time if it means a gain at retrieval time, there is a limit to the efficiency loss that one is prepared to tolerate. We believe that by also resolving on the reduced sequents stored in the knowledge base the system would overstep this boundary.

A reduced sequent will contain a number of indexed formulas. We can further speed up the entire system by also performing part of the computation that is required by the w-unification algorithm at assertion-time. The present implementation of the w-unification algorithm constructs for every used world-symbol the set of accessible worlds for both indices. As far as the world symbols in the world indices of the indexed formulas in the knowledge base are concerned, we can construct the list of accessible worlds at assertion-time.

Whenever a query is made to the knowledge base, we can simply form the sequent $\leftarrow p$ and reduce this sequent. This will yield a list of reduced sequents. In order to prove p, we then have to derive the empty sequent from this list of reduced sequents, and the sequents stored in the knowledge base. The only inference rule that can still be applied is the resolution rule, and we can thus try to resolve the query sequents against any sequents in the knowledge. Clearly, by indexing the sequents in the knowledge base on the basis of which atomic propositions they contain, and on which side, the search for potentially unifying atomic propositions has been speeded up as well. Because we have constructed sets of accessible possible worlds for all world-indices that occur in the sequents in the knowledge base, the w-unification algorithm is somewhat faster as well.

If we combine the modal theorem proving techniques described in this chapter with the technique of assertion time inferencing described in chapter 6, the result is a reasonably efficient knowledge representation system based on modal predicate logic. It is then possible to instantiate the theorem prover for a particular logic that is suitable for a particular class of applications. Thus, in [Jack88c], and chapter 9, we specialise the theorem prover for the modal doxastic logic KD45, where the accessibility relation is serial, transitive and Euclidean. We describe an extension to the pure proof method which enables nonmonotonic reasoning on incomplete doxastic theories, i.e. theories which do not satisfy the usual closure conditions.

8.5.4 Applications and possible improvements

There are a number of improvements that could be made to the system as presently implemented. First, the implementation is restricted to modal logics in which both BF and FB hold. However, we believe that it would be a relatively straightforward matter to extend the system to arbitrary modal predicate logics. The main changes would involve a modification to the representation of propositions to take into account term-indices, and a change to the resolution rule so that it implemented mt-unification rather than m-unification. The change of the representation of propositions is straightforward, while all the components needed, for the implementation of mt-unification, such as an implementation of w-unification, and a routine for testing the compatibility of two unifications, are in place as well. After all, they were also necessary for m-unification.

The final three improvements concern efficiency improvements that can be made. The first improvement is very simple: rather than dealing with non-primitive connectives such as M, $\&$, $\lor$ and the existential quantifier in the parser by means of rewrite rules, we could implement derived inference rules corresponding to these connectives. As the user can see from the appendix, reducing a formula like Mp requires three applications of an inference rule. An additional advantage is of course that the proofs become more natural. The implementation that we use for the experiments mentioned above uses these derived inference rules. In the appendix we use no derived inference rules, and restrict ourselves to the inference rules presented in this chapter.

A second (and more serious) improvement concerns the implementation of the w-unification algorithm. As we have said, the system follows the definition of w-unification more or less directly. For each world symbol that occurs in one of world-indices to be w-unified, it constructs the set of accessible possible worlds. Although the system will test whether two world-indices unify after each (single) step in this construction process, the present implementation of w-unification turns out to be rather inefficient, and slows down the theorem prover quite considerably. We expect that more efficient implementations are possible, and we are currently working on this problem. The need for a more efficient implementation of the w-unification algorithm becomes more pressing when we generalize the logics in which neither BF nor FB hold, as we have to apply the w-unification algorithm more often in these cases.

The final efficiency improvement concerns the control regime. This problem is more acute when the system is used as a theorem prover rather than as a knowledge representation language interpreter. There are two problems. First, we only resolve on reduced sequents. As a result, in some cases the system does a lot of unnecessary reasoning. Consider for example a proposition like $LML(p\ \&\ q) \rightarrow LML(p\ \&\ q)$. If we resolved on non-reduced sequents, then all we had to do would be to apply inference rules R3 and R4 to $\leftarrow |LML(p\ \&\ q) \rightarrow LML(p\ \&\ q)|_0$ before we could apply R1 and derive the empty sequent. As it is, we have to apply a large number of other inference rules before R1 can finally be applied.

[Jack88a, Section 3.3] demonstrates how one could encode control heuristics in a modal meta-language, and then use such heuristics to direct object-level proofs. For example, given a universally quantified subgoal, such as $(\forall x)(p(x) \rightarrow q(x))$, one could have a meta-rule which says "consider the goal achieved if it is known that prototypical individual c of type p has the property q". The idea is that such rules could preempt the operations of an ordinary inference rule, such as R9, which would introduce a skolem function when eliminating the quantifier. The meta-rule represents domain-specific knowledge about a particular individual, e.g. that c is typical of individuals that have p. The resulting proofs involve short cuts, but the short cuts are justified by explicit meta-rules, rather than being hard-coded (and therefore buried) in the interpretation scheme.

A second problem with the present control regime concerns the stage in which the system is trying to resolve reduced sequents against each other. The system constructs all possible resolvents, and hence searches the proof tree at this stage in a breadth-first manner. Clearly, a depth-first control regime at this stage, or a best-first control regime, would greatly speed up the system.

8.6 Related work in automated theorem proving

[Abad86] present a non-clausal resolution proof method for several systems of modal logic. There are different inference rules for different systems, so the method is more complex than ours. The Barcan formula always holds under their semantics, and so the method suffers from the same restrictions as our original presentation. Moreover, it is not clear how this restriction could be remedied. Another problem is that their inference rules may can new connectives, which generates a very redundant search space. Our inference rules only eliminate logical operators.

[Cerr86] presents a modal extension to Prolog called MOLOG. MOLOG uses a modal resolution rule, which replaces the conditions under which two clauses can resolve from a simple unification test to a more complicated test which is dependent on the particular modal logic used. For every modal logic one has to design a new procedure and Fariñas del Cerro restricts himself to S5. MOLOG is therefore less general than our system. Another limitation is that MOLOG restricts the language to modal Horn clauses, where a modal Horn clause can be obtained from a non-modal Horn clause by putting (possibly empty) sequents of modal operators in front of each of the atomic formulas, and putting a (possibly empty) sequent of modal operators in front of the resulting clause. Clearly, this leads to limitations in expressive power. For example, MOLOG cannot represent propositions such as $L(p \rightarrow L(q \rightarrow r))$, $Lp \rightarrow \neg Lq$, or $Lp \rightarrow L(q \vee r)$. In addition, MOLOG does not allow quantifiers to occur in the scope of modal operators. Partly because of this, MOLOG is restricted to domains in which both BF and FB are true.

Another piece of related work is [Kono86a], [Kono86b]. Konolige's treatment of quantification in epistemic logic (e.g. [Kono86a, section 3.3]) differentiates between different kinds of constant. *Id constants* are supplied by a "naming map" defined over the universe of individuals, and they are rigid designators which always denote the extension of of an individual's name in the actual world. This is in contrast with skolem constants, which are non-rigid designators, as in our proof theory. Konolige follows Kripke in extending all valuation functions to cover every individual in a model, so that neither BF nor FB is valid in his semantics. The treatment of quantification in his deduction model is therefore similar to our treatment in a possible worlds model, as long as the naming map is assumed to be partial.

As in Konolige's system, our system assumes that the denotation of a constant is made relative to a particular world, namely the world in which it was introduced. Unlike Konolige, we do not define the value of the denotation function from indexed terms to possible individuals as the term's denotation in the real world. Indeed, the term may not have a denotation in the real world, if BF is not valid. Our formulation also makes explicit the role of the accessibility relation in determining the validity of the Barcan formula.

The matrix proof method presented in [Wall86] generalizes work on the connection calculus [Bibe82b] to modal logic. His system is most closely related to ours, in that formulas are given *prefixes*, in the manner of prefixed tableau systems [Fitt83]. The prefix associated with a formula stands for the worlds in the formula is true. The main difference appears to be that his prefixes do not contain variables, and therefore do not use skolem functions to encode dependencies, as our indices do. Dependencies are encoded in the order of symbols in a prefix, and modal substitutions are derived which render prefixes identical. Wallen then defines two notions of complementarity, one for constant and one for varying domains. The latter encodes the interaction between modal substitutions and first-order substitutions (which render formulas identical). His presentation is not couched in terms of the validity of BF and FB, although any such encoding must invalidate them both for varying domains.

8.7 Conclusion

We present a sequent-based proof method which is suitable for all normal systems of modal predicate logic. One attractive aspect of the proof method is the fact that the inference rules are invariant between different systems of logic. We obtain different modal logics by varying the conditions under which two formulas are considered to be complementary and can therefore be resolved against each other. These conditions correspond to the properties of the prevailing accessibility relation in the underlying Kripke semantics for the logic in question. We enforce these conditions by (i) associating with every formula a world-index which indicates the world or worlds in which the formula holds, and (ii) providing a unification algorithm which returns a substitution of values for individual and world variables if and only if the formulas are indeed complementary. The proof method that results from the combination of the basic inference rules and the unification algorithm is shown to be sound for all normal systems.

Our original semantics validated both the Barcan formula and its converse, which limited the application of the proof method to domains where the universe of individuals is common to all possible worlds. However, in many applications, new individuals may come into existence as we pass from world to world, while extant individuals may cease to exist. The present work releases the proof method from this restriction by (i) associating with each term a term-index which indicates the world in which the term originated, and (ii) elaborating the unification algorithm so that two formulas now unify if and only if they are complementary and their corresponding terms are counterparts. We present a soundness result for the new proof theory. Then we show that the proof method can easily be modified to accommodate logics in which either the Barcan formula holds, and its converse does not, or vice versa.

An implementation of the original proof method is described in some detail, and a number of possible improvements and extensions of the method are discussed. We argue that the method is more tractable than non-clausal methods and more comprehensive than most alternative clausal methods in the literature. The main advantages are the following. First, the cost of determining whether an inference rule is applicable to a sequent is low, since we can usually confine ourselves to examining the logical operators governing formulas in the sequent.

The only exception is the resolution rule R1, where we need to take the
indices of formulas into account. Second, there is no need to perform
complicated syntactic transformations, such as extracting quantifiers,
before inference rules can be applied. Such transformations typically
involve searching through sub-expressions in formulas, and hence incur
the computational overhead of extensive list processing. Finally, none of
the inference rules introduces new operators, unlike those found in some
other proof methods (e.g.[Abad86]).

8.8 Appendix

The following is an example run of the system. Comments are indented.

```
1> *accessibility-restrictions*
nil
```

> Initially, there are no restrictions on the accessibility relation.
> We first prove one of the formulas that is true even in the
> weakest of modal logics.

```
2> (prove '(=>(L(=>(pa)(qa)))(=>(L(pa))(L(q a)))))
successful proof
g864   nil <== nil
  from ((g861 . g863) resolution)
```

> The lay-out of application of the resolution rule R1 is as
> follows. Between >> n >>>>> and -- n -----, we give the
> derivation of the first of the sequents to be resolved. Between
> -- n ----- and << n <<<<< we present the derivation of the
> other sequent. Numbers are used because in the derivation
> of one of the sequents to be resolved, there may have been
> other applications of the resolution rule.

```
>> 1 >>>>>
g861   (((p a) :index (|?w-var1| 0))) <== nil
  from (g859 nec-introduction)
```

> Nec-introduction corresponds to inference rule R8. ?w-
> var1 therefore is a free world-variable

```
g859   (((1 (p a)) :index (0))) <== nil
  from (g856 impl-elimination-1)
```

> Impl-elimination-1 stands for inference rule R4. Common
> Lisp is unfortunately case-insensitive. As a result, the L-
> operator, when it appears in proof traces, is printed in small
> case.

```
g856   nil <== (((=> (1 (p a)) (1 (q a))) :index (0)))
  from (g854 impl-elimination-2)
```

Impl-elimination-2 is inference rule R3.

```
g854    nil <==(((=>(1(=>(p a)(q a)))(=>(1(p a))(1(q a))))
                  :index (0)))
  from (premise)
-- 1 -----
g863    nil <== (((p a) :index (0 (|w-sk2|))))
  from ((g858 . g862) resolution)
>> 2 >>>>>
g858    (((q a) :index (|?w-var0| 0))) <== (((p a) :index
                                              (|?w-var0| 0)))
  from (g857 impl-introduction)
```

Impl-introduction is R2.

```
g857    (((=> (p a) (q a)) :index (|?w-var0| 0))) <== nil
  from (g855 nec-introduction)
g855    (((1 (=> (p a) (q a))) :index (0))) <== nil
  from (g854 impl-elimination-1)
g854    nil <== (((=>(1(=>(p a)(q a)))(=>(1(p a))(1(q a))))
                  :index (0)))
  from (premise)
-- 2 -----
g862    nil <== (((q a) :index ((|w-sk2|) 0)))
  from (g860 nec-elimination)
```

Nec-elimination corresponds to inference rule R7. (w-sk2) is a 0-place world-skolem function, i.e. a skolem world-constant.

```
g860    nil <== (((1 (q a)) :index (0)))
  from (g856 impl-elimination-2)
g856    nil <== (((=> (1 (p a)) (1 (q a))) :index (0)))
  from (g854 impl-elimination-2)
g854    nil <== (((=>(1(=>(p a)(q a)))(=>(1(p a))(1(q a))))
                  :index (0)))
  from (premise)
<< 2 <<<<<
<< 1 <<<<<
t
```

In addition to a user-definable flag which determines whether a successful proof should be printed out, there is a user-definable flag which will print out information during the search of a proof. In particular, it will tell the user which inference rule is currently being applied to which formula. Because of the large amount of information which would normally be displayed, its default value is nil. However, in order to show what is going on in an unsuccessful search of a proof, we temporarily set the value to t.

```
3> (setf *proof-trace* t)
t
```

We now try to prove a proposition that should hold only if the accessibility relation is serial. Because it is not, the proof fails.

```
4> (prove '(=> (L p) (M p)))
Rewrote (m p)
Impl-elimination on (=> (1 (p)) (~ (1 (~ (p)))))
Nec-introduction on (1 (p))
Neg-elimination on (~ (1 (~ (p))))
Nec-introduction on (1 (~ (p)))
Neg-introduction on (~ (p))
Trying to unify
      formula (p)
      with index (|?w-var3| 0)
with
      formula (p)
      with index (|?w-var4| 0)
```

Because the accessibility relation is not serial, the world-indices of the above formulas will not w-unify, and therefore the formulas cannot be resolved against each other.

```
failing proof
nil
```

We now declare the accessibility relation to be serial, and try again.

```
5> (set-accessibility 'serial)
(serial)

6> (prove '(=> (L p) (M p)))
Rewrote (m p)
Impl-elimination on (=> (l (p)) (~ (l (~ (p)))))
Nec-introduction on (l (p))
Neg-elimination on (~ (l (~ (p))))
Nec-introduction on (l (~ (p)))
Neg-introduction on (~ (p))
```

Until now the proof has been like as in the previous case.
However, the accessibility relation is now serial, and therefore
the attempt at resolving the two formulas will be successful.

```
Trying to unify
    formula (p)
    with index (|?w-var5| 0)
with
    formula (p)
    with index (|?w-var6| 0)
Resolve (p) with index (|?w-var5| 0) with
       (p) with index (|?w-var6| 0)
successful proof
g885   nil <== nil
  from ((g878 . g881) resolution)
>> 1 >>>>>
g878   (((p) :index (|?w-var5| 0))) <== nil
  from (g876 nec-introduction)
g876   (((l (p)) :index (0))) <== nil
  from (g875 impl-elimination-1)
g875   nil <== (((=>(l(p))(~(l(~(p))))) :index (0)))
  from (g874 rewrite-rules)
```

The parser rewrites (M p) as (~ (L (~ (p)))). The actual
theorem prover therefore needs to contain no separate inference rules for the possibility operator. (L p) is rewritten
as (L (p)) for purely implementation reasons: it makes the

code corresponding to inference rules R7 and R8 easier to write.

```
g874    nil <== (((=> (l p) (m p)) :index (0)))
  from (premise)
-- 1 -----
g881    nil <== (((p) :index (|?w-var6| 0)))
  from (g880 neg-introduction)
```

Neg-introduction corresponds to R5.

```
g880    (((~ (p)) :index (|?w-var6| 0))) <== nil
  from (g879 nec-introduction)
g879    (((l (~ (p))) :index (0))) <== nil
  from (g877 neg-elimination)
```

Neg-elimination corresponds to R6.

```
g877    nil <== (((~ (l (~ (p)))) :index (0)))
  from (g875 impl-elimination-2)
g875    nil <== (((=>(l(p))(~(l(~(p))))) :index (0)))
  from (g874 rewrite-rules)
g874    nil <== (((=> (l p) (m p)) :index (0)))
  from (premise)
<< 1 <<<<<
t
```

We now try to prove the axiom which holds only if the accessibility relation is transitive. At the moment, the only restrictions on the accessibility relation is that it is serial, and the proof therefore fails.

```
7> (prove '(=> (L p) (L (L p))))
Impl-elimination on (=> (l (p)) (l (l (p))))
Nec-introduction on (l (p))
Nec-elimination on (l (l (p)))
Nec-elimination on (l (p))
Trying to unify
    formula (p)
    with index (|?w-var7| 0)
```

```
with
     formula (p)
     with index ((|w-sk9|) (|w-sk8|) 0)
failing proof
nil
```

> We reset *proof-trace* to nil to suppress some of the infor-
> mation that is being printed out, and set the accessibility
> relation to be transitive as well as serial. Then we try again.

```
8> (setf *proof-trace* nil)
nil

9> (set-accessibility 'transitive)
(transitive serial)

10> (prove '(=> (L p) (L (L p))))
successful proof
g913    nil <== nil
  from ((g904 . g906) resolution)
>> 1 >>>>>
g904    (((p) :index (|?w-var10| 0))) <== nil
  from (g902 nec-introduction)
g902    (((l (p)) :index (0))) <== nil
  from (g901 impl-elimination-1)
g901    nil <== (((=> (l (p)) (l (l (p)))) :index (0)))
  from (g900 rewrite-rules)
g900    nil <== (((=> (l p) (l (l p))) :index (0)))
  from (premise)
-- 1 -----
g906    nil <== (((p) :index ((|w-sk12|) (|w-sk11|) 0)))
  from (g905 nec-elimination)
g905    nil <== (((l (p)) :index ((|w-sk11|) 0)))
  from (g903 nec-elimination)
g903    nil <== (((l (l (p))) :index (0)))
  from (g901 impl-elimination-2)
g901    nil <== (((=> (l (p)) (l (l (p)))) :index (0)))
  from (g900 rewrite-rules)
g900    nil <== (((=> (l p) (l (l p))) :index (0)))
```

```
from (premise)
<< 1 <<<<<
t
```

We show in the next example that BF can be proven.

```
11> (prove '(=> ((all x)(L (p x))) (L ((all y)(p y)))))
successful proof
g921   nil <== nil
  from ((g918 . g920) resolution)
>> 1 >>>>>
g918   (((p |?var13|) :index (|?w-var14| 0))) <== nil
  from (g917 nec-introduction)
g917   (((1 (p |?var13|)) :index (0))) <== nil
  from (g915 u-introduction)
```

> u-introduction corresponds to R10. ?var13 is a free indi-
> vidual variable.

```
g915   ((((all x) (1 (p x))) :index (0))) <== nil
  from (g914 impl-elimination-1)
g914   nil <== (((=>((all x)(1(p x)))(1((all y)(p y))))
                 :index (0)))
  from (premise)
-- 1 -----
g920   nil <== (((p (|sk-f16|)) :index ((|w-sk15|) 0)))
  from (g919 u-elimination)
```

> u-elimination corresponds to R9. (sk-f16) is a 0-place
> individual skolem function, that is a skolem constant.

```
g919   nil <== ((((all y) (p y)) :index ((|w-sk15|) 0)))
  from (g916 nec-elimination)
g916   nil <== (((1 ((all y) (p y))) :index (0)))
  from (g914 impl-elimination-2)
g914   nil <== (((=>((all x)(1(p x)))(1((all y)(p y))))
                 :index (0)))
  from (premise)
<< 1 <<<<<
t
```

We reset *proof-trace*.

```
12> (setf *proof-trace* t)
t
```

The following formula cannot be proven. For every world, there may be an alternative individual that makes the antecedent true. Clearly, the consequent is then false.

```
13> (prove '(=> (L((exists x)(p x)))((exists y)(L(p y)))))
Rewrote ((exists x) (p x))
Rewrote ((exists y) (1 (p y)))
Impl-elimination on (=> (1 (~ ((all x) (~ (p x)))))
                        (~ ((all y) (~ (1 (p y))))))
Nec-introduction on (1 (~ ((all x) (~ (p x)))))
Neg-introduction on (~ ((all x) (~ (p x))))
U-elimination on ((all x) (~ (p x)))
Neg-elimination on (~ (p (|sk-f21| |?w-var20|)))
Neg-elimination on (~ ((all y) (~ (1 (p y)))))
U-introduction on ((all y) (~ (1 (p y))))
Neg-introduction on (~ (1 (p |?var22|)))
Nec-elimination on (1 (p |?var22|))
Trying to unify
     formula (p (|sk-f21| |?w-var20|))
     with index (|?w-var20| 0)
with
     formula (p |?var22|)
     with index ((|w-sk23| |?var22|) 0)
```

Here we see the importance of the occurs-check in determining whether a substitution is acceptable as a unification. The world-indices w-unify, while the formulas unify. However, the two unifications are not compatible.

```
failing proof
nil
```

The converse of the previous formula obviously holds: if there is an individual that always has a property, then there is always an individual that has the property.

```
14> (prove '(=> ((exists x)(L(p x)))(L((exists y)(p y)))))
Rewrote ((exists x) (l (p x)))
Rewrote ((exists y) (p y))
Impl-elimination on (=> (~ ((all x) (~ (l (p x)))))
                        (l (~ ((all y) (~ (p y)))))))
Neg-introduction on (~ ((all x) (~ (l (p x))))))
U-elimination on ((all x) (~ (l (p x)))))
Neg-elimination on (~ (l (p (|sk-f0|)))))
Nec-introduction on (l (p (|sk-f0|))))
Nec-elimination on (l (~ ((all y) (~ (p y))))))
Neg-elimination on (~ ((all y) (~ (p y)))))
U-introduction on ((all y) (~ (p y))))
Neg-introduction on (~ (p |?var3|)))
Trying to unify
      formula (p (|sk-f0|))
      with index (|?w-var1| 0)
with
      formula (p |?var3|)
      with index ((|w-sk2|) 0)
Resolve (p (|sk-f0|)) with index (|?w-var1| 0) with
        (p |?var3|) with index ((|w-sk2|) 0)
successful proof
g866    nil <== nil
  from ((g861 . g865) resolution)
>> 1 >>>>>
g861    (((p (|sk-f0|)) :index (|?w-var1| 0))) <== nil
  from (g860 nec-introduction)
g860    (((l (p (|sk-f0|))) :index (0))) <== nil
  from (g859 neg-elimination)
g859    nil <== (((~ (l (p (|sk-f0|)))) :index (0)))
  from (g858 u-elimination)
g858    nil <== ((((all x) (~ (l (p x)))) :index (0)))
  from (g856 neg-introduction)
g856    (((~((all x)(~(l(p x))))) :index (0))) <== nil
  from (g855 impl-elimination-1)
g855    nil <== (((=> (~ ((all x) (~ (l (p x)))))
                      (l (~ ((all y) (~ (p y)))))))
                 :index (0)))
```

```
    from (g854 rewrite-rules)

      We rewrite ((exists x)(p x)) as
      (~ ((all x)(~ (p x))))

g854    nil <== (((=> ((exists x)(1(p x)))
                                    (1((exists y)(p y))))
                        :index (0)))
    from (premise)
-- 1 -----
g865    nil <== (((p |?var3|) :index ((|w-sk2|) 0)))
    from (g864 neg-introduction)
g864    (((~ (p |?var3|)) :index ((|w-sk2|) 0))) <== nil
    from (g863 u-introduction)
g863    ((((all y)(~(p y))) :index ((|w-sk2|) 0))) <== nil
    from (g862 neg-elimination)
g862    nil <== (((~((all y)(~(p y))))
                        :index ((|w-sk2|) 0)))
    from (g857 nec-elimination)
g857    nil <== (((1(~((all y)(~(p y)))))) :index (0)))
    from (g855 impl-elimination-2)
g855    nil <== (((=> (~ ((all x) (~ (1 (p x)))))
                            (1 (~ ((all y) (~ (p y))))))
                        :index (0)))
    from (g854 rewrite-rules)
g854    nil <== (((=> ((exists x)(1(p x)))
                            (1((exists y)(p y))))
                        :index (0)))
    from (premise)
<< 1 <<<<<
t
```

9 A Modal Proof Method for Doxastic Reasoning

Peter Jackson

Han Reichgelt

9.1 Doxastic theories

The correspondence between modal treatments of doxastic logic and possible world semantics is due to [Hint62]. An agent a believes that P written $L_a P$, in world w iff P is true in every world accessible to a from w. The idea is that the worlds accessible to a in w represent just those hypothetical situations which are consistent with a's beliefs in w, i.e. they are ways the real world could be, given what is currently believed. Hintikka calls such worlds "epistemic alternatives", and describes them as

> possible states of affairs in which a person knows at least as much as — and usually even more than — he knows in the given state (op cit, p.56).

More formally, a doxastic model is a tuple, $M = (W, w_0, R_a, V)$, where W is a set of worlds, $w_0 \in W$ represents the real world, $R_a \subseteq W^2$ is a doxastic accessibility relation with respect to a, and V is a valuation function which associates with every atomic proposition a set of worlds in which it is true. If a proposition P is true at world w in model M, we usually write $M, w \models P$, or just $w \models P$, where M is understood from the context. In a given model, $w \models P$ under the following conditions:

if P is atomic, then $w \models P$ iff $w \in V(P)$;
if P is $\neg Q$, then $w \models P$ iff $w \not\models Q$;
if P is $(Q \vee R)$, then $w \models P$ iff $w \models Q$ or $w \models R$;
if P is $L_a Q$, then $w \models P$ iff $w' \models Q$ for all w' such that $(w, w') \in R_a$.

R_a is generally held to be transitive and Euclidean, but not reflexive. Reflexivity would result in an agent's beliefs automatically being true of the world in which he held them, since for all $w \in W$ we would have $(w, w) \in R_a$. In other words, one could go directly from $w \models L_a P$ to $w \models P$ for any world w, since $L_a P \rightarrow P$ would be a theorem of doxastic logic. But this would rule out the possibility of an agent ever entertaining erroneous beliefs.

Reflexivity is often replaced by seriality, i.e. for every world w there is at least one other world w' such that $(w, w') \in Ra$. This guarantees that there is at least one possible world in which a's beliefs are true, ensuring that an agent does not believe impossible or contradictory things. Thus $L_a P \to \neg L_a \neg P$ is now a theorem.

The transitivity of R_a means that if $(w, w') \in R_a$ and $(w', w'') \in R_a$, then $(w, w'') \in R_a$. This enables a to perform positive introspection, since if $w_0 \models L_a P$ then $w \models L_a P$ for all worlds w accessible to w_0. If a believes that P, then he believes that he believes it, and $L_a P \to L_a L_a P$ is a theorem.

The Euclidean property means that if $(w, w') \in R_a$ and $(w, w'') \in R_a$, then $(w', w'') \in R_a$. This enables negative introspection, since if $w \models \neg P$ for some world w accessible to w_0, then $w \models \neg L_a P$ for every world w accessible to w_0. If a does not believe that P, then he believes that he does not believe it, and $\neg L_a P \to L_a \neg L_a P$ is a theorem.

If R_a is serial, transitive and Euclidean, then the resulting logic is formally equivalent to the modal system KD45, which has come to be regarded as an appropriate axiomatic basis for a logic of belief (see e.g. [Halp85] [Kono85]).

When reasoning about belief, however, we begin not with a doxastic model but with a theory of what an agent believes. Much of our communicative behaviour is based upon our having rudimentary notions of what other parties believe. Although we cannot see the world (and its epistemic alternatives) through someone else's eyes, we can have ideas about what propositions an agent would affirm or deny.

Definition 1 If D_a is a doxastic theory of what an agent a believes, then $L_a P$ for all $P \in D_a$.

For concreteness, we can think of D_a as the contents of a user model in some help system, or in the explanation facility of an expert system. We want D_a to be consistent, but it need not be complete or closed under deductive consequence. Neither shall we impose any introspective closure conditions, such as insisting that $L_a P$ be in D_a if P is.

Nevertheless, extending the model or answering questions about it may involve both deductive and introspective behaviour. Some of our inferences concerning a's beliefs may follow routinely as tautological consequences of D_a. Others might involve default reasoning about typical classes of user, e.g. assuming that a does not believe that P, unless there is evidence to the contrary. Such commonsense inferences can be seen to involve a kind of introspection. Although they are difficult to formalise, they might be extremely useful in deciding what a user should be told in an explanation.

Introspective theories are normally defined in terms of a complete and stable expansion of an initial set of premises (e.g. [Moor85b]). Thus one reasons about an incomplete doxastic theory, such our user model D_a, in terms of an expansion which is the set of all logical consequences of $D_a^* = D_a \cup \{L_a P \mid P \in D_a^*\} \cup \{\neg L_a P \mid P \notin D_a^*\}$. The decision procedure outlined by [Moor88] requires enumerating all possible sets of truth assignments to the propositional constants in D_a^*. Although this can be done off-line, prior to determining whether or not a formula is in a stable expansion of the premises, it requires exponential time. Furthermore, as new information becomes available, this enumeration will have to be updated. In the interests computational convenience, there is a case for considering alternative proof methods which expand the initial premises incrementally and on demand.

The next section describes a proof method that can be applied to stable expansions of KD45 theories, but which fails to perform certain kinds of introspection on theories in which Moore's closure conditions do not hold. We then show that the method can be augmented so that it is applicable to incomplete theories. The final section explains the problem with the pure proof method and provides a rationale for the solution in terms of [Kono85] account of belief introspection. This chapter is an expanded version of [Jack88c].

9.2 The pure proof method

A general proof method for modal predicate logic is described in chapter 8. To recapitulate, the method is sequent based, and formulas in a sequent are indexed according to the worlds in which they are true. The key technique is world unification, in which we require that the indices of complementary literals denote the same possible world under the prevailing accessibility relation. Thus the method takes the underlying semantics into account at unification time; otherwise the axioms and inference rules are the same for all normal systems. Here we shall confine ourselves to the instantiation of the method for propositional KD45.

World symbols are either world constants from the set $\{0, 1, 2, \ldots\}$; world variables from the set $\{u, v, w\}$ possibly with subscripts; or world skolems composed of n-ary skolem functions from the set $\{f, g, h\}$ possibly with subscripts applied to n-ary sequences of world symbols. A world index is a sequence of world symbols $s_1 : \ldots : s_n$, in which s_1 is the end symbol and s_n the start symbol (thus indices are read from right to left). A world symbol that is not a world variable is called ground, as is a world index whose world symbols are all ground. By convention, 0 represents the real world, and will be the start symbol of all indices considered herein.

We define a sequent as $S \leftarrow T$, where S, T are (possibly empty) sets of formulas $P, Q, \ldots$ with associated world indices. The informal reading of $S \leftarrow T$ is that if all the formulas in T are true then at least one formula in S is true. If both S and T are empty, then the sequent is empty.

We have the following axiom schemata, where i is an arbitrary index.

A1. Q_i $\qquad\qquad\quad \leftarrow \quad (P \to Q)_i, P_i$
A2. $(P \to Q)_i \qquad \leftarrow \quad Q_i$
A3. $(P \to Q)_i, P_i \quad \leftarrow$
A4. $P_i, \neg P_i \qquad\quad \leftarrow$
A5. $\qquad\qquad\qquad\quad \leftarrow \quad P_i, \neg P_i$

Let S, T, S', T' be sets of indexed formulas. Then we have the following inference rules.

R1. If $S, P_i \leftarrow T$ and $S' \leftarrow P_j, T'$
and i and j w-unify with substitution σ
then $S\sigma, S'\sigma \leftarrow T\sigma, T'\sigma$.

R2. If $S \leftarrow LP_i, T$ then $S \leftarrow P_{n:i}, T$, where if i is ground, then n is a new world constant, else n is a skolem function $f(w_1, \ldots, w_k)$, where $w_1, \ldots, w_k$ are the world variables in i.

R3. If $S, LP_i \leftarrow T$, then $S, P_{w:i} \leftarrow T$, where w is a new world variable.

Unification of two indexed formulas $P_{m:m-1:\ldots:0}$ and $P_{n:n-1:\ldots:0}$ succeeds just in case world symbols m and n can be shown to denote the same world.

Definition 2 World indices $m{:}m - 1{:}\ldots{:}0$ and $n{:}n - 1{:}\ldots{:}0$ w-unify with substitution σ under a serial, transitive and Euclidean accessibility relation R under the following conditions.

1. If m, n are ground, then $\sigma = \emptyset$ iff $m = n$.

2. If m is ground, and n is a world variable, then $\sigma = \{m/n\}\tau$ iff there is a substitution τ such that $(n - 1, m)\tau \in R$.

3. If m, n are world variables, then $\sigma = \{m/n\}\tau$ iff either there is a substitution τ such that $(n - 1, m)\tau$ or $(m - 1, n)\tau \in R$ or $m - 1{:}\ldots{:}0$ and $n - 1{:}\ldots{:}0$ w-unify with substitution τ.

To illustrate the method, consider two proof attempts in KD45: one of the theorem $L_a(L_a P \to P)$ and one of the non-theorem $L_a P \to P$. In each case, we begin by placing the expression in the scope of negation and indexing it with the real world, 0. Then we apply axiom schemata and rules of inference in an attempt to derive the empty sequent, $\leftarrow$. Sequents are annotated with the axiom schema or inference rule applied, followed by the line numbers of the sequents from which they were derived. A denotes an assumption.

Example 1

1. $\leftarrow$ $L_a(L_a P \to P)_0$ A
2. $\leftarrow$ $(L_a P \to P)_{1{:}0}$ $R2, 1$
3. $\leftarrow$ $P_{1{:}0}$ $A2, 2$
4. $L_a P_{1{:}0}$ $\leftarrow$ $A3, 2$
5. $P_{w{:}1{:}0}$ $\leftarrow$ $R3, 4$
6. $\leftarrow$ $R1, 3, 5$

Thus $1 \models \neg P$ and $w \models P$ for all worlds w accessible from 1. Lines 3 and 5 resolve with unification $\{1/w\}$, generating the empty sequent at line 6. The proof succeeds because world 1 is accessible from itself thanks to the Euclidean property of R in KD45.

Compare this with the failed proof.

Example 2

1. $\leftarrow$ $(L_a P \to P)_0$ A
2. $\leftarrow$ P_0 $A2, 1$
3. $L_a P_0$ $\leftarrow$ $A3, 1$
4. $P_{w{:}0}$ $\leftarrow$ $A2, 1$

Thus $0 \models \neg P$ and $w \models P$ for all worlds w accessible from 0. We cannot resolve lines 2 and 4 to obtain a contradiction, because this would require 0 to be accessible from itself. Yet R is not reflexive in KD45.

9.3   The augmented method

In what follows, recall that the contents of a doxastic theory D_a are true in all possible worlds accessible to a in 0, the real world. More precisely, the set of worlds so accessible is $W_a = \{w \mid (w, 0) \in R_a\}$. Thus every proposition in D_a is implicitly in the scope of the belief operator, L_a.

To determine whether or not a believes a proposition P, we simply add $\neg L_a P$ to D_a to produce the extension $D'_a = D_a \cup \{\neg L_a P\}$ and attempt to derive the empty sequent from D'_a, using only axioms A1-A5 and the inference rules R1-R3. If the contradiction is forthcoming, then we conclude that P is indeed believed. To determine whether a might believe P, we add $L_a P$ to D_a and conclude that P is consistent with a's beliefs if no contradiction is forthcoming.

Let D_d be the set $\{P \to L_d P\}$, representing d's beliefs for some agent d; thus $L_d(P \to L_d P)$. D_d^* is the set $\{P \to L_d P, L_d(P \to L_d P), \neg L_d P, \neg L_d \neg P, \ldots\}$, derived by applying Moore's closure conditions. Introspection on D_d^* is now trivial for a KD45 theorem prover.

Yet the pure proof method does not enable full introspection on D_d itself. For example, $L_d P$ must be inconsistent with D_d, because $\neg L_d P \in D_d^*$. But the following attempt to derive a contradiction from the assertion of $L_d P$ fails, even though there must be a world in W_d at which $\neg P$ is true.

Example 3

1.	$L_d P_0$	$\leftarrow$	
2.	$P_{w:0}$	$\leftarrow$	$R3, 1$
3.	$L_d(P \to L_d P)_0$	$\leftarrow$	D_d
4.	$(P \to L_d P)_{v:0}$	$\leftarrow$	$R3, 3$
5.	$L_d P_{v:0}$	$\leftarrow$ $P_{v:0}$	$A1, 4$
6.	$L_d P_{v:0}$	$\leftarrow$	$R1, 2, 5$
7.	$P_{u:v:0}$	$\leftarrow$	$R3, 6$

As things stand, the best that we can hope for is an infinite loop, beginning with the resolution of lines 5 and 7. The problem is that $\neg L_d P$ is not an ordinary logical consequence of D_d but a nonmonotonic inference based on the fact that P is not a consequence of D_d. Such an inference is nonmonotonic because it is not true for all consistent extensions of D_d.

So we need to show that D_d logically implies $L_d L_d P$ in order to resolve away $P_{u:v:0} \leftarrow$ at line 7. But D_d does not contain $L_d P$, because, unlike D_d^*, it is not closed under negative introspection. $L_a L_d P$ would follow immediately from $\neg L_d P$, since $L_d L_d P \rightarrow L_d P$ is a theorem of KD45, as well as $L_d P \rightarrow L_d L_d P$. (Thus belief in P and belief in one's belief in P are equivalent.)

The augmented proof method deals with the problem at line 7 by (i) assuming the contrary of $L_d L_d P$, and (ii) showing that $D_d \cup \{\neg L_d L_d P\}$ is satisfiable. If we fail to derive a contradiction from the assumption $\neg L_d L_d P$, then we are entitled to reject $L_d L_d P$ and resolve $P_{u:v:0} \leftarrow$ away by an indirect proof, thereby refuting the original assertion $L_d P$. If we do derive a contradiction, e.g. because P is believed, then we cannot reject $L_d L_d P$ or refute $L_d P$.

Let us agree to call this inference rule the "Rule of Assumptions" (RA). We cite with its application the line number of the assumption and the line number of the failure to derive the empty sequent. The proof then proceeds as follows.

Example 3 (continued)

7.		$P_{u:v:0}$	$\leftarrow$	$R3, 6$
	1.1.		$\leftarrow$ $P_{2:1:0}$	A
	1.2.	$P_{t:v:0}$	$\leftarrow$ $P_{v:0}$	$R3, 5$
	1.3.		$\leftarrow$ $P_{v:0}$	$R1, 1.1., 1.2$
	1.4.		$\not\leftarrow$	
8.			$\leftarrow$ $P_{2:1:0}$	$RA, 1.1., 1.4.$
9.			$\leftarrow$	$R1, 7.8$

Indented steps 1.1–1.4 constitute an introspective subproof of $L_d L_d P$. Step 1.2 is allowed because line 5 derives from D_d alone. Line 1.4 records the failure to derive the empty sequent.

Note that lines 7 and 1.1 are inconsistent, but they cannot be resolved because $P_{u:v:0} \leftarrow$ does not derive from D_d alone. In an introspective subproof with assumption A, any contradiction must be derived from nothing but D_d and A. Lines 7 and 1.1 belong to different levels in the total proof, as the different numbering conventions suggest.

In example 3, RA enabled us to derive $\neg L_d P$ from D_d, thereby deriving the consistent extension $D'_d = D_d \cup \{\neg L_d P\}$. Thus we have performed negative introspection incrementally and on demand. This is rather different to imposing initial closure conditions on D_d, which establishes introspective ability by fiat.

Although the pure proof method does provide the ability to progressively close D_d under deduction (courtesy of A1-A5 and R1) and positive introspection (courtesy of R2), R3 is insufficient to progressively close D_d under negative introspection. In the next section, we shall see why this is so.

9.4   Discussion and related work

RA most closely resembles McDermott's rules for searching for a non-committal model in nonmonotonic S4 using a tableau proof method [McDe82a, pp. 47-48]. When LP is labeled true in any world, a new tableau is created in which P is labeled false. If this new tableau cannot be closed, then we can label LP false, thus closing its branch. Similarly, if MP is labeled false, a new tableau is created in which P is labeled true. Failure to close this tableau results in MP being labeled true.

McDermott notes as "curious" (p. 50) that one is allowed to use truth assignments in the current tableau when attempting to prove LP false (or MP true), but not when attempting to prove MP false (or LP true). This is like the restriction that we noted earlier, whereby we are noted allowed to resolve formulas in an introspective subproof with arbitrary formulas in a parent (or ancestral) proof. The explanation is that the restricted cases involve negative introspection, while the unrestricted ones involve positive introspection.

Positive introspection attempts to show that LP by showing that P, i.e. by deriving a contradiction from the assumption $\neg P$. Labeling P false in the new tableau will not generate any spurious contradictions between the new and the current tableau, where LP is already labeled false. Viewed in terms of possible worlds, $\neg P$ in some world accessible from a world w is consistent with $\neg LP$ in w.

Negative introspection attempts to show that MP by failing to show that $\neg P$, i.e. by failing to derive a contradiction from the assumption that P. Labeling P true in the new tableau may generate spurious contradictions between the new and the current tableau, where MP is labeled false. This is because P in some world accessible from w is inconsistent with $\neg MP$ in w.

Both the tableau method that McDermott describes and the sequent based method described herein bear a family resemblance to the method of semantic diagrams [Hugh68]. We differ from the tableau method in that we never have to perform disjunction splitting, thanks to the use of resolution in R1. We differ from the method of semantic diagrams in that w-unification decides which formulas can be copied from world to world.

[Jack88a, section 3.2] demonstrates that negative introspection can be performed by a change of doxastic viewpoint and the application of the contrapositive of the transitivity axiom $L_aP \rightarrow L_aL_aP$, which normally forms the basis of positive introspection. The method is similar to the approach of example 3, where $P_{u:v:0}$ is resolved away by failing to derive a contradiction from $P_{2:1:0}$. Creating the new worlds 1 and 2 (and moving to world 2) involves a change of viewpoint, because we are examining belief in P from another perspective. However, it is not altogether clear why the method works.

The augmented proof method is best explicated in the context of [Kono85] work on belief introspection. Our notion of an introspective subproof is similar to his notion of a recursive call to a belief subsystem. It can also be shown that, given sufficient resources, our pure proof method is both positive and negative fulfilled. This is not surprising, since KD45 describes an ideal introspective agent, as Konolige points out. Yet negative fulfillment corresponds quite closely to what we have called negative introspection. Thus it is worth asking how the pure proof method can fail to do all the introspection that we need.

The reason is as follows. Konolige stipulates that the base set of beliefs for an agent, equivalent to our D_a, be non-doxastic. Thus his negative fulfillment condition (nfu) can be written as follows:

if $D_a \models \neg P$ then $D_a \models \neg L_aP$.

where $\models$ denotes KD45-entailment. However, if $D_a \not\models \neg P$, nfu cannot operate to our advantage. Neither does the presence in D_a of a doxastic formula, such as $P \rightarrow L_aP$, help us draw any conclusions about belief in P using nfu. But Moore's corresponding closure condition

if $P \notin D_a$ then $\neg L_aP \in D_a$

would help, if we could use it selectively.

The augmentation rule is required to perform an incremental expansion of D_a. In the continuation of example 3, we were able to reject the addition of P to D_d because we could consistently add $\neg L_d P$. Thus, in (i) making the assumption $\neg L_d P$; (ii) failing to derive a contradiction in the presence of $P \rightarrow L_d P$; and (iii) concluding that P was not believed, we adopted the principle

if $D_a \not\models L_a P$ then $D_a \not\models P$.

But this is just the contrapositive of the positive fulfillment condition (pfu).

The application of RA resembles a recursive call to a belief subsystem in the following way. An assumption, e.g. $\neg L_d L_d P$ in the introspective subproof of example 3, corresponds to a query, e.g. "is P believed to be believed?". Posing this question turns a negative introspection problem (such as that at line 7 in the example) into a positive one, which the pure proof method is able to solve.

The pure proof method has been fully implemented. The theorem prover is relatively efficient because the number of rules applicable at any given time is small and the cost of determining rule applicability is low. Augmenting the theorem prover to accommodate RA is entirely straightforward in the propositional case. In fact, a further simplification is possible, which effects computational savings. Given that $\vdash_{KD45} L_a P$ iff $\vdash_{S5} P$, we can behave as if R_a were an equivalence relation when performing w-unification on indices, so long as we are only interested in goals that are fully modalised propositions. Hence we need not check whether one world is accessible from another, since this will always be the case.

The problem is with first-order logic, where negative introspection may never terminate due to the semi-decidability of the calculus. Here there seems to be little choice but to restrict the application of R1 in introspective subproofs. Thus [Kono86a, section 7.3.3] achieves resource-limited behaviour in belief windows by allowing only rule-based deduction; one loses completeness but retains some introspective power.

10 Conclusion

In this chapter we review the main issues discussed in this book, and we discuss the possibilities for further research.

10.1 Advantages and disadvantages of an abstract architecture

The main subject of part I this book is Socrates: a logic-based framework for building expert systems. Socrates attempts to provide a general-purpose architecture which is capable of being instantiated along a number of different dimensions. The representation language, the control regime, and even the inference rules can all be varied by the knowledge engineer. The approach differs from that found in expert system shells, in that the programmer has many more degrees of freedom at the design stage. Yet Socrates provides more structure than a high-level programming environment, and strives for a greater degree of uniformity in the representation of both domain knowledge and control knowledge.

We saw that the generality of Socrates confers certain advantages, but also incurs certain costs.

Advantages

- The knowledge engineer can match the expressiveness of the logical representation language to the complexity of the domain knowledge. Thus, if temporal or modal concepts are required, these can be incorporated in a principled way. Sorted logic can be used to represent taxonomic relationships between classes of domain object. The full power of the predicate calculus can be employed, if it is required. Otherwise, less expressive but more tractable languages can be used, e.g. propositional languages and production rules.

- The knowledge engineer can experiment with different control regimes without altering the domain knowledge, by developing alternative meta-theories which direct deduction at the object-level. Such meta-theories can employ a variety of criteria for ranking, rating or scoring hypotheses; determining which criteria are best is often an empirical exercise. Knowledge base partitions can be used to differentiate different kinds of knowledge, which may need to be

applied in different ways, i.e. run under different meta-theories. If
the problem solving goes through a series of well defined stages,
which employ different kinds of reasoning, then the scheduler can
be used to keep track of tasks and subtasks. The idea is to enable experimentation with heuristics of variable grain size without
contaminating the declarative knowledge of the domain.

- The knowledge engineer may wish to manipulate the inferential
  power of the system more or less independently of the expressiveness of the representation language and the heuristics employed for
  proof search. It may be known in advance that certain inference
  rules necessary for completeness are not necessary for the solution
  of the problem, as in the Schubert's Steamroller example. Alter-
  natively, it may be convenient to introduce new connectives or
  operators which capture something important about the domain,
  e.g. "A causes B", or "A immediately follows B". The tools provided for declaring logical constants and their associated inference
  rules and intended to encourage this kind of innovation within a
  uniform framework.

Disadvantages

- In general, the more expressive a logical language is, the less
  tractable is its proof theory. Therefore, we must exercise caution
  when advocating the use of non-standard logics in expert systems.
  Nevertheless, the last few years have a seen some progress in the
  provision of proof methods for modal and temporal logics, and our
  architecture is forward-looking in the sense that we anticipate that
  this trend will continue.

- Meta-level inference can add to computational cost, since the system may need to draw a number of meta-level inferences for each
  object-level step. Clearly, a complex meta-theory only makes sense
  if complexity at the object-level is such that meta-level interpretation effects savings at the object-level. The technology for compiling meta-theories into procedural interpreters is still in its infancy,
  and therefore imperfectly understood.

It should be remembered that Socrates is intended as an environment for specifying knowledge base systems and constructing prototypes,

rather than as a high performance delivery system. When the principles underlying a prototype are well understood, e.g. what knowledge is required to solve the problem, what problem solving strategy is best, there are usually a thousand and one things that can be done to optimise the final program. However, Socrates has no role to play in this process, once the basic behaviour of the prototype is judged to be correct.

10.2   Open problems and further research

In Part II, we saw that partial evaluation could not be taken as a general solution to the problem of meta-level overhead in Socrates. Perhaps no single technique will provide the answer to this source of inefficiency. A more pluralistic approach will probably be necessary, e.g. one which combines partial evaluation with other compilation techniques, such as assertion-time inferencing, and the development of matrix proof methods for non-standard logics.

Another open problem concerns the best way of implementing automated reasoning systems for non-standard logics. One way is to develop an ordinary first-order theory which axiomatises the model theory of the logic; another is to develop a whole new proof theory for the logic in question. This issue is still unresolved in the general case.

We saw in chapter 7 that, if one restricts oneself to purely logical considerations, then modal treatments of temporal logics appear to be superior to first order treatments. Yet from the computational point of view, first order treatments seem to be preferable, even though the resulting formulas can be very complicated. The advantage of the modal proof method outlined in chapter 8 is that it can be applied to any normal system of modal predicate logic.

Another avenue for further research involves the extension to full first-order modal logic with both functions and equality (and perhaps containing definite descriptions). The problem is to find a suitable semantics for equality, or perhaps a number of semantic accounts, which can then be translated into corresponding restrictions on unification. It is possible that we may need more than one semantic account, because the "correct" interpretation of equality may well depend upon the particular application. Thus, theorems such as $(\forall x)(\forall y)\big((x = y) \rightarrow L(x = y)\big)$ may be acceptable in some applications but not others.

The Socrates architecture allows for the attachment of different sets of inference rules to different knowledge base partitions, so one could reason about time in one partition and about belief in another. Further research is required if we wish to combine modal systems to enable reasoning about (say) time and belief in the same partition. Such complications would make the first-order treatment even more unwieldy, while the modal proof method would have to contain more than one kind of world, e.g. epistemic alternatives, past and future states, and so on. The fact that representation languages for reasoning about time, change, causality and so forth may require the use of more than one modality makes the provision of a general purpose architecture for constructing automated reasoning systems all the more important. There are many difficult research issues involved here, and we do not claim to have done anything more than make a start in this direction.

Bibliography

[Abad86]   M. Abadi and Z. Manna. Modal theorem proving. In *8th International Conference on Automated Deduction*, pages 172–189, Springer-Verlag, Berlin, 1986.

[Abel85]   H. Abelson and G.J. Sussman. *Structure and Interpretation of Computer Programs*. The MIT Press, 1985.

[Aiel84]   L. Aiello and G. Levi. The uses of metaknowledge in AI systems. In *Proceedings of the Sixth European Conference on Artificial Intelligence, ECAI '84*, pages 707–717, Pisa, September 1984.

[Aiki83]   J.S. Aikins. Prototypical knowledge for expert systems. *Artificial Intelligence*, 20:163–210, 1983.

[Alle82]   J. Allen. Maintaining knowledge about temporal intervals. *Communications of the ACM*, 26:832–843, 1982.

[Alle84]   J. Allen. A general theory of action and time. *Artificial Intelligence*, 21:121–154, 1984.

[Altm87]   R.B. Altman and B.G. Buchanan. Partial compilation of strategic knowledge. In *Proceedings of AAAI-87*, pages 399–404, American Association for Artificial Intelligence, Seattle, Washington, July 1987.

[Alve83]   P. Alvey. Problems of designing a medical expert system. In *Proceedings of the Third Technical Conference of the British Computer Society Specialist Group on Expert Systems, Expert Systems '83*, pages 20–42, Cambridge, UK, December 1983.

[Atta84]   G. Attardi and M. Simi. Metalanguage and reasoning across viewpoints. In *Proceedings of the Sixth European Conference on Artificial Intelligence, ECAI '84*, pages 315–324, Pisa, September 1984.

[Beet87]   M. Beetz. *Specifying Meta-Level Architectures for Rule-Based Systems*. Technical Report SEKI No. SR-87-06 (Diploma Thesis), Universität Kaiserslautern, Fachbereich Informatik, Kaiserslautern, 1987.

[Bent82]   J. van Benthem. *The logic of time*. Reidel, Dordrecht, 1982.

[Beth59]   E. Beth. *The foundations of mathematics*. North Holland, Amsterdam, 1959.

[Bibe82a]   W. Bibel. *Automated theorem proving*. Braunschweig, Vieweg, 1982.

[Bibe82b]   W. Bibel. A comparative study of several proof procedures. *Artificial Intelligence*, 18:269–93, 1982.

[Bjor87]   D. Bjorner, A.P. Ershov, and N.D. Jones, editors. *Workshop on Partial Evaluation and Mixed Computation*, Avernaes, Denmark, October 1987.

[Bled77]   W. Bledsoe. Non-resolution theorem proving. *Artificial Intelligence*, 9:1–35, 1977.

[Bobr83]   D. Bobrow and M. Stefik. *LOOPS Manual*. Xerox, 1983.

[Bowe82]   K.A. Bowen and R.A. Kowalski. Amalgamating language and metalan-
             guage in logic programming. In K. Clark and S. Tarnlund, editors, *Logic
             Programming*, pages 153–172, Academic Press, 1982.

[Brac85]   R. Brachman, V. Gilbert, and H. Levesque. An essential hybrid rea-
             soning system: knowledge and symbol level accounts of KRYPTON. In
             Proceedings of the 9th IJCAI, pages 532–39, International Joint Conference
             on Artificial Intelligence, 1985.

[Brac87]   R. Brachman. Coping with complexity in knowledge representation and
             reasoning. In *Paper presented at the SERC workshop on Knowledge Represen-
             tation*, Abingdon, UK, April 1987.

[Brow87]   F. Brown, editor. *Proceedings of the 1987 workshop on the frame problem in
             artificial intelligence*, Morgan Kaufmann, Los Altos, Ca., 1987.

[Bund79]   A. Bundy, L. Byrd, G. Luger, C. Mellish, R. Milne, and M. Palmer.
             Solving mechanics problems using meta-level inference. In *Proceedings of
             the Sixth IJCAI*, International Joint Conference on Artificial Intelligence,
             Tokyo, August 1979.

[Bund81]   A. Bundy and B. Welham. Using meta-level inference for selective ap-
             plication of multiple rewrite rules in algebraic manipulation. *Artificial
             Intelligence*, 16(2):189–212, 1981.

[Bund85]   A. Bundy and L.S. Sterling. *Meta-Level Inference in Algebra*. Technical Re-
             port DAI Research Paper No. 273, Department of Artificial Intelligence,
             University of Edinburgh, 1985.

[Cerr86]   L. FarFariñas del Cerro. MOLOG: a system than extends PROLOG with
             modal logic. *New Generation Computing*, 4:35–50, 1986.

[Chan83]   B. Chandrasekaran. Towards a taxonomy of problem-solving types. *AI
             Magazine*, 4:9–17, 1983.

[Chan85a]   B. Chandrasekaran. Expert systems: matching techniques to tasks. In
             W. Reitman, editor, *Artificial Intelligence Applications for Business*, Ablex
             Corp, 1985.

[Chan85b]   B. Chandrasekaran. Generic tasks in expert system design and their role
             in explanation of problem solving. In *the NAS/ONR Workshop on AI and
             distributed problem solving*, 1985.

[Chan87]   B. Chandrasekaran. Towards a functional architecture for intelligence
             based on generic information processing tasks. In *Proceedings of the Tenth
             IJCAI*, pages 1183–1192, International Joint Conference on Artificial In-
             telligence, Milan, August 1987.

[Chan88]   D. Chan and M. Wallace. A treatment of negation during partial eval-
             uation. In J. Lloyd, editor, *Proceedings of the Meta'88 Workshop on meta-
             programming in logic programming*, pages 227–240, Bristol, June 1988.

[Char80]   E. Charniak, C.K. Riesbeck, and D.V. McDermott. *Artificial Intelligence
             Programming*. Lawrence Erlbaum Associates, Hillsdale, New Jersey, 1980.

[Chel80]   B. Chellas. *Modal logic*. Cambridge University Press, Cambridge, 1980.

[Clan81]   W. Clancey and R. Letsinger. NEOMYCIN: reconfiguring a rule-based expert system for application to teaching. In *Proceedings of the Seventh IJCAI*, pages 829–836, International Joint Conference on Artificial Intelligence, Vancouver, 1981.

[Clan82]   W. Clancey and C. Bock. *MRS/NEOMYCIN: Representing Metacontrol in Predicate Calculus*. Technical Report No. HPP-82-31, Stanford Heuristic Programming Project, 1982.

[Clan83a]   W. Clancey. The advantages of abstract control knowledge in expert system design. In *Proceedings of AAAI-83*, pages 74–78, American Association for Artificial Intelligence, 1983.

[Clan83b]   W. Clancey. The epistemology of rule-based expert systems: a framework for explanation. *Artificial Intelligence*, 20:215–51, 1983.

[Clan85]   W. Clancey. Representing control knowledge as abstract tasks and metarules. In M. Coombs and L. Bolc, editors, *Computer Expert Systems*, Springer Verlag, 1985.

[Cohn85]   A. Cohn. On the solution of Schubert's steamroller in many-sorted logic. In *Proceedings of the 9th IJCAI*, pages 1169–75, International Joint Conference on Artificial Intelligence, 1985.

[Davi77]   R. Davis and B. Buchanan. Meta-level knowledge: overview and applications. In *Proceedings of the Fifth IJCAI*, pages 920–927, International Joint Conference on Artificial Intelligence, Cambridge, Mass., 1977.

[Davi80]   R. Davis. Meta-rules: reasoning about control. *Artificial Intelligence*, 15:179–222, 1980.

[Davi82]   R. Davis. TEIRESIAS: applications of meta-level knowledge. In R. Davis and D.B. Lenat, editors, *Knowledge-Based Systems in Artificial Intelligence*, pages 227–490, McGraw-Hill, New York, 1982.

[Davi87]   N.J. Davies. Schubert's steamroller in a natural deduction theorem prover. In S. Moralee, editor, *Research and Development in Expert Systems IV*, Cambridge University Press, 1987.

[Deva86]   P. Devanbu, M. Freeland, and S. Naqvi. A procedural approach to search control in Prolog. In *Proceedings of the Seventh European Conference on Artificial Intelligence, ECAI '86*, pages 53–57, Brighton, July 1986.

[Elfr88]   B. Elfrink and H. Reichgelt. The use of assertion-time inference in logic-based knowledge bases. In *Proceedings of the Eighth European Conference on Artificial Intelligence, ECAI '88*, pages 232–37, 1988.

[Erma84]   L. Erman, A. Scott, and P. London. Separating and integrating control in a rule-based tool. In *Proceedings of the IEEE workshop on principles of knowledge based systems*, pages 37–43, Denver, Colorado, December 1984.

[Eshg86]   K. Eshghi. *Meta-Level Reasoning for Declarative Control*. Technical Report Research Report 86/14, Imperial College of Science and Technology, London, 1986.

[Faga80]   L. Fagan. *Representing time-dependent relations in a medical setting*. PhD thesis, Computer Science Department, Stanford University, 1980.

[Fefe62]   S. Feferman. Transfinite recursive progressions of axiomatic theories. *The Journal of Symbolic Logic*, 27(3):259–316, September 1962.

[Fick85]   S. Fickas and D. Novick. Control knowledge in expert systems: relaxing restrictive assumptions. In *Expert systems and their applications; 5th international workshop*, pages 981–994, Avignon, May 1985.

[Fitt69]   M. Fitting. *Intuitionistic logic, model theory and forcing*. North Holland, Amsterdam, 1969.

[Fitt83]   M. Fitting. *Proof methods for modal and intuitionistic logic*. Reidel, Dordrecht, 1983.

[Fris87]   A.M. Frisch. Inference without chaining. In *Proceedings of the Tenth IJCAI*, pages 515–519, International Joint Conference on Artificial Intelligence, Milan, August 1987.

[Gall79]   M. Gallaire and C. Lasserre. Controlling knowledge deduction in a declarative approach. In *Proceedings of the Sixth IJCAI*, pages S1–S6, International Joint Conference on Artificial Intelligence, Tokyo, August 1979.

[Gall82]   M. Gallaire and C. Lasserre. Meta-level control for logic programs. In K. Clark and S. Tarnlund, editors, *Logic Programming*, pages 173–188, Academic Press, 1982.

[Gall85]   M. Gallanti, G. Guida, L. Spampinato, and A. Stefanini. Representing procedural knowledge in expert systems: an application to process control. In *Proceedings of the Ninth IJCAI*, pages 345–352, International Joint Conference on Artificial Intelligence, Los Angeles, 1985.

[Gall86]   J. Gallagher. Transforming logic programs by specialising interpreters. In *Proceedings of the Seventh European Conference on Artificial Intelligence, ECAI '86*, pages 109–122, Brighton, July 1986.

[Gene80]   M. Genesereth, R. Greiner, and D. Smith. *MRS Manual*. Technical Report Memo HPP-80-24, Stanford Heuristic Programming Project, 1980.

[Gene83]   M. Genesereth and D. Smith. An overview of Meta-Level Architecture. In *Proceedings of AAAI-83*, pages 119–124, American Association for Artificial Intelligence, 1983.

[Gene87]   M. Genesereth and N. Nilsson. *Logical foundations of Artificial Intelligence*. Morgan Kaufmann, Los Altos, Cal., 1987.

[Gord79]   M. Gordon, R. Milner, and C. Wadsworth. *Edinburgh LCF: a mechanized logic of computation*. Volume 78 of *Lecture Notes in Computer Science*, Springer Verlag, 1979.

[Halp85]   J. Halpern and Y. Moses. A guide to modal logics of knowledge and belief: preliminary draft. In *Proceedings of the 9th IJCAI*, pages 480–490, International Joint Conference on Artificial Intelligence, 1985.

[Hank87]   S. Hanks and D. McDermott. Nonmonotonic logic and temporal projection. *Artificial Intelligence*, 33:379–412, 1987.

[Harm87]   F. van Harmelen. *Improving the efficiency of meta-level reasoning.* Technical Report Discussion Paper No. 40, Department of Artificial Intelligence, University of Edinburgh, 1987.

[Harm88]   F. van Harmelen and A. Bundy. Explanation-based generalisation = partial evaluation. *Artificial Intelligence Journal,* 30(3):401–412, October 1988.

[Haug87a]   B. Haugh. Non-standard semantics for the method of temporal arguments. In *Proceedings of the tenth IJCAI,* pages 449–455, International Joint Conference on Artificial Intelligence, 1987.

[Haug87b]   B. Haugh. Simple causal minimization for temporal persistence and projection. In *Proceedings of AAAI-87,* pages 218–223, American Association for Artificial Intelligence, 1987.

[Haye73]   P. Hayes. Computation and deduction. In *Proceedings of the Symposium on the Mathematical Foundations of Computer Science,* pages 105–117, Czechoslovakian Academy of Sciences, 1973.

[Haye77]   P. Hayes. In defence of logic. In *Proceedings of the fifth IJCAI,* pages 559–65, International Joint Conference on Artificial Intelligence, 1977.

[Haye85]   B. Hayes-Roth. A blackboard architecture for control. *Artificial Intelligence,* 26:251–321, 1985.

[Hint62]   J. Hintikka. *Knowledge and belief.* Cornell University Press, 1962.

[Hudl84]   E. Hudlicka and V. Lesser. Meta level control through fault detection and diagnosis. In *Proceedings of AAAI-84,* pages 153–161, American Association for Artificial Intelligence, 1984.

[Hugh68]   G. Hughes and M. Cresswell. *An introduction to modal logics.* Methuen, London, 1968.

[Inte84]   Intellicorps. *The Knowledge Engineering Environment.* Intellicorps, 1984.

[Jack87a]   P. Jackson. *A representation language based on a game-theoretic interpretation of logic.* PhD thesis, University of Leeds, 1987.

[Jack87b]   P. Jackson. Towards an architecture for advice-giving systems. In P. Dufour and A. Lamsweerde, editors, *Current issues in Expert Systems,* pages 11–37, Academic Press, 1987.

[Jack87c]   P. Jackson and H. Reichgelt. A general proof method for first-order modal logic. In *Proceedings of the tenth IJCAI,* pages 942–44, International Joint Conference on Artificial Intelligence, 1987.

[Jack88a]   P. Jackson. On game-theoretic interactions with first-order knowledge bases. In P. Smets, E. Mamdami, D. Dubois, and H. Prade, editors, *Non-Standard Logics for Automated Reasoning,* Academic Press, New York, 1988.

[Jack88b]   P. Jackson and H. Reichgelt. A general proof method for modal predicate logic without the barcan formula or its converse. In *Proceedings of AAAI-88,* American Association for Artificial Intelligence, 1988.

[Jack88c]   P. Jackson and H. Reichgelt. A modal proof method for doxastic reason-
             ing in incomplete theories. In *Proceedings of the Eighth European Conference
             on Artificial Intelligence, ECAI '88*, pages 480–485, Pitman, London, 1988.

[Jans86]   W.N.H. Jansweijer, J.J. Elshout, and B.J. Wielinga. The expertise of
             novice problem solvers. In *Proceedings of the Seventh European Conference on
             Artificial Intelligence,ECAI '86*, pages 576–585, Brighton, July 1986.

[Klee52]   S. Kleene. *Introduction to Metamathematics.* Van Nostrand, New York,
             1952.

[Kono85]   K. Konolige. A computational theory of belief introspection. In *Proceed-
             ings of the Ninth IJCAI*, pages 502–508, International Joint Conference on
             Artificial Intelligence, 1985.

[Kono86a]   K. Konolige. *A deduction model of belief.* Pitman, London, 1986.

[Kono86b]   K. Konolige. Resolution and quantified epistemic logics. In *8th Interna-
             tional Conference on Automated Deduction*, pages 199–209, Springer-Verlag,
             Berlin, 1986.

[Kowa75]   R. Kowalski. A proof procedure using connection graphs. *Journal of the
             ACM*, 22:572–95, 1975.

[Kowa79]   B. Kowalski. *Logic for Problem Solving. Artificial Intelligence Series*, North
             Holland Publisher, 1979.

[Kowa86]   R. Kowalski and M. Sergot. A logic-based calculus of events. *New Gen-
             eration Computing*, 4:67–96, 1986.

[Krip63]   S. Kripke. Semantical considerations on modal logics. *Acta Philosophica
             Fennica*, 16:83–94, 1963.

[Krip72]   S. Kripke. Meaning and necessity. In D. Davidson and G. Harman,
             editors, *Semantics of natural language*, Reidel, Dordrecht, 1972.

[Ladk87]   P. Ladkin. The completeness of a natural system for reasoning with time
             intervals. In *Proceedings of the tenth IJCAI*, pages 462–467, 1987.

[Lair84]   J. Laird, P. Rosenbloom, and A. Newell. Towards chunking as a general
             learning mechanism. In *Proceedings of AAAI-84*, pages 373–377, American
             Association for Artificial Intelligence, Austin, Texas, 1984.

[Leve85]   H. Levesque and R. Brachman. A fundamental tradeoff in knowledge
             representation and reasoning (revised version). In R. Brachman and H.
             Levesque, editors, *Readings in knowledge representation*, Morgan Kaufmann,
             Los Altos, CA, 1985.

[Levi88]   G. Levi. Object level reflection of inference rules by partial evaluation. In
             P. Maes and D. Nardi, editors, *Meta-level architectures and reflection*, North
             Holland Publishers, 1988.

[Lloy84]   J. Lloyd. *Foundations of Logic Programming. Symbolic Computation Series*,
             Springer Verlag, 1984.

[Lloy87]   J.W. Lloyd and J.C. Shepherdson. *Partial evaluation in logic programming.* Technical Report CS-87-09, Department of Computer Science, University of Bristol, 1987.

[Lloy88]   J. Lloyd, editor. *Proceedings of the Meta'88 Workshop on meta-programming in logic programming,* Bristol, June 1988.

[Maes86]   P. Maes. Introspection in knowledge representation. In *Proceedings of the Seventh European Conference on Artificial Intelligence, ECAI '86,* pages 256–269, Brighton, July 1986.

[McCa69]   J. McCarthy and P. Hayes. Some philosophical problems from the standpoint of artificial intelligence. In B. Meltzer and D. Michie, editors, *Machine Intelligence 4,* Edinburgh University Press, Edinburgh, 1969.

[McDe82a] D. McDermott. Nonmonotonic logic II: nonmonotonic modal theories. *Journal of the Association for Computing Machinery,* 29:33–57, 1982.

[McDe82b] D. McDermott. A temporal logic for reasoning about processes and plans. *Cognitive Science,* 6:101–55, 1982.

[Mitc86]   T.M. Mitchell, R.M. Keller, and S.T. Kedar-Cabelli. Explanation-based generalization: a unifying view. *Machine Learning,* 1(1):47–80, 1986.

[Moor82]   R. Moore. The role of logic in knowledge representation and commonsense reasoning. In *Proceedings of AAAI-82,* pages 428–433, American Association for Artificial Intelligence, Pittsburgh, Pa, August 1982.

[Moor84]   R. Moore. *The role of logic in Artificial Intelligence.* Technical Report Note 335, SRI International, 1984.

[Moor85a] R. Moore. A formal theory of knowledge and action. In J. Hobbs and R. Moore, editors, *Formal theories of the common sense world,* Ablex, Norwood, N.J., 1985.

[Moor85b] R.C. Moore. Semantical considerations on nonmonotonic logic. *Artificial Intelligence,* 25:75–94, 1985.

[Moor88]   R.C. Moore. Autoepistemic logic. In P. Smets, E.H. Mamdani, D. Dubois, and H. Prade, editors, *Non-standard logics for automated reasoning,* chapter 4, Academic Press, London, 1988.

[Nii79]   H.P. Nii and N. Aiello. AGE (attempt to generalize): a knowledge-based program for building knowledge-based programs. In *Proceedings of the Sixth IJCAI,* pages 645–655, International Joint Conference on Artificial Intelligence, Tokyo, 1979.

[Nils82]   N. Nilsson. *Principles of Artificial Intelligence.* Springer Verlag, Berlin, 1982.

[Owen88]   S. Owen. Issues in the partial evaluation of meta-interpreters. In J. Lloyd, editor, *Proceedings of the Meta'88 Workshop on meta-programming in logic programming,* pages 241–254, Bristol, June 1988.

[Pere82]   L.M. Pereira. Logic control with logic. In *Proceedings of the First International Logic Programming Conference,* pages 9–18, Marseilles, 1982.

[Prie87]   A.E. Priedites and J. Mostow. PROLEARN: towards a Prolog inter-
            preter that learns. In *Proceedings of AAAI-87*, American Association for
            Artificial Intelligence, Seattle, Washington, July 1987.

[Reic85]   H. Reichgelt and F. van Harmelen. Relevant criteria for choosing an
            inference engine in expert systems. In *Proceedings of the fifth Technical
            Conference of the British Computer Society Specialist Group on Expert Systems,
            Expert Systems '85*, pages 21–30, Warwick, December 1985.

[Reic86]   H. Reichgelt and F. van Harmelen. Criteria for choosing representation
            languages and control regimes for expert systems. *The Knowledge Engi-
            neering Review*, 1(4):2–17, December 1986.

[Reic87]   H. Reichgelt. Semantics for reified temporal logic. In J. Hallam and
            C. Mellish, editors, *Advances in artificial intelligence: Proceedings of AISB-87*,
            Wiley and Sons, Chichester, 1987.

[Reic88]   H. Reichgelt. *An architecture for default reasoning*. Technical Report, AI
            Group Working Paper. Dept of Psychology, University of Nottingham,
            1988.

[Resc71]   N. Rescher and A. Urquhart. *Temporal logic*. Springer-Verlag, Berlin,
            1971.

[Russ05]   B. Russell. On denoting. *Mind*, 14:479–93, 1905.

[Safr86]   S. Safra and E. Shapiro. *Meta Interpreters for Real*. Technical Report No.
            CS86-11, Department of Computer Science, The Weizmann Institute of
            Science, May 1986.

[Scot70]   D. Scott. Advice on modal logic. In K. Lambert, editor, *Philosophical
            problems in logic: Some recent developments*, Reidel, Dordrecht, 1970.

[Shap83]   E. Shapiro. Logic programs with uncertainties, a tool for implementing
            rule-based systems. In *Proceedings of the Eighth IJCAI*, pages 529–532, In-
            ternational Joint Conference on Artificial Intelligence, Karlsruhe, August
            1983.

[Shep84]   J.C. Shepherdson. Negation as failure. In *Alvey IKBS Inference Research
            Theme Workshop 1*, Imperial College, London, September 1984.

[Shoh85]   Y. Shoham. Ten requirements for a theory of change. *New Generation
            Computing*, 3:467–77, 1985.

[Shoh86]   Y. Shoham. Reified temporal logics: semantical and ontological con-
            siderations. In *Proceedings of the 7th ECAI*, pages 390–97, Brighton, UK,
            1986.

[Shoh87]   Y. Shoham. Nonmonotonic logics: meaning and utility. In *Proceedings of
            the 10th IJCAI*, pages 388–393, International Joint Conference on Artificial
            Intelligence, 1987.

[Shoh88]   Y. Shoham. *Reasoning about Change*. The MIT Press, Massachusetts,
            1988.

[Siek86]   J.H. Siekmann. Unification theory. In *Proceedings of the Seventh European Conference on Artificial Intelligence, ECAI '86*, pages vii–xxxv, Brighton, July 1986.

[Silv86]   B. Silver. *Meta-level Inference. Studies in Computer Science and Artificial Intelligence*, North Holland Publishers, 1986.

[Smit82]   B. Smith. *Reflection and Semantics in a Procedural Language*. Technical Report 272, Massachusetts Institute of Technology, Laboratory for Computer Science, Cambridge, Massachusetts, 1982.

[Smul68]   R. Smullyan. *First-order logic*. Springer, Berlin, 1968.

[Ster82a]   L. Sterling. *IMPRESS - Meta-level concepts in theorem proving*. Technical Report DAI Working Paper No. 119, Department of Artificial Intelligence, University of Edinburgh, 1982.

[Ster82b]   L. Sterling, A. Bundy, L. Byrd, R. O'Keefe, and B. Silver. Solving symbolic equations with PRESS. In J. Calmet, editor, *Computer Algebra*, Springer Verlag, 1982.

[Ster84]   L. Sterling. *Implementing Problem-Solving Strategies Using the Meta-Level*. Technical Report DAI Research Paper No. 209, Department of Artificial Intelligence, University of Edinburgh, 1984.

[Ster86]   L. Sterling and R.D. Beer. Incremental flavor-mixing of meta-interpreters for expert system construction. In *Proceedings of the 3rd Symposium on Logic Programming*, pages 20–27, Salt Lake City, Utah, September 1986.

[Stic82]   M. Stickel. A nonclausal connection-graph resolution theorem-proving program. In *Proceedings of AAAI-82*, pages 229–33, American Association for Artificial Intelligence, 1982.

[Swar80]   H. de Swart. Gentzen-type systems for C, K and several extensions of C and K; constructive completeness proofsand effective decision procedures for these systems. *Logique et Analyse*, 23(90-91):263–84, 1980.

[Take85]   T. Takewaki, A. Takeuchi, S. Kunifuji, and K. Furukawa. *Application of Partial Evaluation to the Algebraic Manipulation System and its Evaluation*. Technical Report TR-148, Tokyo, ICOT Research Centre, December 1985.

[Take86]   A. Takeuchi and K. Furukawa. Partial evaluation of Prolog programs and its application to meta programming. In *Proceedings of IFIPS '86*, Dublin, 1986.

[Tarn77]   S.Å. Tarnlund. Horn clause computability. *BIT*, 17:215–226, 1977.

[Venk84]   R. Venken. A Prolog meta-interpreter for partial evaluation and its application to source to source transformation and query-optimisation. In *Proceedings of the Sixth European Conference on Artificial Intelligence, ECAI '84*, pages 91–100, Pisa, September 1984.

[Wall83]   L. Wallen. *Towards the Provision of a Natural Mechanism for Expressing Domain Specific Global Strategies in General Purpose Theorem-Provers*. Technical Report DAI Research Paper No. 202, Department of Artificial Intelligence, University of Edinburgh, 1983.

[Wall85]   L. Wallen. Generating connection calculi from tableaux and sequent
            based proof systems. In *Proceedings of AISB 85*, Warwick University, War-
            wick, UK, 1985.

[Wall86]   L. Wallen. Matrix proof methods for modal logics. In *Proceedings of the
            Tenth IJCAI*, pages 917–23, International Joint Conference on Artificial
            Intelligence, 1986.

[Walt84]   C. Walther. A mechanical solution of Schubert's steamroller by many-
            sorted resolution. In *Proceedings of AAAI-84*, pages 330–334, American
            Association for Artificial Intelligence, 1984.

[Warn83]   D. Warner Hasling. Abstract explanations of strategy in a diagnostic
            consultation system. In *Proceedings of AAAI-83*, pages 157–161, American
            Association for Artificial Intelligence, Washington D.C., August 1983.

[Warn84]   D. Warner Hasling, W. Clancey, and G. Rennels. Strategic explanations
            for a diagnostic consultation system. *International Journal of Man-Machine
            Studies*, 20(1):3–19, 1984.

[Welh87]   B. Welham. Declaratively programmable interpreters and meta-level in-
            ferences. In P. Maes and D. Nardi, editors, *Meta-level architectures and
            reflection*, North Holland Publishers, 1987.

[Weyh80]   R. Weyhrauch. Prolegomena to a theory of mechanised formal reasoning.
            Artificial Intelligence, 13:133–170, 1980.

[Wiel86]   B.J. Wielinga and J.A. Breuker. Models of expertise. In *Proceedings of the
            Seventh European Conference on Artificial Intelligence, ECAI '86*, pages 306–
            318, Brighton, July 1986.

[Will83]   C. Williams. *ART, the advanced reasoning tool, conceptual overview*. Inference
            Corporation, 1983.

Index

abstract architecture, 3, 37
accessibility relation, 179, 210, 229
alphabetic variancy, 102
amalgamated, 27
amalgamating, 26
annotation of propositions, 45
ART, 3
assertion-time inference, 72, 211
backward chaining, 18
bag operators, 43
Barcan formula, 177, 189, 199, 203
barn door rules, 69
BB1, 19, 31
belief, 9
best-first search, 54
bilingual, 25, 27
binary connectives, 43
branching out, 97
breadth-first, 18
built-in predicates, 98
CENTAUR, 21
changing ontologies, 147, 151, 154,
    160, 170, 175
classical predicate calculus, 117
classical propositional logic, 115
closed sequent, 114
commutative connectives, 43
complementary formula, 178
complete, 29
computational adequacy, 14
concrete architecture, 3, 37
conditional branches, 98
conflict resolution, 17
conflict-resolution set, 19
conjunct ordering, 17
connection graph theorem prover, 140
control knowledge, 5
control restriction, 48
control strategy, 51
countermodel, 184
crisis-management systems, 19
cut, 100, 110
data, 94
declarative, 28
default reasoning, 147
default specification, 28
denotation, 190
discrimination net, 45
disjunctive normal form, 126
DOCS, 69
domain, 3
doxastic logic, 229
doxastic model, 229
doxastic theory, 230

dynamic information, 96
elimination rules, 70
empty sequent, 178
empty sort, 39
end world-symbol, 180
end-user, 37
entry formula, 125
epistemic alternatives, 229
euclidean accessibility relation, 180,
    229
evaluable predicates, 42, 52, 107
exact, 29
exist predicate, 162, 175
expert system tools, 2
explanation restriction, 48
explanation, 10
explanation-based generalisation, 106
extensional definition, 41
final set of sequents, 114
first order temporal logic, 154
flounder, 110
FOL, 29
folding, 110
forward chaining, 18, 72
frame-problem, 147
fulfillment, 237
generate and test, 58
GOLUX, 27, 31
ground world-symbols, 180
halting criterion, 106
halting problem, 101, 105
heuristic guidance, 104
Hilbert-type proof theory, 123
hybrid systems, 3
hypothetical reasoning, 44
IMPRESS, 23
inference rules, 47
instantiation, 102
intensional definition, 41
introspection, 231, 234, 237
introspective subproof, 235
INVEST, 65
iterated modalities, 144, 159, 175
KD45, 230
KEE, 3
knowledge base, 43
knowledge engineer, 37
knowledge, 94
Kripke structure, 179
KRS, 28, 31
KRYPTON, 140
lazy evaluation, 58
LCF, 57
locus of action, 15

logic of belief, 230
logic, 4
logical connectives, 42
logical inference, 93
logical language, 38
LOOPS, 3
LP, 24
m-unification, 180, 183
many-sorted logics, 39
meaning postulates, 169–170
MECHO, 23
meta-knowledge, 7
meta-language, 164
meta-level architecture, 7
meta-level architectures, 13
meta-level driven, 26
meta-level overhead, 62, 87
meta-level programming language, 57
meta-logical variables, 49
meta-predicates, 16
meta-variables, 166
mixed computation, 107
mixed-level inference, 18
ML, 57
MLA, 21, 27, 31
modal logic, 8, 179
modal predicate logic, 177
modal temporal logic, 148
modal term-unification, 198
modal unification, 180
Modus Ponens, 47
MOLOG, 215
monolingual, 25, 27
mt-unification, 198
MYCIN, 145
naming relation, 56
natural deduction, 46, 79
negation, 110
NEOMYCIN, 21, 27, 31
no chaining restriction, 48
nonmonotonic logics, 9
object-knowledge, 7
object-level driven, 26
occurs-check, 102
open programs, 95
operational predicate, 106
Or Introduction, 47
ORBS, 19
parent world-symbol, 180
partial evaluation, 87, 140
partial specification, 28
partitions, 43
pattern matcher, 48
PDP-0, 19, 31

persistence, 147
positive heuristic, 29
possible world semantics, 229
possible world, 179
preferred TR-interpretation, 169
PRESS, 23, 31
procedural control, 57
procedural interpretation, 52
procedural, 28
PROLEARN, 109
Prolog, 16, 20, 25, 89–90
Prolog's, 75
proof formula formation algorithm,
    127
proof formula, 125
proof strategy, 38, 51
proof theory, 38, 46
proof tree, 114
PROP, 21
propagating data structures, 97–98
propositional KD45, 232
pseudo-infinite computation, 99
pseudo-infinitely deep computation,
    99
pseudo-infinitely wide computation,
    99
pure meta-level inference, 23
pushing down meta-arguments, 97
quoting mechanism, 27
Reason Maintenance System, 139
recognition procedure, 41
reduced formula, 114
reflect-and-act, 19
reflection principles, 29
reflexive accessibility relation, 179
reified approach, 154
reified logics, 50
reified temporal logic, 164, 175
repeated temporal expressions, 144
representation language, 39
representational adequacy, 14
resolution, 140
retrieval mechanism, 43, 47
rigid designators, 8, 153, 170
Rule of Assumptions, 235
S-M-N theorem, 87
S.1, 21, 27, 31
scheduler, 60
Schubert's Steamroller, 79
segment variables, 49
semantic attachment, 42, 56, 67
sequence operators, 43
sequent based proof method, 177
sequent, 114, 178, 209, 232

serial accessibility relation, 179
set-connectives, 43
shells, 2
side effects, 98
side-effects, 108
signed formula, 114
situation calculus, 155
skolemisation, 50, 185
skolemising by need, 118
slot-value mechanism, 45
SOAR, 19
Socrates, 37
sorted logic, 155
soundness, 62
start world-symbol, 180
static information, 96
STATIONS, 75
stop criterion, 100, 105
streams, 58
strict instantiation, 102
strict, 29
structural knowledge, 40, 155
subtask, 60
subtask-management, 21
symbolic evaluation, 140
symmetric accessibility relation, 180, 207
t-unification, 198
tableau proof systems, 114
TAG, 157
task, 4
taxonomic hierarchy, 40
TEIRESIAS, 19, 27, 31
temporal arguments, 154–155
term unification, 198
term-index, 198
termination criteria, 101
time dependent expressions, 144, 159
TM, 148
TM-interpretation, 151
TM-structure, 150
TR-interpretation, 168
TR-structure, 168
transitive accessibility relation, 180
truth-maintenance, 45
Turing complete, 101
typed quantification, 47
unary connectives, 43
uncertainty, 10
unfolding, 97–98, 111
unification, 40, 101
unifier, 48
unifying composition, 183
universal sort, 39

user profile, 67
value assignment, 193
verification theorem prover, 71
VM, 143
VMT, 19
w-unification, 192, 233
w-unify, 181
what-if reasoning, 44
wide scope quantifiers, 131
wide scope skolem term, 118
wide scope variable, 118
world constants, 232
world diagram, 185
world symbols, 232
world unification, 181
world variables, 232
world-index, 178, 180